STORM OVER ASIA

China and Southeast Asia:
Thrust and Response

STORM OVER ASIA

China and Southeast Asia:
Thrust and Response

ROBERT KARR McCABE

 THE NEW AMERICAN LIBRARY

For Inger

About the Book

Storm Over Asia is a report, not an exhaustive academic analysis. There is room for the latter; I have been struck by the extraordinary lack of source material for my own book. To my mind, this shortage is unfortunate, for I believe that China and Southeast Asia are destined to become, over the next several years, even *more* important than today. And it would seem only logical that we, as citizens of a world in which New York is as close to Saigon as it was to Boston just fifty years ago, should know much much more about the tribes just over the hill.

This book owes much to many people. At *Newsweek,* where I spent five rewarding years, special thanks must go to Osborn Elliott, Robert Christopher, Mert Perry, and Sydney Liu. The late Philip Graham, of the Washington Post Company, and Mrs. Katharine Graham, played a more important role than I can adequately express. Among the journalists from whom I learned much were Takashi Oka of the *Christian Science Monitor,* Seymour Topping of *The New York Times,* Richard Hughes of the *London Sunday Times,* and Derek Davies of *The Far Eastern Economic Review.* Harald Munthe-Kaas, also of the *Review,* played the major role in assembling the bibliography. Until he retired to a Buddhist monastery in 1966, Parke Fulham did much to make the book what it is today. From the academic world, Professors John K. Fairbank and John Lindbeck of Harvard and A. Doak Barnett and Donald Klein of Columbia did their best to help me understand more of what was happening in Asia, and the Fund for Adult Education pointed me firmly toward academia back in 1959. Edith Haggard and Perry Knowlton, of Curtis Brown, Ltd., helped get me started in the author's world, and Robert Gutwillig and

Wendy Weil of The New American Library wrestled with the problems of getting this book into shape.

Mrs. Robert Shaplen, Mrs. Douglas Pike, and S. T. Wong contributed vital pieces of research in Hong Kong, and Steve Andors of Columbia was equally helpful in New York. Miss Philo Wu of Hong Kong and Miss Marion Broderick of New York coped valiantly with the typing chores.

Even more important to the book were the thousands of Asians I talked to over the last ten years, from prime ministers to peasants, all of whom helped me to form my own ideas. In the largest sense, it is to them that this book is dedicated. For all this assistance, I am deeply grateful. But the opinions, judgments, and mistakes of this book are all my own.

This is a book about war, though not a war story, because war and death are cardinal facts in today's Asia. This is a book about peace as well, for the hope of peace and progress is a part of every Asian's dreams. In sum, this is a book about Asia under storm clouds—but it includes, I trust, an implicit promise that the storm is not forever.

Hong Kong, East Hampton, and Manhattan, 1965–67

CONTENTS

STORM
OVER
ASIA

China and Southeast Asia:
Thrust and Response

STORM WARNINGS

Introduction

For centuries the Chinese have polished the art of proverb-making to perfection; to sum up Asia today, the single most apposite might be this: "War Ends, Another Begins." On September 2, 1945, Japan's beaten leaders wound up World War II aboard the USS Missouri in Tokyo Bay. But during their four-year occupation of Southeast Asia and eastern China, the Japanese helped mightily to accelerate the Asian nationalist revolution that erupted in the late forties and still rages today. In Southeast Asia, the basis for revolution had been built before the war by nationalists and communists, eager for independence from their colonial rulers; in China, Chiang Kai-shek's increasingly reactionary posture had force-fed the creation of a generation anxious to support any alternative to the arbitrary, corrupt Kuomintang rule.

In Japan, simultaneously, the military clique that had seized power from the liberals in the mid-1930's was dreaming of a "Greater East Asian Co-Prosperity Sphere," a federation of Asian nations totally subservient to Tokyo's political and economic domination. And once the Japanese armed forces completed their 1941–42 sweep through Southeast Asia, the new rulers supervised the creation of new governments intended to provide a solid foundation for Japanese hegemony in Asia. In a few countries, such as the Dutch East Indies, some leadership already existed; elsewhere, the Japanese ran the show themselves, using local puppets as their tools. By 1945, across Southeast Asia, the framework of colonial rule had been shattered forever, though nearly a decade passed before the foreign powers involved realized it. To the north, in China, the nationalists and the communists locked themselves into a civil war that was to run for the next

[1]

four years. Clearly, the Pacific War represented an all-out effort by Japan to erase Western influence in Asia; in the postwar years, Communist China took over the campaign. And today's Asian agonies testify to the power of this policy.

From 1945 to 1950, the new Asian order was ratified in blood. The exhausted and corrupt government of Chiang Kai-shek held out until 1949, when it was chased across the Formosa Straits into ignominious exile from the mainland. In Southeast Asia, a series of revolutions erupted against the colonial powers that sought to retain their territories. Indochinese nationalists threw in their lot with their communist counterparts in the struggle for independence from France. Indonesia's Sukarno, spurred by heavy doses of encouragement from the Japanese, proclaimed his nation's independence of Holland in 1945 and set out on the long difficult road toward effective self-government. Offered independence within the Commonwealth, Burma politely opted out and began its still-continuing quest for the chimera of "Burmese socialism." Malaya's largely Chinese communists failed to enlist their nationalist Malay counterparts in their revolt and eventually were smashed, but the struggle lasted twelve bitter years and cost thousands of lives. (Three years after the end of the Malayan Emergency, Britain began to pull out, exiting more gracefully than the French and the Dutch, but just as finally.) The Filipinos, given their independence by the United States in 1945, crushed a rebellion led by the Communist Hukbalahap, but only after an eight-year battle. Thailand was the exception: because the Thais had succeeded in escaping colonial rule, they avoided its bloody aftermath, for a time at least.

Today, Southeast Asia has won its independence from the colonizing powers. But however bitter and all-encompassing that struggle may have been, the fact remains that independence as such was only the first faltering step toward true nationhood. Almost without exception, the new leaders had little realization of the realities—and obligations—of power. Indeed, there were barely enough administrators even to determine these needs; the colonial powers, for the most part, had left little more than a hierarchy of clerks behind. Beyond this, there was a grimmer problem: in each new nation, the dedicated and well-organized local communists posed an ever-present threat. Today, these problems still exist, in greater or lesser degree. But economic difficulties are at least as troublesome: perhaps the saddest fact of life in Southeast Asia is that the political revolution has so rapidly outpaced the economic.

In their attempts to overtake the industrialized nations of the developed world, too many Southeast Asian nations have attempted to compress the Industrial Revolution into a matter of hours, ignoring the fact that the first nations to enter this phase of development took nearly a century to pass through it. Granted, the staggering economic progress made by the West since 1945 has made it possible to condense the learning process to some degree. But no one has yet succeeded in synthesizing Instant Industrialization.

The failure of Southeast Asian leaders to close the gap between dream and reality has, quite simply, been calamitous. Speeches, slogans, and bold promises are not enough. And as the contrasts between promises and performances become increasingly obvious, political instability becomes a fact of life. Purely nationalistic appeals no longer carry the same old force. And those communist leaders who were content to work with the nationalists during the first phase of independence began moving into power once the nationalists began to falter, or, more directly, simply shoved them aside.

Beyond these domestic problems, a much more serious threat began to emerge in the early fifties. It was enormous, active, and smart, and it was called the People's Republic of China. Japan's abandonment of its campaign for Asian hegemony created a huge power vacuum; Communist China's foreign policy since 1949 has been dedicated to filling it. From the day they assumed power in Peking on October 1, 1949, Mao Tse-tung and his comrades began to formulate plans for restoring their nation's age-old power and influence in Asia.

By 1951, Chinese "volunteers" were battling United Nations forces in Korea in what turned out to be a fruitless attempt to help the Soviet-backed Pyongyang regime to conquer the U.S.-supported South. But Korea was only the first action in the border areas: at the time, China was fully backed, supplied—and restrained—by the Soviet Union. Since then, Peking and Moscow have parted ways. China no longer receives help from the USSR, and is accordingly free from whatever restraints Moscow may have imposed in the early years. (For several years, there have been recurring reports of serious incidents on the Sino-Soviet border.) Further evidence of Chinese expansionism is offered by the abrupt and bloody war with India in 1962, the conquest of Tibet, the wooing of Afghanistan and India-hating Pakistan, and the pressures upon the tiny Himalayan border states of Nepal and Sikkim.

The major target, however, is Southeast Asia. The area's millions are an obvious and profitable export market for Chinese products, and the great natural wealth of Indonesia and Indochina, Malaya, and Thailand is enormously tempting to Peking. In past centuries, China's influence at times stretched far beyond Asia; New China's dreams today extend to Africa and Latin America—the entire underdeveloped world, to Peking's eyes, must inevitably come under Chinese domination.

To many Westerners, these dreams seem, at best, nonsensical. China, so the argument runs, is nothing more than a mass of peasants cringing under the whip of a dictatorial regime. And the leadership itself at times seems mad: witness the tragic absurdities of the Great Leap Forward, or the Great Proletarian Cultural Revolution, which in 1967 was tearing the country apart. China's economy in 1949 was even less developed than that of Russia in 1917, and even today, that economy can only be described as one of pure subsistence. Beyond this, China has forfeited the friendship of the Soviet Union, the one great power willing to help.

The argument, as far as it goes, has its moments of accuracy. But China must be judged in terms of its potential rather than its present, and that potential is enormous.

Today, there are an estimated 750 million Chinese on the mainland. Until Mao decreed the enormous purge that swept China in 1966–67, the nation had been regimented to a degree never before approached in China's centuries of recorded history; political control reached from Peking down to the smallest hamlet. Despite the confusion common to every totally planned economy, genuine progress was being made: from the period of deprivation that followed the collapse of the Great Leap Forward in the late fifties, food production rose steadily through a period of natural disasters and, judged by Westerners who traveled through China in the mid-sixties, seemed to be continuing its steady rise. The split with Moscow did not have the crippling effect that most experts—including the Russians themselves —expected: China's scientists have produced a series of nuclear explosions and are well on the way toward developing a weapons delivery system.

To the underdeveloped nations in general, and to many Southeast Asians in particular, China's progress carried an urgent message. If the demoralized, scorned, and ineffectual China of 1949 could become a great power within fifteen years, then surely China's methods must be worth imitating. This was China's great appeal—and despite the excesses of the GPCR, it still seems to carry weight. The Chinese have never been underrated by other Asians: their drive, industry, and intelligence have shown the way to Asia for centuries.

And as the storm clouds rolled over Asia in the post–World War II years, the United States was retreating from the position of power and influence it had established throughout the area by 1945. The Pacific Fleet went into mothballs, the soldiers into mufti. After a fruitless attempt to resolve the Chinese civil war, America turned its attention to Europe. The Marshall Plan and the North American Treaty Organization (NATO) absorbed Washington's attention—Secretary of State George C. Marshall failed in China, but his plans for European reconstruction worked well, reinforcing a general American belief that Europeans, rather than Asians, were people with whom they could work. Japan, where General Douglas MacArthur worked to build a democratic, pacifist nation, was the only real area of U.S. interest in Asia.

And then the Korean War erupted, to the stunned disbelief of many in the United States. Few Americans had ever heard of Korea, and, of this minority, even fewer realized there were American troops still stationed there. But for all the surprise, Korea was an easy war to understand; straightforward military invasion is a starkly simple concept. The American response was perfectly in tune: troops, aircraft, and weapons. In contrast to Vietnam, Korea boiled down to badmen versus good guys.

American policy in Asia, in fact, hasn't been much more complex. In 1945, it seems to have been decided that only time would bring solutions to Asia's manifold problems; since then, Washington has devoted itself to buying time, in the hope that eventually a new generation of realistic, effective political leaders would appear. Thus far, the policy has had limited success. Only in Indonesia does it seem that such a new generation has appeared, and it is far too early to tell just how effective Sukarno's successors will be. Nowhere else in Southeast Asia has the change been as sweeping: in truth, the new leaders in Thailand, Burma, and Vietnam seem little improvement over the old.

It is in regard to China, of course, that the wait-and-see policy will meet its most important test. In mid-1967, it was impossible to guess the outcome of the power struggle wracking China at the time. There seemed a chance—and not much more than that—that Mao's successors might be somewhat less single-mindedly intent on extending China's hegemony. But the odds were against it: certainly the so-called opposition to Mao offered little prospect of radical change in foreign policy over the long run. And the very illogic of the struggle in China made it even more difficult to count on Chinese pragmatism as a restraining force, particularly in the context of pressures on its neighbors.

But even given perfect order and tranquility in Peking, would the Chinese thrust take the form of crude military conquest? Probably not. Today, 90 percent of China's population lives on an estimated 15 percent of the country's land. Inner Mongolia and Sinkiang are largely empty; China still must colonize much of its own land area before it becomes necessary to send settlers over the frontiers. But the *Drang Nach Suden* has other and equally compelling motives: primary among them are markets, the creation of satellite tributary states, and, perhaps most important, the preparation of a bleeding ground for Mao's great foe, the United States.

In Southeast Asia, the United States and its allies face an awkward choice. Withdrawal from South Vietnam will, in the course of Asian events, intensify the problems for the other new nations of Southeast Asia. There is a case to be made for the idea that the United States, by reason of its power and affluence, ought naturally to guarantee the independence of its allies. But this is an idea that has drawn intense opposition on the domestic political scene; indeed, a body of opinion has arisen that insists the United States has no right to be in Asia, that the area naturally should be dominated by the Chinese. There was little worry over the path of events in China; there was no concern over the fate of Asians consigned to the harshly erratic despotism of today's China. Specifically, it was argued that South Vietnam had displayed little ability to solve its own problems, and that therefore it scarcely merited American assistance. Besides, America had its own problems, notably that of civil rights, and the Asian war was destroying the battle to ensure those rights for American Negroes.

This argument, it seemed to me, was a product of two factors: first, a general lack of American concern for Asia and Asians; second, a simplistic belief that an end to American involvement in Asia would automatically bring a solution to the civil rights problem. The latter, I believe, can be dismissed out of hand: American Negroes will achieve their rights, fully and freely, not by massive infusions of money but by an acceleration of the long, hard, and patient work of those Americans, both colored and white, who have made significant progress in the years since 1960. Racial diehards won't change their minds as the result of a Supreme Court decision; their children will. And this educative process applies to the problem of American understanding of Asia as well. Our policy in Asia, our progress in the expansion of civil rights, must both evolve based on a mixture of wisdom and passion—and these two aspects are complementary, not mutually exclusive.

I am, I suppose, an Asia-Firster. I have been deeply involved with Asian affairs for the past ten years. During the years I was reporting from the Orient, I watched South Vietnam grow from a minor irritant to an all-engrossing concern in Washington, and I have seen too many close friends in officialdom become deeply embittered because of our policy errors there. Cambodia, as late as 1961, was still reasonably friendly to the United States: today, relations have been severed. Indonesia, toying with a surprisingly credulous Soviet Union that same year, became what amounted to a Communist Chinese satellite and then, in 1965, reversed its path. Change has been just as radical—and as startling—elsewhere. In Southeast Asia, inconstancy has been the sole constancy, skepticism the sole guideline.

For any reporter, these events are pure catnip. Less than two hundred years ago, the West began to struggle through its own political and economic revolutions. In those long-ago times, change was measured in decades: in Southeast Asia today, minutes are the measurement. Reporting this story is the most demanding, and most exciting, assignment in the world of the sixties.

To many in America, Southeast Asia is the end of the line. But in an age when Saigon is less than twenty-four hours by jet from New York, Southeast Asia is as close to Manhattan as was San Francisco in 1946. It will become even closer.

This book is not intended to be a political Baedeker, or to provide a detailed record of Asian events for the historians of the coming decades. It is simply a setting-down of what I saw, experienced, and reported during the years that China and Southeast Asia became a center of world concern.

Its theme is basic to American policy over the coming years. Communist China and Asia can be ignored no longer. The area's importance, already great, will continue to grow. The war in South Vietnam is only part of the Asian story today—there will be many more explosions. We can no longer afford to dismiss Asia and its problems as those of short tan men who revel in intrigue and corruption, who prefer to make love and smoke opium rather than work to determine their own fate. Together, China and Southeast Asia total more than a third of the world's population. These millions are rapidly being led—or driven—into the twentieth century. China, by itself, poses enormous problems of its own; China as the acknowledged leader of this enormous bloc of mankind will shake the world. We ignore it at our peril.

one

THE KILLING GROUND:

Vietnam, Cambodia, and Laos

Sleepy, green, and lovely: that summed up the Saigon I saw first in December, 1957. Pedicabs dawdled along the wide, almost empty streets, and beautiful women in silky bright *ao-dais* fluttered like butterflies past the chic shops on Rue Catinat. At sidewalk cafe tables, Saigon's intelligentsia and white-suited French businessmen sipped eternal aperitifs; the traditional noontime siesta seemed to last all day. The capital of the three-year-old Republic of Vietnam clearly was getting along quite comfortably under President Ngo Dinh Diem. Terrorism? "It still exists," an American official told me. "There've been a few Viet Minh incidents up country, and one of our people was injured by a grenade last spring." But in Saigon, the only real excitement was being provided at the Eden Cinema, where James Dean was scowling his way through *East of Eden*. I had flown in from Angkor Wat on a creaky, ancient Air Vietnam DC-3, and Tan Son Nhut airport beautifully keynoted Saigon's mood those days. Drowsy officials fumbled with passports, the driver of the rickety airport bus was almost impossible to awake, and the desk clerk at the Hotel Continental barely roused himself to check me in before drifting back to sleep. There were plenty of rooms at the monumental old Continental; few tourists bothered to visit Saigon in those days.

Nearly ten years later, I said a temporary farewell to Saigon on my way back to a new job in New York. But the drowsy Saigon of 1957 had long since vanished. In mid-1966, the pedicabs had been shouldered aside by taxis, the lovely women replaced by noisy whores, the sidewalk cafes made untenable by the threat of Viet Cong grenades—only the siesta prevailed, and it was brief and uneasy. Diem was gone. Terror was commonplace. Tan Son Nhut had become the world's busiest airport, and the Hotel Continental was chock-full of American soldiers and correspondents. Saigon in 1966 was a sad, sick city: it had become a war capital and a distinctly unpleasant one. And South Vietnam's pleasant, tranquil country-side was now a battlefield on which Asia's future might well be determined.

The war in Vietnam represents the most violent aspect of a Southeast Asian struggle that began far before World War II, and may well last for many more years. In this struggle are many ele-ments: anti-colonialism, nationalism, communism, and other, more basic problems: poverty, ignorance, hunger, and disease. Together, they constitute Southeast Asia's heritage, and these afflictions are compounded exponentially by common concern over the policies and intentions of China and the Chinese. The major peoples of Indochina —Vietnamese, Lao, and Khmer—were forced south from China many centuries ago by the Hans, who now rule in Peking. And China has remained a significant influence ever since, both in times of peace and times of war. Today, the bulk of the social, political, and cultural institutions of the area testify to this legacy. And this is particularly true of Vietnam.

For more than a thousand years, Vietnam was a Chinese colony. In the third century B.C., Chinese soldiers turned up in Annam, the area known today as Central Vietnam. These troops were the fore-runners of eventual Chinese conquest of Tonkin and Annam (north-ern and central Vietnam). At first, rule was indirect: in 208 B.C., when the Chin Dynasty began to disintegrate, Chinese General Chao To split off China's two southernmost provinces, Kwangtung and Kwangsi, and joined them with the newly conquered regions of Tonkin and Annam to form the kingdom of Nam Viet. In 111 B.C., however, Nam Viet was conquered by the new Chinese dynasty. And for the next 1,050 years, until 939 A.D., Annam and Tonkin were under Chinese domination—an integral part of the sprawling empire ruled from the Dragon Throne.

Down the centuries, however, the Vietnamese retained a distinct sense of their own individuality. Many aspects of Chinese culture found a place in Vietnamese life, but political oppression was steadily resisted. Vietnam's two great heroines, the Trung sisters, took their places in history as leaders of a rebellion that broke the Chinese grasp for three years—from 40 to 43 A.D. But punishment was harsh. The Trung forces were smashed and native officials, who had, up until that time, ruled on behalf of the Chinese, were replaced by Chinese administrators. There were further attempts at rebellion as well, and though they were crushed, it was made clear to the Chinese that Vietnam was not an easy country to rule, just as the French were to discover, in their turn, centuries later.

Vietnamese intractability was only part of the problem for China. Another power with designs on Annam and Tonkin ruled the area now known as southern Vietnam. This was the kingdom of Champa, a state with distinct Hindu origins, which for centuries challenged Chinese hegemony. In 605, for example, China sent a punitive expedition south to chastise the Chams for a series of attacks on Annam, as well as to force Champa to resume the tribute payments dropped 150 years before. The expedition paid off, temporarily: Champa ceased its invasion of Annam and once again paid tribute to the emperor. Then in 780, Champa marched into Annam once more, and China, ruled by the weakening Tang dynasty, was unable to hold off the invaders. In 862, Thai troops swarmed into Tonkin and sacked Hanoi the following year, while the Chams consolidated their hold on southern Annam. The Tang dynasty grew steadily weaker, and finally collapsed in 907. Another Vietnamese attempt to seize independence was inevitable; so was its success. In 939, under the leadership of Ngo Duyen, Vietnam became a sovereign state once more.

Behind them, the Chinese left a double legacy. On the one hand, the Vietnamese had been given sufficient reason to fear and mistrust their huge northern neighbor, and this fear and mistrust has lasted down to the present. On the other hand, the thousand years of Chinese occupation gave Vietnamese culture a distinctly Chinese tinge which has proved equally long-lasting. The Vietnamese language, for example, was written with Chinese characters until the seventeenth century, when European missionaries devised a romanized Vietnamese script. Chinese Buddhism took its place among Vietnamese religions, though over the centuries it has developed peculiarly Vietnamese overtones. Taoism and Confucianism planted deep roots in Vietnam, and the Chinese family system was adopted to great degree by Vietnamese. So was the system of government. The Vietnamese—as any Vietnamese will tell you—remained essentially Vietnamese throughout the long Chinese occupation, but China built the framework for Vietnamese power.

Over the next century, that power came to concentrate in Annam (the "pacified south," in Chinese). A Chinese attempt at reconquest was stopped by the Annamites in 1076, and the ever-troublesome Chams and Thais were held at arm's length. But in the thirteenth century, the situation reversed itself once again. Invading Mongol armies seized power in China, and evidence of the new dynasty's power soon became evident in the south. In 1257, Hanoi was sacked by a Mongol force, which held the city briefly before being chased out by Annamite soldiers. Three years later Kublai Khan assumed the throne in Peking and promptly sent an army south with orders to solidify Chinese power in Southeast Asia. This proved an overly optimistic design. Faced by a common foe, Annam and Champa suspended their own war to unite against the Khan. From 1281 to 1287, a succession of attacking Chinese armies was thrown back.

With the Chinese threat once again in abeyance, Champa resumed its war with Annam. No conclusive victory was won by either side, however, and in 1407 the newly installed Ming emperor intervened to end the fighting by the simple expedient of conquering Annam. This time, the Chinese occupation lasted only twenty-one years: under the command of Le Loi, the Ming troops were expelled in 1428. Le, and his successors, maintained their victorious momentum. By 1471, much of Champa had fallen to the Annamites, and over the next two hundred years Vietnamese colonists moved into the Cham areas of southern Vietnam, in the process expanding Vietnam's boundaries approximately to their location today. China continued to play a role in Vietnamese politics, however: from the sixteenth to the nineteenth century, rival claimants to the Vietnamese throne made a practice of appealing to China for recognition in an attempt to bolster their cases—recognition China was only too willing to give as a means of exerting at least a degree of control over its former vassal state. Finally, in 1803, Nguyen Anh was granted formal recognition as emperor of Vietnam by the Ching dynasty emperor in Peking, on the condition that tribute missions should be sent every two years and that homage should be paid to the Chinese emperor every four years. Thus it was with Chinese support that Vietnam was unified. But by this time another foreign power had appeared on the scene: the French, engaged in trying to outdo the British in the race to open up trade with Asia, began to look covetously at the great economic potential of Indochina.

From the earliest days of their arrival in the Indochinese peninsula, the Vietnamese dominated the other natives of the area—just as they do today. And the outcome of the war in Vietnam seems certain

to determine the future of Laos and Cambodia as well. These two nations, which emerged with Vietnam from the remnants of French
Indochina, have adopted radically different sets of responses to pressure from China. In both nations, however, the responses were largely
conditioned by the immediacies of the interaction between the French
colonial regime, on the one hand, and the Indochinese Communist
Party (ICP) on the other. Cambodia, under the leadership of Prince
Sihanouk as chief of state, chose to reach an accommodation with
Communist China. Laos found itself forced to choose between alignment with the West or disintegration into chaos. Though both Laotians
and Khmers trace their origins back to China, their responses to
modern pressures have differed widely. A glance at their respective
histories helps to explain why.

Both the Laotians of Laos and the Khmers of Cambodia moved
south from China centuries ago, in common with most other Southeast Asians. But the Laotians are linked ethnically with the Thais,
and the area known today as Laos was dominated by the Thai kings
from earliest times down through the incorporation of Laos into
French Indochina in the nineteenth century. The Khmers, however,
do in fact constitute a separate race. For many hundreds of years the
Khmer kingdom of Kambuja dominated the south and west of the
Indochinese peninsula. And at Angkor, the Khmer spirit flowered
into one of the most impressive urban complexes known in the Asian
world. Angkor, in fact, was impressive enough to have drawn praise
from Chinese travelers, whose accounts of their visits provide modern
historians with much of their information about the city and the
kingdom. But Khmers and Chinese had had more than a sufficiency
of previous contact.

The pattern of Chinese interest in the area was set as far back as
the third century B.C., as in the case of Vietnam, when Chinese soldiers
marched into the area. The Kingdom of Funan, a predecessor of the
Khmer rulers, had sent tribute to the Chinese emperors early in the
Christian era. In 484 A.D., one of the last great kings of Funan,
Jayavarman, sent a delegation to Canton to seek Chinese mili-
tary assistance against his foes. His request was refused, but
Funan traders continued to visit Canton and finally, in 503,
Jayavarman's power was confirmed by the Chinese emperor: he
was granted the title of "General of the Pacified South, King of
Funan." His successor continued to send missions to China, but
the procedure evidently stopped in 539. Funan fell into oblivion

shortly thereafter, conquered by neighboring Chenla, an early Khmer dominion. Over the next two centuries, Chenla consolidated its hold over the region, and a succession of Khmer kings contributed to the development of a distinct Khmer culture, which by the tenth century culminated in the building of Angkor. And in 1116 Suryavarman II, greatest of the Khmer kings, began a series of assaults against neighboring states which significantly increased Khmer power in the area. To the east, Champa fell under Cambodian rule, and one historian of the period reported that Cambodia's border stretched south to the sea and west to Pagan (in present-day Burma), though remaining silent on what seem to have been a largely futile series of efforts to extend Cambodian influence to the north and northeast. Suryavarman succeeded—temporarily, at least—in consolidating Khmer power, and Cambodia once again resumed relations with China. His first embassy was received in China in 1116, a second turned up in 1120 and, on the arrival of a third, the Chinese emperor conferred upon Suryavarman the title of King of Chenla. But on his death, his nation went into a decline that saw Angkor sacked and a successor king slain by invaders in 1177. Next on the throne was Jayavarman VII, who smashed rival Champa almost beyond recall shortly after he was crowned in 1181. Once again, Cambodia's borders stretched far—north to Vientiane, west into Thailand and (perhaps) Burma, south to the northern part of the Malay peninsula. And under Jayavarman came the final great burst of building at Angkor. Sadly, however, he tried to build too much too quickly, and thus his great works, such as the Bayon, have not endured as well as some of the earlier temples. Nor was he able to significantly strengthen his nation—on his death, the Khmers began a slow retreat from glory, which ended finally when Angkor was captured by the Thais in 1431.

In the intervening years, relations with China were maintained on an irregular basis. Jayavarman VII's successor had the bad taste to jail officials sent by Kublai Khan, which is understandable in light of the fact that Kublai Khan himself had made a practice of encouraging Thai attacks on the Khmers. For a time, relations improved, but the Khmers avoided too close contact with China in order to sidestep involvement in the continual fighting between troops of the Mongol dynasty and the neighboring kingdom of Annam. And with Angkor's fall to the Thais, Khmer civilization disintegrated. Today, under

Sihanouk, Cambodian efforts to revive the ancient glories have taken on the coloration of modern-day nationalism.

Laos, on the other hand, produced nothing remotely resembling the Khmer achievements. Settled by men who were close kin to the Thais of Nan-Chao (see Chapter II), Laos never amounted to much more than a collection of small fiefdoms until about 1637, when King Souligna Vongsa unified much of the present-day kingdom. But by 1707, Laos had split into two separate states, with capitals at Vientiane and Luang Prabang. The Vientiane leaders had little to do with China: their appeals for assistance went as needed to various rulers in Burma, Thailand, or Annam. Luang Prabang's King Intasom saw fit to send two embassies to China, in 1729 and 1734, but for all practical purposes both sections of Laos remained under Thai influence. In the end, it was only the accession to power in Indochina by the French that wrenched Laos from the status of a semi-autonomous Thai province.

Status as a French colony, for that matter, did little to bring either Laos or Cambodia into the modern world. French interest in Indochina centered in Annam and Tonkin—and later the southern area, which came to be known as Cochin-China. Chinese interest in the area followed a similar pattern, colored by the fact that the Ching Dynasty (which finally collapsed in 1911) entered into a period of decline by the eighteenth century which accordingly cut its interest in Southeast Asia. Trade continued, however, despite the gradual withering of political interest. And Indochina became a place of political refuge for assorted victims and losers in the power struggles back in China. The South, in particular, attracted Chinese immigrants —a trend supported by the fact that while there are an estimated eight hundred thousand Chinese in southern Vietnam today, only about fifty-five thousand live in North Vietnam. And true to the pattern elsewhere in Southeast Asia, the overseas Chinese eventually found themselves in places of heavy economic influence. (The same, it should be added, is true of Chinese residents today in Laos and Cambodia.)

The Chinese, of course, were perfectly attuned to the mood of the other newcomers to Indochina. The early nineteenth century was a time of rapidly accelerating economic interest in Asia on the part of the United States and the major European powers. The British led the way, opening up the coastal ports of China to trade and cementing their position with the treaty that followed the Opium War. By 1842, Britain forced the Ching emperor to grant it the island of Hong Kong in perpetuity, and obtained rights to trade at five coastal ports as well. France, not to be outdone, obtained similar trading rights in 1845. And in 1847, French warships seeking revenge for the slaying of a French priest clashed with four Vietnamese warships off Tourane (now Danang) and sank the lot. Gradually, French contact with Vietnam increased: in 1858, Tourane was occupied, and a year later, Saigon—at that time a relatively unimportant village—was seized to provide a base for the extension of French influence over the potentially valuable lands of the Mekong Delta. Development, however, was slow, and it was not until 1884 that France finally established a protectorate over Vietnam. In the intervening years, vacillation summed up the mood of all concerned. The Vietnamese, hoping to hold off the French, called on China for help, but China refused to act rapidly. The French, who sought access via Tonkin to the southern China market, dithered largely because of heavy opposition at home to expansion in Indochina. It was not until after Vietnam accepted—with distinct reluctance—the French protectorate that China moved. Chinese attacks on French troops in the China-Tonkin border areas were answered by punitive French attacks on Formosa and Foochow. A year later, China finally yielded the last official shreds of its "special position" in Vietnam in a Franco-Chinese treaty signed at Tientsin in June, 1885. For the next fifty years, France was to be the major foreign factor in Vietnam's history.

France's stay in Indochina thus was neither long nor, surprisingly, terribly profitable.[1] Its record as a colonial power was nothing to be proud of, but scarcely as all-encompassingly harsh and oppressive as Vietnamese communist writings indicate. And its half-century of rule in Indochina was barely under way when the man who was to bring that empire down in graceless ruin was born.

No one really knows his name, or the exact year of his birth. But the man known variously as Nguyen That Thanh, Nguyen Van Thanh, Nguyen Ai Quoc, and Ho Chi Minh stands today as one of the world's great revolutionary leaders. He was, and is, an archetypical Asian nationalist-communist. And he was the great individual dynamic that brought about the end of French rule.

Born in central Vietnam on May 19 of either 1890, 1891, or 1892 (sources vary on the year), he was the son of a minor imperial official who had strong nationalist leanings. From his father, he picked up the anti-colonialist ideals that were to guide him at the start of his career. Educated in the local school and later at high school in Hue, he found a teacher's job in Phan Thiet, then moved on to Saigon. In 1912, most sources agree, he shipped out to Europe, drifting from job to job and at one time working under the great French chef Escoffier in London's Carlton Hotel. It was at about this time, according to the late Bernard Fall in *The Two Vietnams,* that he came in contact with a Chinese-sponsored anti-colonialist organization. Somewhere around 1915 or 1916, he signed on another ship, this time for a visit to the United States, and returned to France in 1918. After a brief fling at world politics, as represented by the Versailles Peace Conference of 1919 (and on which he made no impression), he found himself increasingly involved in France's Socialist Party—but more and more attracted by communism. On December 30, 1920, he became a founding member of the French Communist Party.[2]

For the next several years, Ho shuttled between France and the Soviet Union, finally settling in Moscow in 1924 for a year of study before returning to Asia to organize a communist party in Indochina. Working out of Canton, Ho began recruiting potential cadres, sending some to Moscow for training, assigning others to the Whampoa military academy (which at that time included both Chiang Kai-shek and Chou En-lai on its staff) and teaching still others himself. Forced to return to Moscow after the Kuomintang-Communist split in 1926–27, he later traveled through Europe as a party organizer in the late twenties, then returned to Asia—this time to live for a while in the Vietnamese settlements in eastern Thailand.

During this period, Vietnamese nationalism was on the rise. A Vietnamese Nationalist Party had been formed in Canton in 1914, and a series of abortive uprisings against French rule had taken place in succeeding years. Splinter communist parties had been formed in Tonkin and Annam, but none displayed great promise. To end the intramural quarreling which had inevitably developed, Ho called a conference of Vietnamese communists in Hong Kong, and on January 6, 1930, the Indochinese Communist Party was formally created —strangely enough, in a soccer stadium. (First known as the Vietnamese Communist Party, its name was changed in October of the same year to the Indochinese Communist Party (ICP). Today, it should be added, the party's official name is the Dang Lao Dong, or Vietnamese Worker's Party.) For the next five years, Ho and the ICP both experienced difficulties: much of the ICP leadership was jailed in

Vietnam shortly after the party's founding, while Ho himself was imprisoned for six months in Hong Kong and then fled to Shanghai, from which he went on to Moscow. After more training under Comintern auspices, he returned to China in 1937, worked awhile with the Chinese Communist Eighth Route Army, then turned up in Tonkin in 1941 for an ICP central committee meeting. It was at this meeting that the Viet Minh—parent organization of today's Viet Cong—came into existence.

During World War II, Ho's trail fades. Evidently, he spent some time in a Chinese nationalist prison, was released in 1943 after promising to behave, and was allowed by the KMT warlord in Southeast China to join in what was to become the postwar government of Vietnam. According to one source, Ho managed in 1944 to convince the American OSS that he was indeed a nationalist, rather than a communist—and he accordingly received significant American help in establishing a Viet Minh government in Hanoi after the Japanese surrender in 1945.[3] This may or may not be accurate. But when the Japanese surrendered, the Viet Minh government was ready to start functioning in Hanoi—and the Viet Minh was nothing more or less than a front for the ICP. Ho had played his cards well.

There were rivals, of course. The Japanese had granted "independence" to a rickety government, led by Vietnamese emperor Bao Dai, on March 10, 1945, which had its capital in Hue. And it was clear that France had no intention of giving up its position in Indochina, though several months would necessarily elapse before the French returned in force. The Teheran and Potsdam agreements had given the British and KMT Chinese the right to accept Japanese surrenders in Indochina: China was to administer affairs north of the 16th Parallel, while British and Commonwealth forces were to take over in the south. But the Viet Minh moved fastest: on August 19 it seized control of Hanoi, and on August 25, Saigon and much of South Vietnam went under Ho's authority. Bao Dai, clearly outmaneuvered and already stigmatized as a Japanese puppet, dropped out of competition. On September 2 in Hanoi, the Viet Minh proclaimed the independence of the Democratic Republic of Vietnam (DRV).

The record of Kuomintang occupation is a sorry one. First, the Chinese Nationalist generals allowed the Viet Minh to gain a foothold in the north, which it never really lost—even after the return of the French. Then, to compound their bungling, they allowed their troops to loot and steal at will, thus ensuring that the old hatred of China and the Chinese would be well and truly reawakened. In their greed they allowed Ho's men to purchase from them a sizable stock of arms, which provided a solid base for the creation of a "people's army." To the South, the Viet Minh had much less luck with the British, who though they were largely intent on turning Saigon over to the French with a minimum of delay, managed to prevent the Viet Minh from gaining the same solid foothold they had already obtained in the north. In November, Ho dissolved—on the surface—the ICP, clearing the way for KMT-approved elections in January, 1946. The results, given the pressures of the time, were predictable: a united front government controlled behind the scenes by Ho and his fellow Communists. A month later, the KMT agreed to withdraw its army of occupation, opening the doors for the return of the French to northern Vietnam.

For a time, French and Viet Minh leaders attempted to reach an agreement. France offered tentative recognition to the Hanoi government, and Ho traveled to Paris to sign a formal treaty. But negotiations broke down, at least partly because of a series of blunders back in Vietnam by subordinates, both French and Vietnamese; and after a series of bloody incidents in Tonkin, the country was plunged into war in December, 1946. Details of the fighting have been set down elsewhere,[4] and it is pointless to repeat them once again. Summed up, the war was a tragedy for both sides. France fought to retain a colony it had effectively lost long before, and the cost, in money, talent, and lives, was enormous. Ho and the Viet Minh, on the other hand, at least had the satisfaction of smashing their white opponents in battle, but they lost heavily as well. Because Ho and most of his leading officials were northerners, many leading southern nationalists found themselves either fighting for the French or at the very least playing a passive role, and thus communist hopes of bringing all nationalists together under the Viet Minh banner were shattered by the endemic regionalism that still plagues the nation. More than this, the Geneva Accords of 1954 split Indochina into a series of weak and fragmentary states. North Vietnam lost the agricultural resources of the south, which were—and are—vitally important to its economy. It lost its first and perhaps only chance to unite all Indochina under its rule, when Laos and Cambodia came into full existence. South Vietnam was left with little to work with: politically, Cochin-China under the French had been the least developed of the three Vietnamese regions, and there was little top leadership talent available. Because industrial development had been concentrated in Tonkin, there was little beyond agriculture to sustain the economy. And while North Vietnam had at least a viable, well-trained army, South Vietnam had little with which to defend itself. Laos in 1954 should have been placed under mandate: almost completely without a national tradition or nationalistic leaders, with only a primitive economy, Laos badly needed expert guidance. Only for Cambodia were there advantages in Geneva's ratification of its independence. Blessed by a reasonably able leader, a national tradition, and a functioning, though unsophisticated, economy, Cambodia has managed to survive reasonably well.

Ho, it seems clear, expected South Vietnam to fall into his hands quickly and painlessly. Bolstered by the Geneva promise of nation-wide elections and certain that *any* South Vietnamese leader would fail to solve the massive problems of the infant nation, Ho seems now to have sat back and simply waited—though he was cynical enough to ensure that a sizable cadre of Viet Minh remained behind in the south after the bulk of the guerrillas were repatriated to Hanoi. For once, however, events failed to go his way.

Out of nowhere, almost literally, appeared a chunky, stolid little man named Ngo Dinh Diem. Son of a respected Mandarin who served the imperial court at Hue, brother of a leading nationalist slain by the Viet Minh in the purge of recalcitrant nationalists in 1946, Diem had served briefly under the figurehead emperor Bao Dai as minister of the interior back in the thirties, and had built up a respectable administrative record. But Diem was as anti-French as Ho and the Viet Minh leaders, and he quit his post in protest against the rigid French control over his work. He spent the thirties and early forties as a scholarly recluse, refusing offers of posts under the Japanese. In 1945, he turned down a similar offer from Ho, then resumed active politicking after the lapse of more than a decade by working for the return to power of Bao Dai. But his efforts failed, and Diem dropped politics once more. In 1950, he visited the United States briefly, then returned in 1951 for a longer stay. Soon adopted as a protégé by, among others, New York's Francis Cardinal Spellman, Diem made a deep impression on several high-ranking Americans. In 1953, after a series of speeches in the States, Diem went to Belgium and took residence in a monastery. A year later, Bao Dai asked him to return to Vietnam as his prime minister.

Wisely, in view of later events, Diem held off acceptance, arguing that the French presence in Vietnam would not allow him a free hand. But with the signing of the Franco–South Vietnamese independence accords in June, 1954, the way was clear. He returned to Saigon in late June, grimly intent on assuming full power. Backed by the French (albeit reluctantly) by the Americans, and by Bao Dai, he settled into authority with the ease of the traditional mandarin he had been all his life. The prospects he faced, however, were grim beyond description.

No one in those uneasy days expected Diem to last. The Republic of South Vietnam, it seemed obvious, had been created only to salve Western consciences—as a temporary haven for those opposed to the communists led by Ho. Saigon and much of the outlying area was under the direct control of one or another of the powerful and corrupt political-religious sects and bandits who had withstood all French attempts to bring them to heel. And the republic, clearly, was desperately short of political, economic, and military leadership.

But incredibly enough, Diem came out on top. With a combination of force and the silver bullets of bribery,[5] he crushed the private armies of the sects and underworld. Out of the wealth of his long-time nationalistic contacts, he produced enough able men to staff his government. Potential warlords among the military were whisked into exile. And in 1955, in one of the most carefully rigged elections ever held in Asia, a nationwide referendum confirmed Bao Dai's ouster by better than 98 to 1. Diem was on his way.

Over the next four years, South Vietnam prospered. In 1956, Diem rammed a constitution through the rubber-stamp national assembly and emerged as the republic's president. Prices were stable. Agricultural production increased: South Vietnam was well on the way to reestablishing itself as Asia's rice bowl, just as it had been up to 1939, and rubber production also continued to earn solid chunks of foreign exchange. The industrial sector began to blossom as well.

But in Hanoi, trouble was brewing for Diem. The Geneva Accords had provided for all-Vietnam elections in 1956. Diem, understandably unwilling to put his infant regime to the test of a popular vote, refused to participate, arguing that South Vietnam had not signed the accords. (France, in its role as the custodial power, had signed for the then-nonexistent republic.) Ho, who had counted on the peaceful accession of South Vietnam, came to realize that unification could only be achieved by conquest. Slowly, carefully, and patiently, he set his plans in motion.

On his side were some genuine assets, notably the presence in the south of hard-core Viet Minh elements that had gone underground instead of accepting transfer to the north in 1954. Beyond this was a degree of personal popularity, based on the mistaken impression Ho was more nationalist than communist. Added to all this was his enormous talent for organization, polished by years as a conspirator and proven in the war against the French. And despite Diem's very real achievements in the south, the Saigon republic shaped up as a fairly soft target.

The government of South Vietnam was solid enough to progress slowly on its own, but there were some very weak points as well. Diem never managed, for example, to make much of an impression on the peasantry: remote and cold, he was the antithesis of "Uncle Ho." His administration was staffed largely by close friends and relatives, and the key power slots were filled by members of his immediate family, notably brother Ngo Dinh Nhu, for Diem trusted no one he did not know intimately. And Diem himself simply did not compel popular allegiance—a vitally necessary element in the early development of any new nation. The Americans, who had taken over the role of supporting power from the French after the Geneva Accords, made errors of their own. Perhaps the most glaring single mistake was to build up a South Vietnamese army that was beautifully trained and equipped to fight a war of movement such as World War II—but which was almost completely ignorant of the principles of guerrilla war. (In the middle and late fifties, of course, few Americans dreamed such a war was in the offing.) And there was little or no interest in attempting to persuade Diem that a bit more warmth might help him maintain his rule: on the surface, things looked rosy enough. True, there was the problem of terrorists, but until 1959 this was dismissed as largely the work of "bandits."

By 1959, however, the rosy tinge had begun to take on the color of blood. The incident rate shot up alarmingly, and along the Rue Catinat the eternally disaffected liberals and intellectuals increased their criticism of Diem's autocratic rule. To counter the terrorists, Diem instituted the first of several equally luckless programs aimed at bringing increased security to the countryside. This was the *agroville* project, which was intended to create secure nuclei of government control in the rural areas. The first, at Vi Thanh, was completed by March, 1960, and more than a dozen more were established by the fall. On the face of it, the *agrovilles* seemed a good idea: hopefully, the peasants would flock into these islands of security, emerging by day to work their fields while their families would profit by the schools, markets, and medical facilities near their home. Best of all, the *agrovilles* would shield the peasantry from contact with the communists. But the peasants proved distinctly unready to abandon fields their families had tended for generations, and the clumsy attempts at forced relocation worked in favor of the Viet Cong. At the same time, the number of terrorist incidents had begun to rise alarmingly.

In 1960, for example, an estimated twelve hundred civilians and sixteen hundred policemen and soldiers had been killed by the VC—clear evidence that governmental security was poor. And disaffection was rising in Saigon as well. In November, 1960, dissident paratroop officers mounted an abortive coup d'etat and for thirty-six hours held Diem captive in the presidential palace. But the coup failed, largely because the bulk of the army and civilian opposition leaders as well failed to rise in its support. Loyal troops, in fact, finally crushed the revolt. Diem, cold and unflappable, rode out the storm, finally winning his release by pledging that the coupmakers would not be punished. Incredibly enough, he was believed, and the coup leaders promptly paid the price for their credulity in prisons or in exile. And in April, 1961, Diem staged another of his patented "elections," which saw him returned to the presidency with 88 percent of the votes.

Six months later I returned to Saigon after nearly four years' absence. The city had changed: a gloss of prosperity now lacquered over the still-evident charm. Tiny blue-and-white Renault taxis had begun to replace the pedicabs, motorscooters were everywhere, and the hotels were bustling. Along Rue Catinat, crewcut Americans conspicuously ill at ease in sportshirts and slacks mingled with the crowds. But the restaurants were as superb as ever, and the girls as lovely. And talk was still free in the sidewalk cafes: "Diem is a monster," a university teacher told me, "and his brother is worse." Terrorism was on the rise: in November, 1961, alone, the Saigon government admitted a total of 1,195 soldiers killed, wounded, or missing. (In May, the losses had been half that total.) And American interest had deepened. Vice President Lyndon Johnson had bustled through, pausing long enough to hail Diem as "the Churchill of Asia," and he was followed by retired Gen. Maxwell Taylor, sent out by President John F. Kennedy for a complete and thoughtful appraisal of the situation.

From Taylor's recommendations, and others as well, Washington decided that South Vietnam's fight for continuing independence was viable. More weapons, more helicopters and strike aircraft, and more American advisers, were to be the answer to Viet Cong subversion. From this point on, the United States was irrevocably committed to the support of South Vietnam—and to Ngo Dinh Diem in the bargain. It was apparent to most Americans in Vietnam at the time that substantial government reform was necessary, but it was equally apparent to Diem that American officials had lost their leverage. And when U.S. Ambassador Frederick E. Nolting, Jr., attempted to press the urgency of reforms on Diem, in the course of November negotiations over the form of the increased aid, Diem blew up. In the captive Saigon press, notably the English-language *Times of Vietnam,* angry bursts of vituperation appeared, assailing this interference in the affairs of a sovereign country. In what was evidently an attempt to avoid a direct attack on Washington, the *TVN* singled out Robert Trumbull, the capable Southeast Asian bureau chief for *The New York Times* at that time, and assailed him for reporting what it called "the gossip of the Rue Catinat" instead of making a "reasonable and intelligent evaluation of the situation." But buried well down in the article was a key sentence: "Preservation of the national integrity at this juncture in Vietnam requires certain controls which a nation at peace with her neighbors can afford to fear but which a nation at war cannot afford to forget." It was the traditional excuse of a dictatorship, which in fact the Diem regime long since had become.

Over the next few weeks, before heading over to Cambodia, I dug deeper into Vietnam's problems. The political disaffection was obvious, and equally apparent was the futile attempt by American Embassy spokesmen to present Diem as the only possible savior for South Vietnam. Privately, several diplomats had severe reservations, and it was one of these contacts who summed up the American position as "Sink or Swim With Ngo Dinh Diem." The American commitment was absolute and complete by the late fall of 1961, and it was clear that no amount of criticism, from whatever source, would change it. But the longer I stayed in Vietnam, the more apparent the shakiness of the regime became.

Late in November, for example, I flew to Pleiku in the Central Highlands with Richard Hughes of London's *Sunday Times.* At that time, Diem was making enormous efforts to rally the Montagnards of the Highlands to the government's cause, and both Hughes and I were deeply interested in his progress. It was clear that success in persuading the Montagnards—non-Vietnamese tribesmen boasting a Stone Age culture at best and living athwart the Viet Cong infiltration routes into the south—could be of enormous significance in clamping down on the flow of arms and men to the enemy. We were shown Montagnards, of course, moving in smooth bronze columns into government sanctuaries. But from our Vietnamese escorting officers, we perceived a deep scorn for the tribesmen. Traditionally, the Vietnamese have had little to do with the Montagnards; and even today there are few Vietnamese living in the Highlands. Diem himself, who prided himself on his ability to manage the Montagnards, regarded them as "moi" (savages). To me, the attempt to win Montagnard allegiance seemed halfhearted at best. And that halfheartedness was beautifully representative of the situation as a whole: Diem and Nhu seemed to feel that speeches produced realities, and that follow-through was unnecessary.

In Hanoi, the opposite was true. And by late 1961, Hanoi's cadres were flowing steadily into South Vietnam under the aegis of the Mat Tran Dan Toc Giai Phong Mien Nam Viet Nam, better known as the National Front for the Liberation of South Vietnam. It was founded on December 20, 1960, and most of its key men were southern communists who'd gone north after the 1954 accords. From its very beginnings the National Liberation Front (NLF) was an effective weapon. "It was an organizational steamroller," says one source, "nationally conceived and nationally organized, endowed with ample cadres and funds, crashing out of the jungle to flatten the GVN."[6] In many ways, it was a typical "popular front," including within its ranks not only hard-core Viet Minh Communists but also peasant leaders, Cao Dai and Hoa Hao sect members, students, politicians, and Montagnards. Their common denominator was a hatred for Diem, who as early as 1959 had succeeded in alienating a fatal proportion of the people he ruled. And for each group of the alienated there was a receptive organization within the Liberation Front: the Farmers' Liberation Association, for instance, was paralleled by similar units for women, workers, youth, students, cultural workers, Buddhists, teachers . . . the list goes on and on. At the heart of the Front was the People's Revolutionary Party (PRP), the equivalent of Ho's Lao Dong Party in the north. Officially, the PRP came into existence in January, 1962; in reality, it is simply the renamed southern wing of the Lao Dong, and it has made no secret of its standing as *primus inter pares* within the Front. In statement after statement, it has called itself the "vanguard of the NLF, the paramount member."[7] Nor has it made any secret of its communist nature, before or after 1962. And Lao Dong party documents give a clear picture of the NLF's origins. In January, 1960, for example, North Vietnam's defense minister Vo Nguyen Giap declared: "The North has become a large rear echelon of our army. The North is the revolutionary base for the whole country."[8] In September, 1960, at the third congress of the Lao Dong Party in Hanoi, a party resolution proclaimed: "To ensure the complete success of the revolutionary struggle in South Vietnam, our people there must strive to establish a united bloc of workers, peasants, and soldiers to bring into being a broad united front . . ."[9] It seems something less than coincidental that the NLF came into existence only three months later.

Throughout 1961 and 1962, the NLF built up its organization across South Vietnam. Terrorism—on both sides—became commonplace. But while Diem's forces pressed ahead with largely pointless military exercises against the Viet Cong,[10] the NLF concentrated its efforts on teachers, village leaders, and police, with a single deadly aim: to eliminate South Vietnam's political infrastructure and replace it with one of its own. By mid-1962, the efforts were beginning to pay off: the NLF dominated an estimated 60 percent of South Vietnam's land area, and about one-third of the population.

In Saigon, Diem himself was beginning to show the strains of his long struggle, despite the fact that he had won, for the time being, his long battle for major increases in American aid. Close friends reported in late 1962 that he no longer had the remarkable stamina of earlier years, that he was quick to lose his temper and equally quick to mistrust subordinates. In February, 1962, two young Vietnamese Air Force fliers bombed his official residence, and though Diem and the Nhus survived, they were severely shaken. Despite this evidence of Diem's growing unpopularity—and there was much, much more data available along these lines—Washington continued its all-out support. U.S. Ambassador Nolting, and most of the senior embassy officials, made no secret of their distaste for journalists who hinted Diem was something less than perfect. And General Paul D. Harkins, who arrived in Saigon in 1962 to head the U.S. military mission, was equally enthusiastic about Diem. By November, 1962, there were ten thousand American soldiers in Vietnam—a clear violation of the Geneva Accords, and one which earned the U.S. the criticism of the

International Control Commission (ICC). But by this time, the ICC was largely ineffectual: both North and South Vietnam had generated so many violations of the accords that the ICC was reduced to producing reports which were interesting reading but carried no weight. For South Vietnam, 1962 marked the end of the prologue to war. But for Laos, it was a much better year: a settlement seemed at hand.

That June, as the Vietnam war continued its slow but steady escalation, the three warring Lao factions (Pathet Lao, neutralist, and right-wing) reached agreement on a coalition government. It was a considerable achievement, for the fighting, though small in scale, had seemed almost literally unendable. Through no fault of its own, Laos by 1962 had become a place of East-West confrontation. And the left-wing Pathet Lao, aided by North Vietnam, the Soviet Union, and Communist China, had made alarming gains.

In 1962, however, after the vital North Vietnamese supply routes to the south had been secured, the Pathet Lao momentum slowed. The mildly pro-Western right-wingers managed to cling to the Mekong banks, which constitute the only areas of particular agricultural value in the country, and on which the bulk of the population resided. With the opposing forces at a standstill, the time was ripe for settlement. And a month after the Pathet Lao, the rightists, and the neutralists had agreed on the form of a national government, the Fourteen-Nation Conference on Laos agreed at Geneva on accords guaranteeing the neutrality of the tiny, landlocked country. Though the post-62 years were to produce a fair share of problems for the Vientiane government, Laos since has staggered along free of the enormous problems that plague South Vietnam. And that is, beyond doubt, a considerable achievement.

It becomes even more impressive once it is realized that Laos, as a nation, barely exists. In late 1966, for example, there were two, or perhaps three, governments and 1.8 (or perhaps 2.5) million people, only about half of which are ethnic Lao. There are more Lao in Thailand (7 million) than in Laos. The Vientiane government of Prime Minister Prince Souvanna Phouma controlled at best 30 percent of the territorial area—though in population terms Vientiane rules about 70 percent of Laos. The history of Laos over the past decades explains many of the country's problems—but offers little in the way of solutions.

The kingdom of Laos we know today took shape late in the

nineteenth century as the French pushed westward from their bases in Tonkin and Annam. In 1893, Thailand renounced its claims to all territory on the left bank of the Mekong, and in a series of decrees put forth by the French in 1897–99, Laos was incorporated into the Indochinese Union—a grouping which also included Cochin-China, Annam, Tonkin, and Cambodia. In 1899, a French chief resident was assigned to Vientiane, and under him province commissioners ruled. The old kingdom of Luang Prabang retained much of its identity, but southern Laos was governed wholly by the French. Under French administration, Laos enjoyed stability but not much else—there was little interest in development. (By 1945, for example, only 1 percent of the population was receiving elementary education, and only 200 Lao were enrolled in secondary schools.) Political development, unsurprisingly, was almost nil; the educated Lao constituted a tiny minority and, with only a few exceptions, showed little interest in such intangibles as independence. Laos remained isolated, a dreamy world governed by Frenchmen charmed by the people and their way of life, just as it had been for decades.

World War II, inevitably, changed all this. By July, 1941, Japanese occupation troops moved into Laos, and Thailand, reviving its once-relinquished territorial claims, annexed (with Japanese approval) part of the province of Champassak and all of Sayaboury. Until early 1945, the French continued to rule in Laos. In April, however, the Japanese took over and pressured King Sisavang Vong into declaring his kingdom independent, a declaration he retracted in August, after the Japanese surrender.

In effect, however, the seeds of Lao independence had already taken root. Four years before, the Lao Issara (Free Laos) movement had been formed, under the leadership of Prince Phetsarath, a leading member of the royal house of Luang Prabang. Phetsarath himself was an able, dedicated man, and working closely with him were two men who matched his qualities. They were Princes Souvanna Phouma and Souphanouvong, half-brothers, who went on to play pivotal roles in the events of the next decades. Late in 1945, dismayed by the vacillation of the king, Phetsarath proclaimed all Laos unified as an independent kingdom. For the next several months, aided by Chinese occupation authorities, the Lao Issara dominated the country's politics, but in the spring of 1946, with the withdrawal of the Chinese forces, French troops fought their way north and seized Vientiane on April 24. For Phetsarath, it was the end: he and the other Lao Issara leaders took refuge in Thailand. For his organization, however, it was only the beginning.

Once back in control, the French found themselves making a series of gestures that only added impetus to the idea of Laotian independence. In an agreement signed in August, 1946, France acknowledged Laos as a racial and cultural entity, under the leadership of the Luang Prabang dynasty. A constituent assembly produced a constitution in December, 1946, and three years later Laos was recognized as an independent state, with certain qualifications. In 1953, as the French position crumbled in Tonkin under the assault of the Viet Minh, France granted full independence to Laos.

The Lao Issara, during this period, went through an evolution of its own. With strong encouragement from the Thai government, then headed by Pridi Panamyong, a Lao Issara government was set up in Bangkok, headed by Prince Phetsarath. But as is all too often the case with exile governments, the Lao Issara split, and Souphanouvong emerged as leader of the left wing. By 1949, the Thai enthusiasm cooled, at least partly because Pridi had been deposed, and conservatives within the Lao Issara decided the qualified independence granted Laos in 1949 was sufficient reason to return home. Souvanna himself took office in 1950, after the right-wing prince, Boun Oum, stepped down as prime minister. Phetsarath, founder of the Lao Issara, deferred his return to Vientiane until 1957. He died two years later, his active role in politics long finished.

Souphanouvong, however, refused to join the new government. In 1949, he had been dropped from the government-in-exile for demanding closer cooperation with the Viet Minh against the French, and with the dissolution of the Lao Issara in 1950, he moved on to Vietnam, then to Communist China. With the help of Vietnamese communists, he formed a resistance government, with himself as prime minister and foreign minister, and in late 1951 moved his forces—a few Lao and many Viet Minh—across the border into Laos, scattering the royal troops with ridiculous ease. In April, 1953, after French troops had helped stop his invasion, Souphanouvong set up his capital in Sam Neua, capital of the northeast province of the same name. And as the fighting in Vietnam moved toward a climax, Souphanouvong's Pathet Lao (Land of Lao) troops tightened their grip on the northeast.

The 1954 Geneva Accord put an end to the fighting in Laos as well as in Vietnam. Under its terms, the Pathet Lao was allowed to continue to control Sam Neua and Phong Saly pending a political settlement—a settlement which was not reached until 1957. During the intervening three years, the Pathet Lao continued to build its strength, aided both by Ho Chi Minh's Hanoi government and the Chinese communists in Peking. Under the 1957 settlement, control over the northeast provinces was restored to the royal government, and the Pathet Lao armed forces were to be integrated into the national army. But it became painfully clear almost instantly that Souphanouvong had no intention of keeping his promises.

The coalition government formed in November, 1957, as a result of the agreements, proved equally chimerical. Souphanouvong and the Pathet Lao—or Neo Lao Hak Xat, as the left-wing force had renamed itself—were awarded four governmental portfolios in the government, which was headed by Souvanna Phouma, and in the elections of May, 1958, the NLHX picked up 40 percent of the vote, largely because Souvanna's variegated supporters failed to organize themselves. Souvanna resigned within a month, and the successor government excluded the NLHX—a move that produced a perfectly understandable increase in anti-government "incidents" by the Pathet Lao and led eventually to the defection, in May, 1959, of half of one of the two supposedly integrated Pathet Lao battalions. In Vientiane, Souphanouvong was immediately jailed.

From that point on, the situation worsened almost automatically. Control of Sam Neua and Phong Saly went back into Pathet Lao hands, and the Vientiane government, in desperation, called for United Nations help in turning back what it called armed Pathet Lao attacks, supported by North Vietnamese troops, on the isolated government posts in the area. From both Hanoi and Peking came shrill cries aimed at keeping the UN out of Laos, and a brief lull in the fighting ensued. But it lasted for only a few weeks—and the dramatic November visit of UN Secretary-General Dag Hammarskjold did little to damp down the fires. Vientiane's civilian government floundered helplessly, and the inevitable happened: on December 31, 1959, the army took control, pending new elections.

The army takeover, as it turned out, lasted only a few days. But it was important for two reasons: first, the army thus received its first taste of power—a taste it was to satisfy later with more determination. Second, it marked the emergence of General Phoumi Nosavan, who was to play a key role in the events of the next several years. Phoumi, a graduate of the French War College, was a strangely flabby little man at first glance, and the heavily accented French he poured forth at machine-gun speed was almost impossible to understand. But first glances can be deceiving: Phoumi was a tough, clever, and determined officer—and he had, in those days, the enthusiastic backing of the CIA. In the sleepy political climate of Vientiane, even *one* of these assets makes a man stand out clearly. And when the generals, under heavy pressure from the British and French ambassadors, returned power to the civilians early in January, 1960, Phoumi emerged as defense minister—the only officer to stay in power.

The civilian government that emerged, under the leadership of the aging Kou Abhay, was committed to the staging of general elections that spring. But when polling day rolled around in April, 1960, what resulted was one of the phoniest elections in history. Frightened by the proven power of the NLHX to organize voters, the government went all out to purchase victory: strong Pathet Lao candidates were gerrymandered out of the picture, others were forced to drop out by clever redrafting of candidate qualifications. Civil servants and soldiers were ordered to vote for government candidates or face the loss of their jobs. And to sew things up completely, some sources report, CIA agents handed out large sums of money to village leaders. It goes without saying that the government candidates won; in Sam Neua, a Pathet Lao bastion, the NLHX candidate got 13 votes to his government opponent's 6,508. As one old Vientiane hand commented, "it was proof positive that the West can stage-manage an election just as efficiently as the communists can."[11] To no one's surprise, Phoumi emerged as deputy premier and defense minister in the new government. Souphanouvong, all hopes of further collaboration with Souvanna ended, walked out of detention and kept right on going, turning up in Sam Neua five months later after a three-hundred-mile hike.

By that time, however, the politicking in Vientiane had taken a new and totally unexpected turn. In August, a tiny little captain named Kong Le, backed by a battalion of paratroopers, had seized power in Vientiane with absurd ease. His aim was clear—an end to all "foreign interference" in Lao affairs. And the foreigners most directly confronted were the Americans, notably the U.S. Army military men and agents who were trying, without much luck, to turn the royal army into a force capable of opposing the Pathet Lao. Kong Le was not a communist. But he was indeed a nationalist, and an effective one. "I am tired of seeing Lao fight Lao," he announced, and to lead the political side of his crusade he called on Souvanna, back from a term as ambassador in Paris. With this backing, a new government came into power, headed by Souvanna and including, for a few days, Phoumi Nosavan.

Phoumi, however, rapidly developed second thoughts: he flew off to the southern capital of Savannakhet and formed an anti-coup committee, dedicated to the new government's overthrow. Attempts by Souvanna to arrange a settlement came to nothing: Phoumi began to build up his strength, enlisting the aid of Prince Boun Oum, the southern kingpin. And the Pathet Lao, quick to take advantage of Souvanna's weakness, edged back into the political picture, calling for a resumption of negotiations on the question of their participation in Souvanna's government.

Throughout the fall, a series of polarizations occurred. The Americans early in the game decided Phoumi was the best bet against the communists and began making this clear by word and deed. The Pathet Lao gradually convinced Kong Le—who was not notably sophisticated—that they were true Lao patriots with only Souvanna's best interests at heart. Souvanna himself, faced by Phoumi's growing strength, edged closer to the Pathet Lao, thus further distressing the Americans. Meanwhile, the Russians, who had just opened an embassy in Vientiane, began shipping fuel and weapons to Kong Le's troops in Vientiane. Across Laos, a series of military actions flared. And Souvanna, early in December, finally realized there was no way out: on December 9, he turned over power to his army commander and flew to exile in Cambodia. Four days later, the Battle of Vientiane erupted.

From December 13 to 16, Kong Le's troops battled the forces of Phoumi, led by General Kouprasith Abhay. It was, from the beginning, an unequal battle—Kong Le's forces were outnumbered and outgunned. And finally, they withdrew, clearing the way for the assumption of power by Phoumi and Boun Oum. Early in January, 1961, Boun Oum took over as prime minister, with Phoumi as deputy premier and defense minister once again. Kong Le, now allied with the Pathet Lao, moved into control of the strategic Plaine des Jarres some 100 miles northeast of Vientiane, well supplied by a Soviet airlift of material from Hanoi.

Souvanna's next move was clear. In February, 1961, he flew from the Cambodian capital of Phnom Penh to Khang Khay on the Plaine, where he was greeted by Kong Le and the three pro–Pathet Lao ministers of his last government. The third Lao capital began to function. Khang Khay, by several accounts, was a place of bright optimism: around Kong Le had rallied the brightest and hardest-working of the Lao youth, and the town's mood was far more cheerful than that of Vientiane. But there was a dark side as well. Dour Pathet Lao troops were everywhere, and there were reliable reports that North Vietnamese regulars had begun to move across the border and down toward the Plaine.

Against this sort of opposition, Phoumi's plans to retake the Plaine began to look more and more hopeless. That spring, the left-wing forces mounted a major offensive that forced Vientiane's troops back at every encounter. It is sad but true that Lao troops fear Vietnamese soldiers almost as much as they fear the ghosts and demons that still live today in Lao folk tales. And the mere report that Vietnamese regulars were across the next hill was enough to send a royal unit flying. As Phoumi's men fell back, a stream of alarmed reports began flowing to Washington. For President John F. Kennedy, freshly installed in office and deeply occupied with the Bay of Pigs preparations, it was an unwelcome—and perturbing—situation. Kennedy's solution was to employ the classic tactic of carrot and stick. On one hand, he made it clear that the U.S. wanted "a truly neutral government" in Laos, "not a cold-war pawn." Through diplomatic channels, the message was pressed on Khrushchev, in the certain knowledge he would pass the word on to Hanoi and Peking. On the other hand, he quietly ordered all preparations made for the landing of American troops in the area. Kennedy's message got through: on May 3, 1961, a general cease-fire went into effect, and the struggle for Laos shifted into the political arena.

First at Ban Namone, in Laos, and then in May at Geneva, the talks went on. Ominously, the fighting continued, though on a much-reduced scale. After a long siege, the Pathet Lao overran a pro-Western strongpoint at Padong, near the Plaine des Jarres. In late May, two Air America[12] helicopters were downed, killing two; aboard one ship was NBC cameraman Grant Wolfkill, who was taken prisoner by the Pathet Lao.[13] At Geneva, proceedings opened on a sour note for the Americans—over their strong protests, a Pathet Lao delegation was seated, to the applause of the North Vietnamese and Chinese representatives. After a month featuring a conspicuous lack of progress, the first break occurred: Souvanna, Souphanouvong, and Boun Oum, meeting separately at Zurich, reached general agreement on the form of a new coalition. From then on through the end of the year, however, no progress was made: the principals themselves returned to Laos, and prospects were bleak.

Early in 1962, the Pathet Lao began mounting another offensive, this one aimed at Nam Tha, in the northwest. More specifically it was aimed at Phoumi, whose reluctance to agree to a coalition government had become a major stumbling block to a settlement. Phoumi crumbled first: in March, it was made perfectly clear by the United States that any more foot-dragging was totally unwelcome, and Phoumi began to cave in. In May, his troops were routed at Nam Tha by Pathet Lao and North Vietnamese forces. There was no follow-up; none was really necessary. In June, the three princes conferred once again, this time on the Plaine des Jarres. On June 11, final agreement was reached on the coalition: Souvanna was to become prime minister, Phoumi and Souphanouvong his deputies, and Boun Oum retired from politics. Both deputy prime ministers retained veto power—a power that quickly won for the so-called Government of National Union its "troika" nickname. The cabinet, of course, was carefully divided between neutralists, leftists, and right-wingers. American reaction was split: although Averell Harriman, with full backing from Kennedy, played a key role in bringing about the agreement, there were skeptics who were sure Laos would be totally communist-controlled within six months. With this latter group, the Chinese seemed to agree: Radio Peking called the settlement "a heavy blow to the aggressive policy of U.S. imperialism," although the same commentator urged "sharp vigilance" against the possibility of further American deviltry. In late July, the fourteen Geneva nations signed the official protocol. Laos was "neutralized" from this point onward, or so said the optimists.

For the rest of 1962, Souvanna struggled with his unwieldy troika. After a fashion, it did in fact provide a degree of stability, and certainly the possibility of total political collapse receded into the middle distance. Vientiane lapsed into torpidity: when I first visited the capital in early 1963, shabby pedicabs monopolized the dusty streets, and the few autos barely ran, hammered into decrepitude as they were by the torture-track roads. Scabby mongrels sprawled everywhere: outside the town's one active bar, squads of half-clad shoeshine boys fought to tear shoes from unwary drinkers. Vientiane truly was, as I reported then, a sort of Miltown-on-the-Mekong. And Souvanna, for all his ability, was getting nowhere in his efforts to bring the Geneva promises to fruition. Essentially, these aims were national reunification, the evacuation of foreign troops, elimination of foreign interference, and the establishment of neutrality. In every area, however, his efforts were stymied by the Pathet Lao. Souphanouvong's forces clung to their hold on the northwest, at least five thousand North Vietnamese troops remained in Laos although all Americans had left, southeast Laos was still used by North Vietnam to supply the Viet Cong in South Vietnam, and Communist China was moving into the far northern borderlands.

More immediately dangerous, the Pathet Lao, in early 1962, embarked on a campaign to subvert the neutralist troops on the Plaine. In mid-February, PL guns cut down Colonel Ketsana Vongsanavan, Kong Le's chief of staff, as he was obeying nature's call behind his house on the Plaine. Kong Le, mutual friends told me, was deeply angered, but there was little he could do: his six thousand troops on the Plaine were surrounded by PL artillery and soldiers. Silver bullets eliminated another Kong Le aide. Colonel Deaune Sisovath, convinced by the Pathet Lao that he should have Ketsana's job, was coldly turned down and went over to Souphanouvong, accepting a healthy payoff in the process. Neutralist troops, dependent on supplies flown to the Plaine by Soviet aircraft, were beginning to have trouble obtaining food. Kong Le himself, after a period of trying to cooperate with the Pathet Lao, finally began to speak out on his problems. "Physically they are Lao," he charged in December, "but their spirit is foreign. They follow the policy of foreigners." In Laos, this is very nearly the supreme insult.

As the splits widened, the story of Chinese activity in northern Laos finally surfaced. Under agreements signed by Souvanna and the Chinese in January, 1962, the Peking government agreed to build a road linking the town of Phong Saly and Nam Tha—a necessary link, for Phong Saly at the time was completely cut off from the rest of the country by mountains and jungle. Instead, the Chinese proceeded to link Phong Saly with Meng La, in China's Yunnan Province. Then came word of two more Chinese roads in the area, one from Meng La to Nam Tha, in Laos; the second from China's Mang Meng to Muong Sing in Laos. From the two Lao towns, passable roads link northern Laos to Ban Houei Sai on the Thai border. Clearly, the roads might well hold interesting military significance—and Western intelligence sources in Vientiane had no qualms at all about telling reporters there was trouble ahead. China, of course, labeled such reports "ravings" and "sheer fabrication." The United States, shrilled *People's Daily,* "aims to disrupt the unity of the Lao patriotic forces and create confusion in Laos." All in all, it was an illuminating first trip, and a Lao friend summed it all up for me as we flew south to Bangkok: "We have a government which doesn't govern, an army which doesn't fight. The Pathet Lao wants to imprison us all, and our future is uncertain. But at least we have peace, and for this blessing we are grateful."

Two months later, the "peace" he spoke of began to unravel. Early in April, Foreign Minister Quinim Pholsena was assassinated by a neutralist guard at his villa in Vientiane. Originally regarded as a close friend of Souvanna's, Quinim in the months since the 1962 settlement had moved sharply closer to the Pathet Lao. Officially, the murderer was labeled "mentally unstable"—and no more satisfactory solution has yet been offered. Two weeks later, Police Colonel Kanthi Sisoupanthong was shot dead in Vientiane. A close friend of Quinim's, he also was known to be pro–Pathet Lao. For Souphanouvong, this was enough: he fled Vientiane for Khang Khay.

Simultaneously, Kong Le's military situation on the Plaine des Jarres began to deteriorate. After a series of incidents, compounded by the defection of more neutralist troops to Colonel Deaune, the tension between Kong Le's forces and the Pathet Lao produced several small but bitter firefights, and Kong Le pulled his forces back into the western third of the Plaine. The fighting continued, however, and Kong Le came under increasingly severe pressure, particularly because by now the North Vietnamese contingent on the Plaine had expanded significantly.

In Peking, the reasons for the new outburst of trouble were clear: "The Kennedy administration is the chief culprit provoking the armed conflicts among the Lao . . . trying deliberately to subvert the Lao Government of National Union." For the Soviet Union, however, it was a different story: disgusted with the failures of Asians to behave as ordered, the Russians finally gave up any pretense of caring what happened. In mid-May, Moscow withdrew Soviet airlift pilots and mechanics from Laos, lamely explaining that "if we continued to help only one faction, we may be accused of interfering in Laos' internal affairs."[14] The truth of the matter seemed to be, however, that the North Vietnamese, under Chinese pressure, simply told the Russians their services were no longer needed—and the

Russians were perfectly ready to leave. "I believe," a senior Western ambassador told me in June, "that the Russians sincerely hoped things would go well after the 1962 agreements were signed." Less than a year later, the Soviet Union seemed thoroughly disabused of such expectations. Perhaps the most succinct symbol of the Russian position was the big black bear that dwelt behind Vientiane's Settha Palace Hotel in those days: he was big and black, his claws were powerful, and he seemed strong—but he was in a cage.

When I returned to Vientiane in June, nothing seemed to have changed, despite the growing crisis on the Plaine. The same two smiling elves unloaded baggage from our plane at Wattay Airport in the usual ninety minutes, and the same polite customs officials raised eyebrows at Western impatience. (By this time, I had discovered that the quickest way out was to unload my own baggage and take it directly to the car, thus bypassing all officials concerned. No one seemed to mind.) At the Hotel Constellation, there was the usual warm welcome from Maurice Cavallerie, Vientiane's one indispensable man, who could—and would—arrange nearly everything. Few correspondents were in town, but the Constellation Bar was still roaring every evening: "You could do worse," a friend once told me before I flew off to Laos for the first time, "than simply sit at the front table on the right and just listen for a week." The Constellation was a combination of "21," Bleeck's, and Toots Shor's—diplomats, correspondents, spies, Air America pilots, government advisers, and whores all made it a point to stop in before supper. And sure enough, Maurice had something helpful to tell me this time.

Souvanna, it turned out, was giving a press conference just down the road. And for the first time, in stark contrast to his usual caution, he was speaking out forcefully against the Pathet Lao and the North Vietnamese. Accusing Souphanouvong of producing "completely false propaganda and systematically deforming the facts," he declared that the NLHX might well tell the co-presidents of the Geneva Accords (Britain and the USSR) "of the unarguable presence of North Vietnamese troops in Pathet Lao areas. The information given by refugees and our troops is formal on this subject. These are not Lao soldiers." That statement, made on June 6, 1963, was a watershed in Lao politics: from that point onward, Souvanna's ideas of neutralism began to die. "Souvanna had hoped Souphanouvong could eventually be persuaded to work with him," a high-ranking American diplomat told me. "There was a genuine fondness between them; they are half-brothers and very close. But it's obvious now that Souvanna has become very discouraged."

Up on the Plaine, Kong Le's troops were in increasingly serious trouble. Once supplied by the Soviet airlift from Hanoi, the neutralist forces had come to depend more and more on U.S. material flown in by planes of the Royal Lao Air Force. The monsoon was threatening to break any day, which would cut air supplies sharply. Beyond this, Pathet Lao artillery (manned by expert North Vietnamese gunners) commanded Kong Le's sole airstrip. Unsurprisingly, neutralist morale was low.

Phoumi, in contrast, was sitting pretty. Souvanna's problems meant little to him: "He can afford to wait," a senior British diplomat said. "There's no reason for him to attempt a coup now." It seemed reasonably certain that Phoumi would slide into the prime-ministership if Souvanna decided to quit—and Phoumi was well aware of the possibility. For the third member of the triumvirate, life was growing increasingly more difficult: Souphanouvong retained his chairmanship of the NLHX, but Western intelligence sources were increasingly certain that real power was held by two others. They were Nouhak Phoumsavan, a sharp-featured, sharp-witted former shopkeeper who had belonged to the old Indochinese Communist Party; and Kaysone Phomvihan, half-Vietnamese and half-Lao, the leading Lao communist. Both men were members of the North Vietnamese Lao Dong (Workers') Party, and were almost certainly running the NLHX on Hanoi's behalf. Souphanouvong was becoming little more than a figurehead.

In mid-1963, though few observers in Vientiane seemed to realize it at the time, a major polarization had begun: Souvanna and the neutralists were moving to the right, forced in that direction by the intransigent policies of the Pathet Lao. And as Souvanna shifted his ground, the basis of the coalition government—leftists, neutralists and rightists—began to vanish. Slowly but inevitably, the idea of coalition began to be replaced by one of basic left-right confrontation. And over the next three years, that was precisely the line followed—though given the intricacies of Vientiane, there were several unsuspected turns.

Over the balance of the year, however, there was little radical change. In September, there was a brief outbreak of fighting in Vientiane between Phoumi's troops and the small Pathet Lao unit left behind in Vientiane to guard the two remaining Pathet Lao government ministers. But fast action by the Russian, British, and American ambassadors stopped the fighting quickly, and the capital slipped back into somnolence. In November, the neutralists and the Pathet Lao renewed their skirmishing on the Plaine after the monsoon ended, obeying what had by that time become a tradition, but casualties were few. (It should be remembered that "battles" in Laos usually produce few casualties: at no time did fighting on the Plaine or elsewhere ever near the intensity of the struggle in Vietnam.) A month later, Laos produced its fourth political assassination of the year. The victim was Colonel Leuang, Souvanna's chief intelligence officer, who was machine-gunned near his Vientiane home. It was generally believed Leuang was slain by the Pathet Lao, but no proof was ever offered.

Four months later, another political eruption shattered Vientiane's calm. Right-wing army officers, led by General Kouprasith and backed by National Police General Siho Lamphouthacoul, attempted to seize power from Souvanna. Striking before dawn on April 19, they placed Souvanna under house arrest and carted at least three ministers off to Kouprasith's headquarters at Camp Chinaimo, five miles outside the capital. (Phoumi was not included in the junta.) Though there were several bursts of firing, casualties were few—and it soon became apparent that the junta was in much greater difficulty than it had bargained for.

U.S. Ambassador Leonard Unger, accompanied by the French and Australian ambassadors and the British chargé d'affaires, first met Souvanna briefly to assure him of their continued support, then spent an hour with Kouprasith and Siho. In their talks, they made it harshly clear that unless the junta backed down, Western support would end abruptly and completely. By the time I managed to get back to Laos—three days after the coup—the tension had eased considerably. (Airplane connections between Laos and the outside world tend to dissolve when coup d'etats are under way.) The junta had bowed to Western pressure, at least to the degree of allowing Souvanna to retain power, but retained its proprietary interest in government. As one high-ranking Western diplomat put it: "A rather amorphous group now has the opportunity to express its views."

The major casualty, in fact, seemed to be Phoumi, and there was one school of thought at the Constellation Bar that maintained he had been the real target of the coup-makers. He had, in fact, committed several prize bungles over the past six months, most notably the opening of gambling casinos in Vientiane and other cities, which turned out to be distinct financial drains. Not that the general populace won: I can testify that the games were rigged unbelievably crudely, having dropped 5,000 Kip in five minutes at one table. But Phoumi's managers were as crooked as their tables; they kept most of the profits themselves. Another sore spot was Phoumi's gold monopoly, exercised through his personally controlled Bank of Laos, which netted him an estimated $500,000 a year. This did not endear him to less-strategically placed officers. Shortly after the April 19th affair, it became known that Phoumi's hand-picked army chief of staff had been replaced by a general known to be opposed to him; Phoumi's star, in fact, had begun to wane.

So had Souvanna's, or so it seemed at the time. His neutralist forces had been merged forcibly with the Royal Army, and shorn of this independent support, the prince lost much of his former flexibility. As far as the Pathet Lao was concerned, Souvanna now was a rightist. Souphanouvong, after a meeting with Souvanna at Khang Khay, put it this way: "Prince Souvanna Phouma claimed that he is the leader of both right-wing and neutralist forces and is in power, but the fact is that he is under the control of the Kouprasith-Siho group." Souvanna was less talkative after the meeting, saying merely that he had informed the NLHX of certain political changes: "The atmosphere was very friendly," he added, in what was probably the misstatement of the year.

The Pathet Lao response came with totally un-Laotian speed. Speaking for Souphanouvong, Phoumi Vongvichit demanded that the "Kouprasith-Siho ringleaders be severely punished" and that "the situation in Vientiane be restored to that of before April 19." It seemed clear, however, that even the Pathet Lao had little hope this would happen, that in fact the prospects for a "liberation government" were growing fast. By the spring of 1964, the pro-communist forces were claiming to have set up provincial governments along the entire eastern border, in a chain extending from the Chinese frontier south to North and South Vietnam. It was precisely this fact which severely perturbed the Thais, who had played a key role in the April coup.

Throughout 1963, the Bangkok government had grown increasingly annoyed with Souvanna's policies. The Thais had never been particularly enthusiastic about the 1962 accords and the consequent coalition government, feeling, with some justice, that they needed a strong Lao government to serve as a buffer between the impoverished, subversion-ripe Thai Northeast and North Vietnam. Before the death of Thailand's Prime Minister Field Marshal Sarit Thanarat in 1963, the links between Thailand and Laos were firm: Sarit and Phoumi were second cousins—and there is reasonably believable evidence to the effect that Sarit contributed heavily to Phoumi's slush fund. Certainly Sarit's death marked the beginning of Phoumi's decline. The April 19th coup attempt, which the Thais supported,[15] hurt Phoumi considerably, which is perhaps another indication of the cost to Phoumi of Sarit's death.

As if to underline the intensified Pathet Lao distaste for Souvanna, new fighting erupted on the Plaine. Kong Le's troops, outnumbered and outgunned, were forced completely off the Plaine, and Pathet Lao forces mounted a second offensive, this one southeast toward the important Mekong town of Pakse. For a time, a military disaster seemed in the making. But the Pathet Lao stopped before crossing the 1962 cease-fire line, and dedicated themselves to consolidating their sizable gains. Souvanna's next great military problem, surprisingly, involved the U.S.

For some months, U.S. jet reconnaissance planes had been photographing military movements in the Pathet Lao–controlled portions of Laos. In early June, a Pathet Lao antiaircraft unit—almost certainly manned by North Vietnamese—bagged a U.S. recon jet over Phonesavan, on the Plaine. Predictably, the U.S. then assigned armed escort jets to the recon flights, and the communist guns promptly picked off one of the escorts. Next day, U.S. jets strafed the gun positions and in the process damaged some buildings on the Plaine—including the Chinese Communist "embassy" at Souphanouvong's headquarters. Peking reacted almost instantly, with the expected loud protest, but Souvanna proved much less predictable.

In an interview after the downing of the escort jet, he told Reuters reporter Ernesto A. Mendoza he had not authorized the use of American escorts—and he added that the reconnaissance flights would stop. Then he flew off to see the King in Luang Prabang. U.S. Ambassador Unger, an intelligent and effective diplomat, was left holding the bag: he told curious newsmen that the photo flights weren't scheduled to continue "forever" and added that Souvanna had told him nothing about wanting the flights halted. A day later, Souvanna returned from Luang Prabang to produce a statement which calmed everyone except the Pathet Lao. "I have no objection to the continuation of armed escorts," he said, adding that the Laotian air force could not provide quite so effective protection. As far as stopping the flights was concerned, Souvanna was even more benign: it turned out he had called them off only "temporarily" to bring about "calm in the operational zone," and he said he had asked Unger to forward a request for renewed flights. "It is perfectly legitimate," he said, "that we survey the movements of the Pathet Lao and the Viet Minh who have committed acts of aggression against the neutralist forces."

Politically and militarily, Laos remained comparatively tranquil through the rest of 1964. There were the inevitable brief flareups on the fringes of the Plaine, where Kong Le's troops still held their ground, but no major thrusts developed. Souvanna's attempts to bring Souphanouvong and the Pathet Lao back into the coalition government continued, but they were halfhearted: Souvanna's reorganized government began to function reasonably well.

Early in 1965, however, political pressures produced another crisis. This time around, the culprit was Phoumi, who mounted a final bid for power. He had managed, through the turbulence of 1964, to cling to his post as deputy prime minister, but his powers were steadily chipped away. In February, 1965, backed by Police General Siho, he attempted a coup against Souvanna. But after ten hours of gunfire in the streets of Vientiane, Phoumi fled into the jungle. A week later, he and Siho turned up in Thailand to claim political asylum, which was granted. When last heard of, Phoumi was languishing in south Thailand, far from Vientiane.

With Phoumi and his fellow intriguers on the shelf, Souvanna's political problems eased considerably. The military threat of the Pathet Lao continued to exist, however, and national elections had to be deferred. In their place, limited elections were held in July to elect a new National Assembly, and Souvanna emerged as prime minister once more. (Souphanouvong, somewhat surprisingly, was allowed to retain his post as deputy prime minister despite the fact he had not appeared in Vientiane since 1963. Souvanna, it seemed, wished to preserve the fiction of Pathet Lao participation in the government, in order to leave open the door to eventual reconciliation.)

The steadily increasing political tranquility was matched by a lessening of military pressure as well. Pathet Lao attempts to wipe out government guerrilla forces in Sam Neua Province failed, and in

March, a Pathet Lao thrust against an officers training school at Dong Hene in southern Laos was turned back after fighting produced an estimated 200 Pathet Lao dead. In this battle, government forces captured nine North Vietnamese soldiers, who were paraded before foreign observers in Vientiane as hard evidence of Viet Minh activities in Laos. Overall, however, there was no major Pathet Lao offensive for the first time in several years. It was clear that Laotian and American bombing of the Ho Chi Minh trail complex had had some effect on Pathet Lao potential—but in view of the rapid escalation of the war in South Vietnam, it seemed reasonable to theorize that the Hanoi government was concentrating all its efforts in the south, rather than diverting men and material to the Lao front.

And that, in fact, seemed to be the case. By mid-1967, Laos had dropped almost completely out of the headlines. Late in 1966, nationwide elections were held which returned Souvanna to power once more—and this time the voting was much more representative than the limited polling of 1965. Even the isolated Meo guerrilla tribesmen, who have fought the Pathet Lao on their own ground for the past four years, were able to vote: government helicopters picked up their ballots from their remote hilltop villages. Aside from the ritual press attacks on the U.S. imperialists and their lackeys in Vientiane, even North Vietnam and Communist China seemed to be paying little attention to Lao events. Laos, in fact, had become a backwater of war, its fate dependent on events in South Vietnam over which it had no control.

In that backwater, Laos was not alone. Equally subject to the whims of larger powers was the Khmer kingdom of Cambodia, ruled by His Royal Highness Samdech Preah Norodom Sihanouk Upayuvareach. But while Souvanna, once a neutralist, found himself forced by Pathet Lao intransigence to accept American support, Sihanouk, in the late fifties and early sixties, swung the other way. As Communist Chinese power and influence increased, Sihanouk decided the best hope for Khmer survival lay in an understanding with Peking

By any standards, Sihanouk is a colorful and compelling leader. Neither mercurial (an adjective he despises), a playboy (a role he shed long ago), nor a cynical opportunist, he is, in his own terms, a realist. And Cambodia's peculiar, left-leaning brand of neutralism is nothing more or less than the political expression of his realism.

Inside Cambodia, there is little dissent from this policy. Abroad, sentiments are different.

The fact that many foreigners seem unable to understand his policy annoys the prince: press criticism, for instance, is the signal for a stream of fiery denunciations. The "Anglo-Saxon" press, in particular, has come in for much more than its share of Sihanoukgrams, and on occasion "Anglo-Saxon" reporters have been banned from the kingdom. But within Cambodia, Sihanouk faces few difficulties: no other Asian leader commands the enthusiastic degree of support that he does, or enjoys a closer rapport with the people he rules. Despite his royal lineage, he makes a habit of close contact with the Cambodians: newspapers regularly carry shots of "Monseigneur" sweating with a shovel at a construction project, bashing a volleyball past a helpless opponent, or accepting genuine homage from villagers in a tiny outback hamlet. He takes enormous pleasure in oratory: his squeaky voice carries a witty bite that his listeners love. And the Phnom Penh press regularly features hortatory articles—signed or unsigned—by the prince, who doubles in brass as his country's Walter Lippmann. Complex, controversial, and charismatic, he stands today as one of Asia's most interesting political personalities.

Sihanouk was born on October 31, 1922, son of Prince Norodom Suramarit, and succeeded his grandfather as Cambodia's king on April 23, 1941. The French, who controlled Cambodia in those days, selected Sihanouk (then a student in Saigon) in preference to the late king's eldest son, who appeared to be an embryo anti-colonialist. "Sihanouk seemed to the French to be more pliable, weak-willed, and accommodating," one source reports.[16] But the French, clearly, were wrong. During Sihanouk's first years on the throne, however, there was little indication of just how wrong they had been: Sihanouk, after all, was only eighteen years old when he took the throne.

He inherited leadership of a people who had fallen into decline long before. As noted earlier, the Khmers had dominated much of what is now South Vietnam, Laos, and Thailand between the tenth and fourteenth centuries. By the early nineteenth century, however, much of Cambodia had been swallowed up by Thais and Vietnamese, and in 1863, Cambodia became a French protectorate. Though the French staved off further political disintegration, they did little to build up Cambodia beyond establishing plantations: educationally and socially, Cambodia was ignored almost as completely as was Laos.

Perhaps the single most positive contribution France made to Cambodia was the painstaking reconstruction of the ancient capital of Angkor, buried for four hundred years in the western jungles.

Despite Cambodia's backwardness, however, a tiny nationalist movement came into existence in the years just before the outbreak of World War II. Led by Son Ngoc Thanh, who was half-Vietnamese, it pursued a cautious anti-French line. With the fall of France in 1941, and the consequent Japanese occupation of Indochina that followed, the movement gained momentum. But Thanh overestimated the degree of Japanese support for his movement: when he led a revolt against the French in 1942, the Japanese allowed the French to squelch it. Thanh fled to Bangkok, and later was allowed to travel to Japan. In early 1945, as it became obvious that Japan was about to lose the war, the Japanese occupation leaders removed French administrators from power and substituted their own men—a pattern they followed elsewhere. Thanh was named Cambodia's foreign minister. Two months later, he arrested the other ministers and took over as premier. That was his first and last real chance at power, however: he was seized as a Japanese puppet at the war's end and exiled to France for six years.

Meanwhile, Sihanouk made it clear *he* was determined to play the leading role in Cambodian affairs. On March 12, 1945, he declared Cambodia's independence from the French, and on January 7, 1946, France and Cambodia signed an agreement acknowledging Cambodia's status as an "autonomous state" within the French Union. That autonomy, however, existed only on paper: France retained overall authority, though the Cambodians were somewhat mollified by French action in forcing Thailand to return the two western provinces it had annexed, with Japanese approval, early in the Pacific war.

For some Cambodian nationalists, that was not enough. Several thousand of Thanh's followers fled to the western jungles in 1946, formed themselves into the Khmer Issarak (Free Khmers), and tried to oust the French by force. Their aims were shared by Viet Minh units in eastern Cambodia, and for a brief period the two groups worked together. By 1947, however, most of the Khmer Issarak took advantage of an amnesty and laid down their arms, while the Viet Minh turned to concentrate on the "liberation" of South Vietnam.

After long negotiations, France went a step further toward granting Cambodia full independence: on November 8, 1949, King Sihanouk won acknowledgment of Cambodia's independence—but France clung to a measure of control over foreign and military policy. This was a solution satisfactory to no one except the French, and Cambodian politics entered upon four years of instability. In 1951, after Sihanouk's more militant political opposition swept the elections, Son Ngoc Thanh was allowed to return. He promptly began agitating against the king, in the process reactivating the Khmer Issarak. French officials, realizing at last that Thanh's return was a mistake, made plans to arrest him, and he promptly took to the jungles once again. Compounding Sihanouk's difficulties was a sudden upsurge in Viet Minh activity. In the face of continuing trouble both from the Viet Minh and the Khmer Issarak, Sihanouk saw only one course: he dismissed the unruly government and took full control himself. Steadily, the situation worsened, and in January, 1953, Sihanouk left for Europe, ostensibly for a month's vacation.

As it happened, however, he began a direct offensive against the French, arguing that refusal to grant Cambodia full independence would guarantee eventual French defeat by the Viet Minh. Paris dithered, however, and Sihanouk left with only the sour satisfaction of having lunched with President Vincent Auriol. Sihanouk returned briefly to Phnom Penh, then left the capital, vowing never to come back until independence was complete. Anti-French sentiment blossomed, for Sihanouk had retained his enormous popularity with the masses, and finally, in October, Sihanouk returned to his capital. His case was won. On November 9, 1953, the Cambodians celebrated the achievement of complete independence. Promptly, Sihanouk took to the field to lead his troops against the Viet Minh.

The fighting continued until the signing of the Geneva Accords on Indochina in July, 1954, and in early 1955, Sihanouk submitted himself to the electorate. Approval was overwhelming: the referendum produced 925,812 votes in his favor and 1,834 against. Sihanouk's response was characteristically startling: he abdicated, formed his own political party (the Sangkum Reastr Niyum, or Popular Socialist Community) and led the Sangkum to overwhelming victory in the national elections that September. Explaining his decision to abdicate, he said the monarch was "a prisoner of a rigid system which prevented him from acting freely." In truth, he acted freely from that point onward.

His foreign policy, for example, has been particularly uninhibited.

From 1955 through about 1960, Cambodia remained almost totally nonaligned, despite heavy pressure from both the communist bloc and the west. During that period, however, he paid three visits to Peking (in 1956, 1958, and 1960), and he was evidently much impressed by what he saw. After 1960, Cambodia began leaning toward Peking, for what to Sihanouk were simple reasons of survival. "It is improbable that we will succeed in dissociating our future from that which awaits all Asia," he told me in December, 1961, "and that future is dark." It was an obvious reference to China's increasing influence in Indochina, and he proceeded to make his views even clearer. "I wish to emphasize," he added, "that I have never wished for the victory of communism in Asia, but I must admit it seems inevitable to me because of the errors in this region by the free world and its partisans."

The "partisans" Sihanouk referred to were Thailand and South Vietnam. Cambodia, underpopulated and fertile, is wedged between these two hereditary enemies like a succulent chunk of *brie,* and the history of Cambodian relations with its two neighbors indicates clearly that Sihanouk's policy has realistic roots.

But to believe, as Sihanouk says he does, that Thai or Vietnamese hostility toward Cambodia can be turned off by a simple command from the United States is something else again. There are, no doubt, some American officials who would enjoy that sort of control. But the fact is that, wishful thinking aside, the United States simply doesn't have that degree of authority over the Thai and South Vietnamese governments.

Cambodian-Thai difficulties can be traced back for centuries: the incorporation of Cambodia's two western provinces into Thailand in 1941 was not particularly startling, inasmuch as the Thais, over the years, have cast covetous eyes at their Khmer neighbors almost as a matter of reflex. The current hostility dates back to 1958, with the failure of binational talks over the ownership of Preah Vihear temple, on the frontier. Diplomatic relations were broken off, the border closed, and the controlled Thai press immediately mounted a campaign for the re-annexation of the provinces of Siemreap and Battembang.

In 1959, Cambodia took the issue to the International Court of Justice at The Hague, and two years later, the Thais, after challenging the Hague court's jurisdiction, grudgingly announced they would go along with the court's decision. Meanwhile, tensions eased: in

1960 the two nations resumed diplomatic relations. But in 1961, during a visit to Tokyo, Sihanouk trumpeted that Thailand and South Vietnam posed more of a threat to Cambodia than the communists— and the Thai response was acerbic. Once again Cambodia broke relations with Thailand; once again the Thais closed the border.

For the Thais, more trouble was in store. In June, 1962, the World Court ruled against Thailand in the temple dispute, and Bangkok was furious. Interior Minister Prapas Charusathien vowed that any "invaders of Thai territory" would be shot out of hand. Finally, Thai tempers cooled, and there was a fall-off in name-calling. Diplomatic relations, however, remained nonexistent.

Early in 1966, there was another flareup. Vague reports in Bangkok indicated a "free Cambodian" army had attacked Cambodian posts on the Thai border. Son Ngoc Thanh's name was bandied about again, and all indications were that certain right-wing elements in Thailand were backing the "insurgents." Just who was involved, however, remained unclear—and from the speed with which the fighting died, it seemed obvious that whoever was behind it all had been told to stop.

Much more worrying to Cambodia, however, are its uneasy relationships with the Vietnamese of Saigon, Hanoi, and the Liberation Front. Sihanouk and Cambodians in general mistrust the Thais, but they deeply fear the Vietnamese, in common with the Lao. And every border incursion draws screams of angry protest from Phnom Penh—protests, it should be admitted, that are too often justified. As far as can be determined, however, these incursions (airstrikes, usually, though in some cases South Vietnamese troops have crossed the ill-defined border in pursuit of Viet Cong units) are not deliberate. More important is the question of Viet Cong bases in Cambodia. And a host of investigations by neutral observers and American reporters has failed to uncover proof of the charge, commonplace in Saigon, that Sihanouk shelters the VC. In October, 1965, for example, *New York Times* correspondent Seymour Topping[17] made an on-the-spot investigation, on Sihanouk's invitation, and found that several areas, cited as VC bases or supply trails by American and South Vietnamese sources, showed no evidence of having been used for such purposes. He did add, however, that "there are some remote jungle areas of the Cambodian Vietnam border that are impossible to check for Viet Cong activity, and it is doubtful that even the Phnom Penh government knows what transpires there."[18] Other correspondents have reported along similar lines. It seems fair, in summary, to say that Sihanouk is simply unable to control these border areas, which were, in fact, long-time Viet Minh strongholds during the days of the French war in Indochina.

Another long-standing Sihanouk complaint against the United States and South Vietnam is the existence of the Khmer Serei, which, he asserts, is an armed band of Cambodian rebels funded by American agents, and dedicated to his overthrow. For several years, a Khmer Serei radio in South Vietnam broadcast propaganda into Cambodia and, particularly during the Diem regime, Cambodian rebels surfaced periodically in Saigon. In early 1965, while I was visiting a Special Forces outpost in Vietnam's Tay Ninh Province (on the Cambodian border), I spotted Khmer Serei propaganda painted on rock near the camp, evidently put up by the ethnic Khmers operating under Special Forces direction. By 1966, however, much of the Khmer Serei agitation seemed to have died off—presumably at the urging of the American diplomatic establishment.

Given Sihanouk's fear of Thai and South Vietnamese aggression, combined with the somewhat uncertain posture of the United States in Southeast Asia during the early sixties, his swing toward Communist China is understandable. I made this point emphatically in a 1962 article for the *Far Eastern Economic Review,* a Hong Kong publication, and sat back to wait for the usual wrathful explosion from Phnom Penh. (Sihanouk makes a habit of seeing that critical press pieces are answered rapidly and forcefully.) This time, the explosion was comparatively mild—and while he took the article to task on several points, my explanation of his pro-Peking policy passed unchallenged. Instead, a commentary in *Neak Cheat Niyum* (*The Nationalist*), concluded that though the article "did not give a complete picture of the actual situation in Cambodia, it did definitely compliment Sihanouk on his policies." As a rule, it might be noted, *Neak Cheat Niyum*'s critiques are written by Sihanouk himself.

Sihanouk's faith in Communist Chinese support, in fact, was made clear to me during that 1961 interview: "In the socialist world," he said, "the country which supports us in any circumstances is Peoples' China." To the Chinese themselves, his words were much more flowery. Consider, for example, a Sihanouk speech in Peking, given in December, 1960, at a time when the disintegration of the Great Leap Forward was perfectly apparent: His visit, he said, gave him "an opportunity to admire your considerable new advance which is the greatest proof of what can be achieved by a people as a result of their courage, tenacity, confidence and unity."[19] *Peoples' Daily,* Peking spokesman for the Communist Party, replied in kind. Citing the recent signing of a Sino-Cambodian friendship and mutual non-aggression (*sic*) treaty, the lead editorial said: "The Chinese people have always profoundly admired the firm stand taken by Prince Sihanouk . . . in pursuing the policy of peace, neutrality and independence." And it added: "China and Cambodia will always live together in peace and unity, the Chinese and Cambodian peoples will forever remain close to each other as brothers and share each other's weal and woe."[20]

By early 1963, three Chinese Communist-donated factories were in operation in Phnom Penh, and several more were under construction. Sadly for Sihanouk, difficulties were plentiful. At the plywood factory at Dey Eth, for instance, production was at less than 50 percent of capacity, and quality was poor: the plywood had a tendency to fall apart within a month or so. To cap it all, the material was selling at three times the cost in Phnom Penh of Hong Kong–made plywood. A paper mill at Chhlong was in only slightly better shape, but a textile factory at Kompong Cham was producing on schedule. By 1964, Sihanouk closed the plywood factory, and the others were floundering. Despite these problems, Sihanouk continued to tighten ties with China, and in late December, 1963, he threatened publicly to negotiate a formal alliance with Peking if the Western powers refused to consider his plan for the guaranteed neutralization of Cambodia.

Four months later, when no Western action seemed to be forthcoming on this point, Sihanouk sent a military mission to Peking to negotiate arms purchases, and Sihanouk himself followed in time to celebrate China's National Day on October 1. On this visit, however, he suffered a setback. Frustrated in his search for Western guarantees of his frontiers, he asked the Chinese government for a formal alliance. The Chinese refused, urging him instead to retain his neutral pose—though Sihanouk received verbal promises that China would tolerate no territorial infringements. That pledge was repeated on November 8—Cambodia's Independence Day—by Foreign Minister Chen Yi. And military aid continued to flow. By the fall of 1964, Cambodia had received 1,600 light and heavy automatic weapons, 100 trucks, and 60 heavy weapons, including mortars, recoilless rifles, and rocket launchers. On Sihanouk's return from Peking, he announced that China had offered enough light and heavy armament to equip 20,000 men (two-thirds of the Cambodian army), as well as three MIG jet fighters and seven other planes, anti-aircraft artillery, and three patrol boats.

Through 1965, as the war in neighboring South Vietnam grew hotter, Sihanouk clung to his pro-Chinese position. In May, when Cambodian-American diplomatic relations ended, Premier Chou En-lai cabled the prince to promise "that should U.S. imperialism dare to spread the flames of aggressive war to the peace-loving kingdom of Cambodia, the Chinese people absolutely will not stand idly by."[21]

Although Cambodia's relations with China prospered through the early sixties, Sihanouk's efforts to ensure similarly warm relationships with the Viet Cong and the Pathet Lao were unfruitful. During his 1964 visit to Peking, for instance, both North Vietnam and Liberation Front representatives whom he contacted there flatly refused to sign any guarantee of Cambodia's frontiers. The following March, Sihanouk convoked a Conference of Indochinese Peoples (which included Viet Cong and Pathet Lao delegations) to seek a solution to the Vietnam problem. In essence, Sihanouk hoped to produce a guarantee of South Vietnam's territorial integrity in return for an American withdrawal from that country. Communist China, however, made it clear that no promises were to be offered the Americans prior to withdrawal, and the conference thus became a failure before it got under way. Sihanouk refused to read his introductory speech, which contained this proposal: instead, he had it printed and passed out to the delegates. In a statement to a foreign educator, he made the reasons for his policy quite clear: "The Viet Cong believe that each day they are getting closer to victory. If the Viet Cong go on fighting, the Americans will, too. But the American position is hopeless, so eventually they will leave without any previous guarantees as to the non-communism and territorial integrity of South Vietnam. What does this mean? That Cambodia will be face to face with communism along her entire eastern border. This will be very dangerous for Cambodia, which does not want to become communist. And for us in Cambodia, of all possible communisms, Vietnamese communism is the worst."[22]

As Sihanouk led his nation into ever-tighter relations with China, Cambodia's links to the United States withered accordingly. And United States policy, in fact, gave the prince plenty of opportunities for irritation. There was, for example, the covert encouragement of the Khmer Serei and the exiled Son Ngoc Thanh. There was the plot against Sihanouk allegedly assisted by an American diplomat named Victor Matsui. There was the United States ambassador who allegedly showed up at an airport reception for the returning prince wearing shorts and a sport shirt and accompanied by his bulldog, breaching protocol to a degree that infuriated Sihanouk—the dog, it appears, was considered an insult. More important was what appeared to be a total American unwillingness to recognize that while Sihanouk's policies were something less than intransigently anti-communist, this fact did not make him a communist himself. America's Cambodia policy in the late fifties and early sixties had an uncomfortably Dullesian ring to it: if Sihanouk isn't for us, Washington seemed to think, he must be against us.

For Sihanouk, the last straw seems to have been the assassination of Diem in early November, 1963. There are unverifiable reports that Sihanouk was convinced Diem was slain by the Americans because of his refusal to follow Washington's orders, and that Sihanouk was convinced the same fate was in store for him. True or not, the fact is that Sihanouk renounced American economic and military assistance within a few weeks of Diem's death. (At the time, U.S. aid to Cambodia was running at more than $20 million a year.) Then, in December, another dispute erupted: confused reports from Phnom Penh seemed to indicate that Sihanouk had ordered a celebration in connection with the assassination of President John F. Kennedy, and Washington made an immediate protest. Sihanouk denied the story, saying the rejoicing had been ordered to mark the death of Thai Prime Minister Sarit Thanarat, a longtime foe. But he added: "Let us then hope for an early break in relations between the United States and ourselves."[23] To underscore his statement, he withdrew Cambodia's ambassador in Washington—and all but one of the embassy's staff. Over the next year, relations continued to crumble: in March, 1964, the American and British embassies in Phnom Penh were looted by a mob of demonstrators. And the Vietnam war continued to spill over onto Cambodian soil. Cambodia refused to accept Vietnamese—and American—explanations that the incidents were caused by map-reading errors. In December, United States and Cambodian emissaries met in New Delhi for nine days of talks aimed at settling differences—but the meetings ended in failure. Sihanouk blasted the Americans for their "systematic bad faith."

The final break came four months later. *Newsweek,* in an issue dated April 5, 1965, reported in the course of a long article on Cambodia that Sihanouk's mother, Queen Kossamak, "was said to be money-mad and reportedly runs a number of concessions in town, plus a string of bordellos at the edge of the city." Strangely enough, in light of the later uproar, initial Cambodian reaction was favorable to the piece. But in late April, a Phnom Penh mob smashed the windows of the U.S. Embassy and trampled on the American flag in protest. Sihanouk, explaining the three-week lag, said that his people had "just learned" of the article. On May 4, Cambodia broke diplomatic relations with the United States, stating that "the American government has, in fact, let one of the most important American publications, *Newsweek,* discredit Cambodia."[24] Sihanouk added a second reason: he cited a recent bombing of a Cambodian village, in which at least one person was killed, and recalled that he had sworn previously to break relations "if a single Khmer life is lost after a new aggression."[25] It seemed clear that the *Newsweek* piece simply provided an added pretext for the breakoff, given the absurdly slow reaction time. Saddest of all, however, was that the report of the Queen's peccadillos was almost certainly on target. Four years before, reasonably reliable sources told me the Queen made a habit of skimming 10 percent off the top of Red Cross funds.

Corruption, in fact, was one of Sihanouk's endemic domestic problems. Just before my visit in 1961, he had summoned his ministers for an angry lecture on precisely this point, while an audience of startled foreign diplomats and journalists looked on. Sihanouk's sincere opposition to corruption was unique, in Asia at least; I know of no other Asian leader who feels as strongly on this point.

Internal crises, however, are rare. In 1963, for example, Sihanouk fired his entire cabinet for inefficiency—but he allowed himself to be persuaded to stay on as head of state and promptly put together a new team of ministers. Faced with problems of this sort, Sihanouk has a habit of submitting himself to his people—and in view of his genuine personal popularity, he risks little. Perhaps his most effective single gambit is the open-air Sangkum Congress. Once a year, on the average, he sets up an al-fresco meeting in Phnom Penh to which hamlets across the country are invited to send delegates. Point by point, he discusses their complaints and makes his rulings, debating with critics freely and wittily. It is an impressive show. In one of these Sangkum Congresses, he offered to debate leaders of the

Pracheachon (Communist) Party and demolished them almost effortlessly. The local communists, in fact, seem to worry Sihanouk not at all. "They are few in number," he told me on one occasion, "and their influence on the masses is nil."

Cambodia, all in all, is an almost indecently pleasant place, given the fact that it is surrounded by nations more or less at war. Phnom Penh is one of Southeast Asia's most charming cities: clean and quiet, with good restaurants and lively enough nightclubs, it stands in strong contrast to raucous Saigon, just thirty-five minutes away by air. With a sizable annual rice surplus, a reasonably steady economy, and stable domestic leadership, Cambodia is blessed above and beyond most other Southeast Asian nations. It is Sihanouk's own peculiar tragedy that he still must seek what he can never have—absolute guarantees of his nation's future independence. The solution, quite simply, is out of his hands.

In South Vietnam, 1963 began ominously. South of Saigon, on January 2, two thousand ARVN soldiers, supported by American advisers, helicopters, and armored personnel carriers (APCs), seemed about to close a trap on an estimated two hundred Viet Cong dug in along a treeline. But the ARVN were unable to press their attack home—time and again, the APCs rumbled toward the treeline, then veered away.[26] The Viet Cong downed five choppers and killed three Americans; ARVN losses were heavy. Late in the day, the Viet Cong broke out of the trap with embarrassing ease. American officers and reporters on the scene called it a "disaster."

In Saigon, however, sentiments were different. Ap Bac, said the South Vietnamese spokesmen, was a triumph—and this appraisal was echoed by the press officers of MACV (U.S. Military Assistance Command in Vietnam). Inevitably, correspondents who disagreed were accused of fomenting VC propaganda—but by that time Western reporters were used to it. The "press war," as it came to be called, was a deeply interesting story, reflecting as it did the unwillingness of American diplomatic and military officials to dig for facts beneath the rose-tipped prose of Diem's information apparatus.[27] Briefly, there were three major obstacles confronting foreign correspondents in Saigon: MACV, the U.S. Embassy, and the Diem government. The first two were overcome easily enough—each correspondent managed to develop his own source net. But Diem and Nhu posed a different problem; only a few correspondents were truly plugged into the government, and none, to my knowledge, had ready entree to the Ngo family. This was a pity, for the true story of just what happened from day to day in ornate Gia Long Palace now will never be known.

Even without a pipeline to the palace, however, enough was known about the Ngos to provide at least a basis for argument. They were mandarin to the core, with all the aloofness and coldness that the term implies. They were Catholic, while the bulk of the population was Buddhist. And they were at least a half-century out of step with the times, particularly in contrast with communist techniques of organization and control. Diem, in particular, seemed still to believe in the Confucian theory of government by example—and never came to realize that no one was watching.

In the spring of what was to be the last year of his life, Diem evidently was running out of steam. Energetic and relatively adaptable when he came to power almost ten years before, he became increasingly withdrawn during his years in power. Squirrel-cheeked, chunky, and impassive, he had little gift for arousing popular enthusiasm. Twice in recent years, he had put down military attempts to oust him from power, but he seemed to have little energy left for the new crises of 1963: toward the Buddhists, for example, his policy seemed confined to saying that the Buddhists had nothing to complain about because all their rights were guaranteed in the constitution. His few public appearances were brief, mechanical posturings, without meaning because he deigned to give them none. In political war, where charisma is vital, this was a fatal flaw. Even close associates admitted he had grown less and less interested in politics, more devoted to administration. Unmarried and ascetic, he was increasingly inclined to leave public appearances to his brother, Political Counsellor Ngo Dinh Nhu.

A hollow-cheeked, intense visionary with a penchant for French metaphysical poetry, Nhu by 1963 had become the most public figure of the regime. Most of the lines of power rested firmly in his gracefully gesturing hands. For all practical purposes, most of my Saigon sources agreed, he controlled government finances, the national police, and much of the military. He headed a powerful political organization called the Can Lao Nhan Vi Cah Mang Dang (Personalist Labor Revolutionary Party), which amounted to a private intelligence network which specialized in smoking out liberal elements and included in its membership nearly every government official of the time. The Can Lao, in fact, was Nhu's answer to the political threat posed by the communists—it was shockingly similar in purpose to the Lao Dong

Party of Ho Chi Minh, combining as it did both political and administrative primacy. And again paralleling Hanoi's techniques, Nhu organized and led the Revolutionary Youth Movement, a paramilitary organization designed to ensure the continuation of the regime's power. He was the high priest of that strange foggy ideology called Personalism—Saigon's counter to the ideals of communism. Nhu argued his policies well; he was, in many ways, a brilliant man. But his arguments sprang from unrealities; he built a structure without foundations.

Much more to the point was his wife, the ineffable Madame Nhu. Strong-willed, hot-tempered, and—when she wanted to be—uncomfortably fetching, she became, in 1963, the extremist of the family on the Buddhist issue, and the fact she came of a devoutly Buddhist family in Hanoi seemed to make little difference. In her capacity as a National Assembly deputy, she rammed through a series of puritanical laws that outlawed contraception, outdoor cafes, dancing, and even the "sad songs" beloved of the Vietnamese. She tried, with considerable lack of success, to suppress Saigon's bar girls. She commanded in fact, if not on paper, the Women's Solidarity Movement and the Women's Paramilitary Force as well, and saw nothing funny in our amusement at the sight of dainty Saigon socialites tripping about the streets in ill-fitting blue fatigue uniforms and fragile high-heeled shoes. Madame Nhu, in short, was a harpy—and a most flamboyant one.

In strong contrast to the ebullient Madame Nhu was Archbishop Ngo Dinh Thuc, Diem's oldest living brother. (Ngo Dinh Khoi, the oldest, was murdered by the Viet Minh in 1945.) Dignified and dour, Thuc was much in evidence in Saigon in 1963, though his seat was in Hue: it was clear that he was counseling Diem during the Buddhist affair. The clan's youngest brother, Luyen, kept well out of the picture. As South Vietnam's ambassador to Britain, Luyen was both physically and philosophically the most remote Ngo.

Brother Canh, however, was very much in the picture. His headquarters were at Hue in Central Vietnam, and he functioned as the region's leader—though as far as official Saigon was concerned, Canh was simply taking care of his aged mother. Few Americans ever came in contact with him—he made a point of pretending to be remote from everyday concerns. One American who had met him, however, described him as "sort of a ward boss. He looks after his own people, and does it damn well. Nobody gets in his way. His own secret cops are the toughest in the country." There were recurring reports of friction between Canh and Nhu, based on Nhu's expanding power in the capital, but nothing was ever proved.

Also regarded as part of the family was Madame Nhu's father, Tran Van Chuong, Saigon's ambassador to the United States. His wife was South Vietnam's observer at the United Nations. Chuong, however, broke with Diem in mid-1963 over the handling of the Buddhist crisis.

Early in the year the major focus of attention was Nhu's strategic hamlet program. Adapted in part from British experiences in putting down a long and bloody communist rebellion in Malaya, the hamlet program was intended to establish a complex of fortified villages across South Vietnam. In theory, the hamlet concept was sound: if it worked, it would deny the Viet Cong access to the peasantry and to the food they produced. American backing for the program was extensive: in 1963, for example, about 75 percent of the total $190 million in economic aid was directed toward the program's support. "In many areas," said Rufus Phillips, the United States aid official directly in charge of the program, "strategic hamlets have proven themselves an effective vehicle for winning the support of the population. This is a battle for loyalties—and we have finally found a technique that works." Other Americans in Saigon were more restrained. "Some hamlets run like trains," said one friend, "but others don't. You can't get an accurate cross-section—there are about six thousand hamlets now; you could visit one hundred and not get a true picture." And a senior aid official, while backing the program in general, admitted that administrative snarls hampered the program's effectiveness and added that the Diem government displayed no intention of untangling the difficulties. There was no question of the depth of Nhu's commitment to the program; but somehow, his ideas didn't seem to take hold in peasant minds.

Nhu himself was optimistic. "One thing is certain," he told me in April. "The Vietnamese people now have much more confidence in themselves, and the concept of the strategic hamlet has played an important role in developing this. Now we have completed about sixty-six hundred hamlets, and by the end of the year we should reach our goal of about eleven thousand." He paused, inhaled deeply on one of the Bastos Rouge cigarettes he smoked incessantly, carefully rubbed off the fresh ash, and continued. "But of those completed so far, only about twenty-five percent are working as well as they should." He glanced quickly at me, presumably expecting a gasp at his frankness. No gasp: the day before, I'd been told, by an excellent source, that 10 percent was nearer to the truth.

Then, with the speed of one of Saigon's summer storms, the strategic hamlet issue was displaced as the capital's major concern. On May 8 in Hue, government troops fired into a crowd of Buddhists demonstrating in front of the radio station, and nine were killed. It was the beginning of the end for Diem and his family—and very nearly for South Vietnam as well.

The roots of the problem, inevitably, were tangled. Of South Vietnam's population of about 51 million, an estimated 11 million are technically Buddhists—but only 4 million could be called practicing religionists. (The rest were ancestor-worshippers, for the most part, and Buddhist only in the most general sense.) It was true, however, that Diem favored Catholics over Buddhists for government positions: a Catholic himself, he trusted his co-religionists. More important, Vietnam's Catholics usually were better educated, and were more likely to be anti-communists; accordingly, they were much more likely to be picked for official posts. Catholics, in fact, constituted a *de facto* elite. In the first years of the Saigon government, there was little religious persecution, but as the Catholic refugees who had streamed south after the 1954 settlement began to consolidate their positions in the south, frictions inevitably occurred between them and the southern Buddhists. Gradually, on the part of the Buddhists, a feeling of religious persecution began to build up.

In Hue, site of the ancient capital of Annam and for centuries a center of Vietnamese Buddhism, anti-Catholic feelings were particularly strong. It was a logical spot to anticipate trouble, but Diem, in typical style, chose to ignore it. For several weeks before the incident itself, pressures had been building up rapidly. At stake were the celebrations of Buddha's 2507th birthday, festivities which all but coincided with a Catholic celebration in honor of Hue Archbishop Ngo Dinh Thuc—Diem's brother.

Protesting what he viewed as increased Catholic oppression of Buddhists, Central Vietnam's Buddhist leader, Thich Tri Quang, refused to send Thuc a routine message of congratulations. The Saigon government, presumably at Thuc's suggestion, then resurrected a law banning display of religious flags and ordered that it be enforced to the letter—though Catholic flags were still flying. Tri

Quang, defying the order, told his followers to display their flags, and the province chief backed down. But as Tri Quang prepared to deliver a radio speech on the issue of religious persecution, he was told his speech was forbidden. On May 8 the Buddhists staged an angry mass rally at the radio station.

Government troops, under command of Major Dang Sy, a Catholic, raced to the scene. Sy's orders to disperse were ignored, and he called on his troops to fire teargas and blanks at the crowd. They failed to move, and Sy fell back on live ammunition. The carnage followed.

Hue is a lovely, placid city, and its residents are charming. Hue's young ladies, in fact, are known for good reason as Vietnam's prettiest. But Hue in the wake of the May 8 incident was an ugly place. "These people are passive and slow to react," said a North Vietnamese who had come south in 1954. "But now they are bitter, and they will not change." An American resident put it more strongly. "Never in a million years will these people accept this government," he told me shortly after the incident. "They are devout Buddhists, and they feel they've been hit below the belt."

Diem's first reaction was tragically predictable: the Viet Cong was responsible for the rally, the Viet Cong did the killing—it was the same old theme. And government spokesmen were quick to point out that, after all, the incident had occurred in Hue, not in Saigon, and thus wasn't really important. Radio Hanoi was much quicker to realize just how significant it all was: day after day, word of the incident was channeled into the South. The commentary was straightforward—exaggeration was unnecessary.

Three weeks later, two other reporters and I were strolling home from lunch at Brodard's, a small, brassy restaurant once favored by the press. Saigon in those days dropped almost instantly into siesta after lunch, and we were about to join the rest of the city in slumber. But as we neared the plaza before the whitewashed, tin-roofed opera house that served as a home for the National Assembly, we were mildly surprised to notice a stir. (This was well before Saigon adopted the street demonstration as an expression of sentiment, and Radio Catinat had predicted nothing of great interest that day.)

But there before us, almost noiselessly, rank on rank of saffron-robed monks filed into the plaza, seemingly from nowhere. They carried signs, in English, French, and Vietnamese, protesting government repression. We rubbed our eyes—surely, Brodard had drugged our iced tea. We raced for cameras, then watched, still incredulously, to see just what the government was going to do.

As it happened, there was no immediate response. The sun beat down on the four hundred shaven heads, bounced off the white buildings of the Hotels Caravelle and Continental. Sporadically, a tuneless Buddhist chant arose, then died. Finally, a few riot police arrived, then more, but they did nothing but stand and watch. "Keep an eye on the rooftops," said a wire service man. "The Viet Cong could turn this into a massacre with just one grenade." A few pedestrians showed up, took one hasty glance, and fled. The banners (in English) fluttered in the light breeze: "We Are Ready to Sacrifice Ourselves for Buddhism," read one. Another said: "The National Assembly and Government Must Grant Us Religious Equality." Minutes turned into hours. A rumor spread that the bonzes planned a forty-eight-hour protest. Palace Guardsmen in jungle camouflage uniforms joined the police, and roads leading to the area were blocked off. Finally, after three hours, the bonzes filed away without incident.

The Buddhist leaders, showing a nice feeling for public relations, had chosen their site well. The square, Cong-truong Lam Son, was at the intersection of Le Loi and Tu Do (formerly Rue Catinat), two of Saigon's busier streets. Facing the square were two of Saigon's three major hotels, and a block away was the headquarters of the United States Information Service (USIS). Two major MACV billets were within a block. No location could have better guaranteed maximum exposure to Americans—Lam Son was Saigon's crazybone.

By this time, the Buddhist leadership had formulated five demands. They asked the government to cancel the order banning public display of the Buddhist flag; to give Buddhism special status paralleling that accorded catholicism; to stop arresting Buddhists; to guarantee freedom to preach and practice Buddhism, and to compensate families of those killed and wounded at Hue as well as to punish the officials involved. Diem's first response was to ignore the Buddhist demands and label the leadership "insolent and impolite" for staging the demonstration. A few days later, however, he caved in to some degree: the Hue province chief and his security aide were quietly sacked. But that was all: on the other demands, Diem refused to budge.

Then came the next shock. As Diem and Thuc attended a mass for the soul of Pope John XXIII in Saigon's Basilica, a seventy-three-year-old Buddhist monk named Thich (Reverend) Quang Duc calmly turned himself into a human torch a mile away. Like the Lam Son protest, the immolation was neatly planned: Quang Duc and three high-ranking bonzes seated themselves in a small green car and drove slowly toward the offices of Cambodia's representative in Saigon, heading a procession of about a thousand yellow-robed monks. At the intersection before the offices of the Cambodian representation, Quang Duc stepped out, seated himself at the center of the streets, and an assistant poured an estimated four gallons of gasoline over his head. Quietly, other monks seated themselves in a circle around him—at a safe distance—and watched quietly while Quang Duc struck a match and burst into flames.

As the flames leaped high, and black oily smoke filled the air with the stench of burning flesh, the bonzes alternately chanted and prayed. Quang Duc's body remained upright for about ten minutes. He had not uttered a sound. After the body toppled, fellow monks covered it with sacred yellow cloth, then lifted the corpse off the melting asphalt, leaving a few shreds of blackened flesh behind. White-uniformed police, trying to hold back the crowd of about five thousand Vietnamese, wept; at one stage, policemen tried to rescue Quang Duc but were forced back by the bonzes. Once again, placards in English were held aloft by the Buddhists: "A Buddhist Priest Burns Himself for Our Religion," said one.

To this, even Diem reacted. He took to Radio Saigon that afternoon to urge the population to "view the facts with composure and examine the situation with clearsightedness," words hardly calculated to soothe listeners. He added, untruthfully, that negotiations with Buddhist leaders were continuing and said: "Buddhism in Vietnam finds its fundamental safeguard in the Constitution of which I am personally the guardian." The Buddhists were unimpressed: "We will continue the struggle until the last drop of our blood is shed," Thich Duc Nghiep, the Buddhist spokesman, told me. "At least four nuns have pledged themselves to incinerate themselves soon if our demands are not met." Duc Nghiep's predictions usually could be discounted by about 50 percent—but this one turned out to be more accurate than usual: Before the coup of November 1, seven monks and nuns followed Quang Duc's example.

Outside Saigon, while thousands of Vietnamese jammed Xa Loi Pagoda for memorial ceremonies, the war rumbled along. Three days after Quang Duc's death, another American adviser died in a Viet

Cong ambush, bringing the year's total to nineteen. (For all of 1962, only twenty-three Americans were killed in action.) At the American Embassy, officials committed to "sink or swim with Diem" were seriously concerned: one high-ranking officer told me the Buddhist protest was "heartbreaking"—because everything, he believed, had been going so well until it erupted. And late that week, Diem began to yield, ever so slightly, to Buddhist pressure: the bonzes won permission to fly their flags publicly as well as a pledge for complete religious equality. Negotiations continued.

Conditions in Saigon worsened. Five days after Quang Duc's death, a brief but fierce street riot between police and Buddhists caused one death and an estimated one hundred injuries. The Buddhist leaders made it clear that they expected American help: "The problem can be solved only by the Americans," one bonze told me, "because Diem will do nothing. Diem is a puppet of Washington, just as Ho Chi Minh is controlled by the Chinese and the Russians." Until this time, the U.S. Embassy had been getting almost all of their information on the Buddhist movement from Diem officials and American journalists. "The Buddhists have a pretty fair publicity organization," one diplomat told me comfortably. "We get copies of all their pronouncements." After the first sacrifice, however, the embassy began seeking its own information—but there was still an evident reluctance to think about policy changes. Ambassador Nolting, who finished his tour in July, summed up his view of the Buddhists this way: "The trouble with this damn thing, if I may speak frankly, is that everybody focuses on a tiny aspect of it. I myself, I say this frankly after almost two and a half years, have never seen any evidence of religious persecution."

At Xa Loi Pagoda, which had become headquarters for the Greater Buddhist Association of Vietnam and thus a major check point for the press, the crowds continued to flock in. On a garish altar lay a charred gray-blue hunk of flesh, enclosed in a glass case. "This Is the Immortal Heart of Thich Quang Duc, Which Cannot Be Burned" read a sign. Leaders continued to maintain that their movement was non-political, though many of the younger bonzes seemed to have more than sutras on their minds. And while the leaders did their best to win over the press, their efforts were marked by fits of suspicion. I was accused of working both for the CIA and Nhu—on the same day—for asking impolite questions.

Nhu and his wife took an increasingly tough line on the Buddhists. The English-language *Times of Vietnam,* Madame's mouth-piece, began hinting that the Buddhists were in the pay of the Viet Cong: "When a communist in the cloth of a bonze is arrested," one editorial asked, "is it discrimination against Buddhists or is it protection of public security against subversion?" There were reports from usually reliable sources that while the Nhus and Thuc remained adamantly opposed to compromise, Diem himself seemed to favor a more flexible line. Verification was impossible. And the Buddhists themselves braced for a crackdown. In a quiet interview one night, Tri Quang showed me a copy of a telegram one of his agents had intercepted. Sent to leading Saigon and province officials, it ordered them to "prepare public opinion for a new attack against the Buddhist movement. Follow, investigate and prepare to purge all Buddhist elements which have been dissatisfied, including high army officials and ranking civil servants." Even after the government and the Buddhist leadership had signed an agreement which partially met Buddhist demands, Nhu secretly ordered his Republican Youth cadres to fire off protests to Diem.

By early August, it was clear that Nhu, not Diem, was making government policy on the Buddhist question. Saigon's rumor mill, always hyperactive, went into overdrive: Nhu was planning a coup against Diem, Nhu was plotting with Hanoi to oust the Americans, Nhu was going to smash the Buddhists by murdering their leaders, Nhu had ordered his secret policemen to assassinate American correspondents—the list seemed endless. Then, on August 21, Nhu ended much of the reason for speculation.

Late that night, after a surprise declaration of martial law, the Nhu-controlled Special Forces units smashed into pagodas in Saigon, Hue, and other cities as well. At least three hundred bonzes were thrown into prison, many more were wounded, and several were killed. All Buddhist files were seized, and a roundup of sympathizers began. Saigon was stunned.

But only briefly. It became clear that Nhu had miscalculated. For one thing, some Buddhist leaders escaped. Tri Quang, for example, took refuge in the U.S. Embassy. For another, Vietnam's students, who until this point had refrained from action for fear of spoiling their careers, suddenly entered the picture. In both Saigon and Hue, huge student protest strikes were called, and street demonstrations began. To Nhu, this was intolerable. Within two days, at least fifteen hundred students had been arrested and hustled off to prison—among them the sons and daughters of many army officers and government officials, Catholic and Buddhist alike. It became clear the Buddhist affair was no longer an elementary religious confrontation. Instead, Nhu found himself confronted by a rebellion of the Vietnamese people against their government.

At this stage, the United States finally began to act. Washington's new ambassador, Henry Cabot Lodge, stepped off an air force jet at Ton Son Nhut as a light shower settled the dust on the tarmac. "Let's hope it's an omen," an embassy friend told me. Lodge's airport statement was noncommittal, unsurprisingly, but reporters noted with some interest that he made a point of greeting the press. Almost immediately after Lodge's arrival, Washington announced its decision to suspend part of its food aid to Vietnam. And in a Voice of America broadcast beamed to Saigon, "American officials" were quoted as saying that ARVN leaders were not responsible for the pagoda raids; instead, blame was cast on Nhu and his personal forces. Madame Nhu reacted by accusing the Americans of cutting off food for Vietnamese babies, but no one seemed to be listening any more. U.S. Embassy officials, including many who had enthusiastically backed policy until the pagoda raids, were furious. Typical was a senior AID official, who told me: "We should damn well have shut down operations after the pagoda raid. The Vietnamese have developed a nasty arrogance toward us in the past few years; they think they can kick us in the teeth and make us like it. It's about time we got tough."

In fact, Lodge *was* getting tough. In personal talks with Diem and Nhu, he made it clear that Nhu was no longer considered useful. In a cautious but meaningful statement to me, he noted that United States policy was "to help the republic of Vietnam win and maintain its freedom from communist terrorism. Anything advancing this," he said, "we support; anything hindering this, we oppose." It was obvious that he considered the government's Buddhist policy as something to be opposed. This wasn't clear, however, to many Vietnamese. Most despaired of any effective United States action: "I think your Mr. Lodge will back down," a young businessman told me. "Nhu is too powerful."

Through early September, the terror continued. High school students, who joined in the demonstrations after Nhu clamped down on universities, were arrested as well. The few civic leaders and public figures who had escaped imprisonment in the past now jammed prison cells: many were tortured, and several died. Nhu, his policy hardening fast, scented a coup, and he was determined to smoke out the plotters. To a small group of reporters who interviewed him in early September, however, he seemed almost relaxed. He laughed off reports that the CIA was plotting a coup, for example: "It's an internal matter for the U.S.," he shrugged. "We are not surprised by attempted coups. Countries such as ours are all volcanic, and you must have a stomach strong enough to take it. Gentlemen who wear stiff collars cannot get along here." And then he tossed a bomb in our laps: "If it would be in the interest of American-Vietnamese solidarity, my wife and I would step down with joy, not with resentment. We have no political ambitions." Madame Nhu, with whom I talked the next day, was equally mild: "We do not consider ourselves irreplaceable," she said. "If there were no war, we would be happy to live in our own home." Asked about a recent statement by President Kennedy to the effect that the Saigon government seemed to be out of touch with its people, she asked playfully: "What changes does Mr. Kennedy want us to make? Unless he is specific, we may make mistakes."

By this time, however, the family had been made perfectly aware of White House thinking, which had been faithfully relayed by Lodge. As an embassy source put it: "You can sum up our policy in five words—get rid of the Nhus." The problem was one of means, not ends. Judgments were complicated by the fact that Washington seemed terribly confused about events. Embassy reporting, which up until the pagoda raids had discounted the possibility of change, reversed itself rapidly with Lodge's arrival, but both the Pentagon and the State Department were evidently puzzled by what was happening in Saigon. Two weeks after Lodge's arrival, for instance, two high functionaries (a Marine general and a former embassy political counsellor) flew in from Washington. Over the weekend they questioned nearly every United States government employee in Saigon on his sentiments about American policy. "We were asked how we felt about the Nhus," said a senior AID administrator, "and we backed dumping them one hundred percent." (Back in Washington a week later, Kennedy read their reports, then asked quizzically: "Did you guys visit the same place?")

Obviously, U.S. official opinion in Saigon was less than unanimous. Both MACV and CIA leaders opposed attempts to force Nhu out. CIA Station Chief John Richardson was extremely close to Nhu and his wife: "My husband considers him as a brother," she told me. It was far from coincidental that in early autumn, Richardson was reassigned. MACV, under General Paul Harkins, was strongly opposed to any change at all, on the theory that the military situation would crumble almost instantly. Ignored in this analysis was the fact that the war was going very badly indeed, a fact of which most correspondents were painfully aware. The Buddhist crisis, and the government's handling of it, had had severe repercussions throughout the army's ranks.

With this in mind, Defense Secretary Robert McNamara and JCS Chief General Maxwell Taylor arrived at Tan Son Nhut in late September. Ostensibly, their mission was solely to appraise military progress, but inevitably they were briefed on the rapidly deteriorating political situation as well. On their return to Washington, however, McNamara and Taylor reported that while the political situation was "deeply serious," the major task of the United States military could be successfully completed by the end of 1963. Senator Richard Russell, after a closed session with McNamara, called it a "cautiously optimistic" report—a phrase that echoed other American appraisals dating back to 1954 and was still, unhappily, being used in 1967.

Lodge, on the other hand, continued to pursue a tougher line. In his first public statement, he answered Madame Nhu's description of young United States advisers as "little soldiers of fortune" by labeling it "a shocking statement . . . It is incomprehensible to me how anyone can speak so cruelly. These men should be thanked and not insulted." No American ambassador had ever talked so harshly to the Nhus: it seemed an omen of greater straightforwardness to come.

Events, however, had already begun to outpace American policy. Three coup plots were well under way, and the pagoda raids had given each added momentum. The most far-reaching—and the one that eventually succeeded—was led by three high-ranking generals: Tran Van Don, Duong Van Minh, and Le Van Kim. A second, which eventually joined forces with the first, was designed by tiny Dr. Tran Kim Tuyen, for several years Nhu's intelligence chief; Colonel Do Mau, an army intelligence officer; and later, Colonel Pham Ngoc Thao, a former Viet Minh leader who joined Diem in 1954. The third plot, most bizarre of all, was masterminded by Nhu himself; he planned a false coup which would result in a bloody purge of army officers he felt were hostile to him and eventually would result in his triumphant return to power. All three plots, as it happened, came to turn on the flawed personality of a single man.

He was Brigadier General Ton That Dinh, commander of the ARVN's III Corps area (which surrounds Saigon) and military governor of the capital under the martial law imposed by Nhu at the time of the pagoda raids. Rash and conceited, Dinh was, as a French friend put it, a "carbon copy of the French 'paras' in Algiers. He even wears his hair 'en brosse.' " He was also considered completely loyal to the regime and, for some months, while the other generals laid their plans, had been bracketed by them with General Huynh Van Cao, IV Corps commander, as prime targets for assassination once the coup was under way.

After the attacks on Xa Loi and other pagodas, Dinh began boasting that he, and he alone, had saved the country from "international adventurers"—including both the Viet Cong and the Americans in this category. With this in mind, Don—a very keen and cool man—went to work. He managed to persuade Dinh that he deserved better things of the regime, that in fact he really ought to be given the Interior Ministry. Dinh snapped at the idea: he went to Nhu and Diem and made what amounted to a demand for the post. Nhu was shocked, and shipped Dinh off to Dalat for a rest, hoping he would cool off. Instead, Dinh grew even angrier. Don threw out more bait: it was in the national interest, he told Dinh, that he act. Would he join a coup plot—particularly if he were assured the minister's post if it succeeded? Dinh was hooked: his switch was crucially important, for the troops he commanded were in the immediate area of the capital and thus would play the single most important role in any fighting that became necessary, as well as provide a shield against any forces further away that might remain loyal to Nhu and Diem.

Meanwhile, Don enlisted more support. The commanders of I and II Corps, in central Vietnam, came over to his side. (They were, respectively, General Do Cao Tri and General Nguyen Khanh, of whom much more would be heard.) And in a series of meetings with an official American contact, Don received word that the United States would not oppose his efforts. In October, Don managed to convince the Tuyen–Do Mau group that they should join forces. The stage was set—if Dinh could be relied upon.

But Dinh had slipped up. In an attempt to fend off intervention by the IV Corps troops of General Cao in the Mekong Delta, he had sent his deputy, Nguyen Huu Co, to talk with some of Cao's officers. Nhu heard of it, summoned Dinh to his office, and confronted him with the story. Thinking quickly, Dinh blamed it all on Co, then pledged his assistance to Nhu. With that, Nhu briefed Dinh on his own false coup, and put it in Dinh's hands.

This was all Dinh needed. He shifted most of the Vietnamese Special Forces, loyal to Nhu, out of the capital, telling Nhu this was done in connection with his countercoup plans. To replace these units, he brought in his own men, again with Nhu's approval. Shortly after noon on November 1, the coup began.

For Don, there were some awkward moments. Talking with me two days later, he recalled that as the coup was about to ignite he was at the airport saying farewell to Pacific Fleet Admiral Harry Felt. "We thought he'd never go," Don said. But that hitch was insignificant: across Saigon, the coup was going like clockwork. Marines seized police headquarters, Radio Saigon, and the post office. Pro-Diem officers, including the colonel in charge of Special Forces, were arrested. And outside the palace, Don's troops and armor had opened fire on presidential guard units. Inside, Nhu and Diem slowly began to realize that the coup—if it was really theirs—wasn't going as planned. A series of frantic phone calls to Dinh, whom they still considered loyal, failed to go through. Alarmed, Nhu radioed an appeal to all troops to rally to the rescue. No one replied. Instead coup leaders called on the brothers to surrender. Diem then telephoned Lodge, who urged him to give up and pledged every effort to be sure he and Nhu would be honorably treated. Diem hung up.

By now, fighting had spread to the presidential-guard barracks, about a mile from the palace. Late that evening, an all-out assault began, and the battle raged for almost twelve hours. At the American Embassy, embassy officers watching the night fighting decided to inform Tri Quang, still a refugee in the chancery, that a coup had begun. "Do you think I'm deaf?" he asked. Finally, after an enormous expenditure of ammunition but remarkably few casualties, the guard units surrendered. Rebel units poured into the palace, searching for Diem and Nhu. They were nowhere to be found.

Long before the battle ended, they had left the palace through a secret tunnel, and been driven to the home of a rich Chinese businessman in Cholon. Early the next day, Diem telephoned Don's headquarters and offered to surrender. From that point on, the story becomes unclear. The most authoritative account says that an APC

(Armored Personnel Carrier) was sent to pick them up, that while Diem climbed aboard immediately, Nhu hung back, then evidently grabbed for the pistol of an escorting officer, and was shot dead instantly. Diem, according to this source, died in the fusillade. Another report said the brothers were killed on orders of the coup leaders. In any case, their bodies were taken to army headquarters and buried in the courtyard, in unmarked graves.[28]

The people of Saigon seemed stunned. After an initial burst of celebration, they drew back. "We are happy," said a young teacher, "at least it's a change. We don't know what will happen next but now at least we have hope." At the battered Gia Long Palace, thousands of Saigonese moved slowly past, gaping at the destruction. Pretty girls in multi-colored silken *ao-dais* offered food and soft drinks to the soldiers on guard, fathers hoisted children on their shoulders for a better view, and older boys frolicked atop the tanks. The bars and restaurants along Tu Do did a roaring trade, and dancing was resumed—even the twist was being performed, and knowledgeably at that. (Evidently, Madame Nhu's ban on dancing hadn't been completely obeyed.) At Xa Loi, the faithful knelt to give thanks, and freed bonzes chatted happily with their friends. But running through every conversation was a feeling of fear for the future.

At Joint General Staff headquarters, the coup leaders rapidly put together a junta government. At the head of it was Duong Van Minh, an officer who commanded wide respect within the army and outside it as well. Next in line were Don, a wealthy aristocrat who had graduated from France's St. Cyr, and Le Van Kim, perhaps the most intelligent of the three. Former Diemist officers and officials were arrested. Madame Nhu and Archbishop Thuc, fortunately for them, had left the country shortly before the coup, but brother Canh remained. (After a long period in custody, he was shot.)

The new leaders inherited a host of problems. Militarily, the country was in serious trouble, and the Viet Cong in November mounted a widespread offensive to take advantage of the coup-caused confusion. Strategic hamlets fell apart. The Buddhists began to criticize the junta for retaining, as premier, Diem's former vice-president, Nguyen Huu Tho. And Dinh, despite his key role in the coup—or perhaps because of it—was widely mistrusted in his new job as security minister. Dinh added nothing to his stature by reportedly saying, after the coup: "On August 21, I was governor of Saigon and loyal to Diem, on November 1, I was governor of Saigon and fighting against Diem, maybe in the future I'll be governor of Saigon and fighting against the Americans." More encouraging was the reappearance of opposition politicians, jailed and tortured by Nhu long before: among them were Phan Khac Suu and Phan Quang Dan.

"At base, the coup has changed everything and nothing," I reported at the time. "The same problems still exist as far as the war is concerned: it still remains to be seen whether the generals can enlist the popular support Diem never obtained." A Vietnamese friend put it another way: "It's a question of whether these people, whose brains have atrophied after nine years of not being allowed to make decisions, can now make the right choices." Peking and Hanoi seemed exultant: "U.S. imperialism cannot save itself from defeat in South Vietnam by installing new stooges there," chortled an article in *Peking Review,* and Radio Hanoi echoed this view.

Two months after the coup against Diem, the triumvirate of Minh, Don, and Kim still had not been able to get South Vietnam off the ground, and once again rumors of coups began to flow. Food prices soared, and Premier Tho was blamed for this as well as other, even more disagreeable manifestations such as strikes and demonstrations. Just about the only positive move had been to force Ton That Dinh out of his command of III Corps in early January. But there was increasing unrest among the lesser military leaders who had supported the coup, but had not—they felt—profited accordingly. One of these men was stocky, aggressive General Nguyen Khanh: all he had received for his trouble was a reassignment from command of II Corps, in the Central Highlands, to I Corps, in Central Vietnam. For Khanh, this simply wasn't enough. He wanted action, for one thing, and I Corps was tranquil in those days. Beyond this, he wanted power—and his headquarters, at Danang, was a long way from Saigon.

There were other disgruntled officers as well. One was Do Mau, whom Don had tucked away in the Ministry of Information. Another was Tran Thien Khiem, who had replaced Dinh as III Corps commander in Saigon, in what seemed to be a demotion from his first post-coup posting to the general staff. But the "demotion" gave him command of the so-called "coup troops" in Saigon—and events began to march almost immediately.

After a series of frantic flights and telephone calls between Danang and Saigon, Khanh struck. At 2 A.M. on January 30, the junta leaders—with the exception of Minh—were scooped up by Khanh's men. Off to house arrest in Danang and later Dalat went Don, Kim, Dinh, and Mai Huu Xuan, the first three charged with collaboration with the French in an effort to neutralize South Vietnam, the fourth accused of unspecified "abuses" under the Diem regime. Khanh installed himself as premier, Khiem was placed in charge of the armed forces, and Minh—as a result of intense American pressure—became chief of state. In an attempt to win himself a sizable block of civilian support, Khanh brought back from Paris the long-exiled Nguyen Ton Hoan, a Catholic and a key figure in the intensely nationalistic Dai Viet party. Hoan became one of three deputy premiers: the other two were Do Mau and Harvard-educated economist Nguyen Xuan Oanh. Hoan's Dai Viet affiliation, in fact, provided a tip-off to Khanh's thinking; there was a distinct Dai Viet coloration to a large proportion of his choices for primary and secondary cabinet posts. Almost immediately, the Buddhists began to grumble once more. Several of the Dai Viet officials, they charged, had also belonged to Nhu's old Can Lao organization as well. But Khanh, from the very beginning, received all-out American backing, and with what amounted to a blank check in his pocket, he shrugged off the Buddhists and began his attempts to cope with a formidable series of problems.

As it turned out, one of Khanh's greatest assets in American eyes was his willingness to take advice. Personal appearances? Khanh swooped across the country, trying his best to charm everyone in sight. Strategic hamlets? Khanh drew up a wide-ranging pacification plan and tried his best to get it rolling. Land reform? Khanh ordered new plans drafted. In response to American hints, Khanh even tried to settle the problem of the Dalat generals, whom he had ousted in January. He staged a brief, embarrassing trial in Dalat, at which the flimsy charges of French collaboration were not mentioned, and the generals drew only a simple reprimand. They were commanded to remain in Dalat, however, and Minh, at least partially out of loyalty to his old comrades, continued to sulk, just as he had done since Khanh's January coup. But Khanh seemed to be making the right moves.

Somehow, nothing much happened.

In April, Khanh began to run into trouble. His Dai Viet support began to fade with the resignation of Interior Minister Ha Thuc Ky, and the Viet Cong stepped up the military pressure. In mid-month, after three days of fighting near Kien Long in the delta, at least three hundred ARVN troops were killed and an additional two hundred civilians killed or wounded. And in ominous counterpoint, religious friction began to build. In an effort to still Buddhist charges that his government leaned toward the Catholics, Khanh ordered a trial for Major Dang Sy, the luckless Catholic who in May, 1963, ordered his troops to fire on Buddhist demonstrators in Hue. Sy was sentenced to life imprisonment, and by the end of June, seven more ex-Diem officials drew similar terms for anti-Buddhist actions. Sy's punishment sparked widespread Catholic demonstrations, and Khanh's calls for nationwide unity in the face of the deepening Viet Cong threat were largely ignored.

Almost certainly, it was at about this time that Khanh began a serious reconsideration of his power bases, which for all practical purposes was a combination of Catholics, Dai Viets, and the Can Lao. When *Newsweek*'s Francois Sully and I talked with him in June, he did his best to play down his difficulties, but admitted he "was trying to arrange a solution behind the scenes." Only later, however, did it become apparent that Khanh was preparing to shed his old backers wholesale.

His decision to shift ground was spurred by action in another quarter. At the end of June, Lodge resigned as ambassador to join in Republican campaigning. His departure was something less than surprising: Lodge had been Kennedy's man in Saigon, and from the assassination onward Lodge's role had steadily lessened in importance. His relations with Khanh were excellent, but he was no longer able to free-wheel as easily as in the days of the coup and its aftermath. And Lodge's departure was a signal for the entry onto the scene of a brand-new U.S. team in Saigon.

General Maxwell D. Taylor, Lodge's replacement, left his post as chairman of the Joint Chiefs of Staff—an enormously important job—to become ambassador. Taylor knew Vietnam well: his recommendations to Kennedy in 1961 were the basis for the expanding United States commitment there, and he had returned on several occasions since then. With Taylor, as deputy, came the able U. Alexis Johnson, a former ambassador to Thailand, who until then had been serving as undersecretary of state. And General Harkins was replaced by General William C. Westmoreland, one of the top American soldiers. It was quite a team.

Peking was obviously impressed. Foreign Minister Chen Yi

warned that the Chinese "would not stand idly by" while the Geneva Accords were ignored. President Lyndon Johnson replied just four days later, saying the United States was "prepared to risk war" in Southeast Asia to help South Vietnam keep its freedom. But Peking still sounded confident: *People's Daily,* for example, recalled that Taylor had commanded the Allied 8th Army in Korea "which had been beaten black and blue by the Korean and Chinese peoples forces." Hanoi's party organ, *Nhan Dan,* noted that "Harkins and Lodge have failed. Taylor cannot help but slide into the rut of his predecessors."

Khanh's base of support was obviously shrinking. Minh was a much more popular figure, and the chunky premier, eternally suspicious, couldn't help recalling that Minh and Taylor had been frequent tennis partners during the ambassador's previous visits to Saigon. (Privately, Khanh sneered at Taylor as "the tennis player.") Anxious to find an issue that would rally his dissolving popularity, Khanh seized on the theme of national unification, and at a mass rally in Saigon he called for an expansion of the war to North Vietnam: "Bac Tien" (March North) was his battle cry.

This was the last thing Taylor wanted to hear, and he set to work to calm Khanh down. American policy, he reportedly told Khanh, was to pacify South Vietnam, not to reunify Vietnam by force of arms. Khanh's reply was both blunt and negative: he told Taylor that *he* made policy in Vietnam, not the United States. Late in July, Khanh seemingly backed down—but it seemed little more than a gesture.

On August 2, 1964, North Vietnamese torpedo boats attacked the U.S. destroyer Maddox in the Tonkin Gulf. Evidently, the Maddox was supporting an attempt to land South Vietnamese infiltrators in the North, though this was never publicly stated. In any case, the attack was brief, and neither the Maddox nor the North Vietnamese craft suffered much damage. Two days later, however, the Maddox and another U.S. destroyer, the C. Turner Joy, were attacked again, and this time the battle lasted for three hours. Two of the North Vietnamese boats were sunk. In Saigon, American officials seemed mystified: "The attacks make no real sense," a top embassy official told me. It was theorized that Hanoi had hoped for an enormous propaganda coup in the sinking of an American destroyer, to match the recent Viet Cong sinking of a U.S. aircraft carrier in the Saigon river—but that scarcely seemed reason enough. In any case, there was no doubt about the U.S. response: Johnson ordered raids on North Vietnamese PT boat bases. On August 5, carrier-based jets destroyed or damaged twenty-five PT boats, erased an oil depot at Vinh, and shot up anti-aircraft installations. Two American jets were lost and two more damaged. It was, of course, a major escalation of the war—and it had been provoked by what seemed to be a gross miscalculation on Hanoi's part. More U.S. naval units moved toward the Tonkin Gulf, and Communist China sent fifteen Mig jets to Hanoi.

The attacks had a totally unexpected side effect: Khanh profited enormously. His "Bac Tien" policy suddenly looked much more intelligent to many Vietnamese, and Hoan's Dai Viet coup plotters received a severe setback. Khanh moved quickly to consolidate his gains by declaring a "state of emergency," which, while ostensibly aimed at preparing for retaliatory action by the Viet Cong or the North Vietnamese, actually was intended to squelch further his opposition. And while Khanh's relations with Taylor remained cool, there was little doubt that the United States was still backing him.

Then, at a time when Khanh seemed at the height of his power, he committed a calamitous blunder. On August 16, he summoned the press to Vung Thau, a sun-drenched seacoast resort south of Saigon, for an "important announcement." We waited for some six hours outside his vacation house, Villa Blanche, for something to happen, while embarrassed aides drifted back and forth explaining that "unforeseen delays" were holding things up. At last, we were allowed inside to watch the generals of the Revolutionary Military Council first vote unanimous approval of a new constitutional charter, which gave a president near-dictatorial powers, then elect Khanh president. Khanh produced a surprised smile for the photographers as the results were announced, but the effect was marred by the fact that a plaque reading Chu-Tich (President) stood in front of his seat all through the voting. Then, in a brief press conference, Khanh announced: "We've made a big step forward."

It proved, almost instantly, to have been a great leap backward. "It's Diemism without Diem," commented an angry Saigon teacher. "Khanh betrayed Minh," said another Vietnamese friend. "We can never trust him again." Pressures began building up almost instantly. U.S. officials, who had approved the Vung Thau charade, were taken aback by the violence with which the charter was attacked in Saigon. And on August 20, Buddhist leaders across the country cranked up an all-out attack on Khanh. Student demonstrations began in Saigon, and Buddhist activists moved to join them. So did the Viet Cong, and Saigon's hostility spread rapidly to Hue, Danang, and other major cities. Khanh tried to temporize, but affairs had gotten out of control. The demonstrations, by August 23, had turned into bloody riots.

Two days later, twenty thousand angry demonstrators besieged the prime minister's office to demand that the Vung Thau Charter be withdrawn. Khanh, courageously, emerged to confront the crowd and denied that he wanted to become a dictator. Shortly afterward, he seemingly surrendered: he announced that he was resigning and that the charter would be abrogated. Saigon's demonstrators, by this time in a state of frightening hysteria, paid no attention. The riots continued and, on Khanh's orders, little was done to stop them. (Reportedly, he feared that some rioters would be killed by any repressive actions, which is what had happened the year before, and that the deaths would provoke even more dangerous clashes.)

For the next three days—it seemed like three years—Saigon was ruled by the mobs. There were brief spells of quiet, but then another screaming crowd of youngsters—older people stayed home—would pour out of the slums and smash headlong into another. At midday on the twenty-seventh, I had come back from one of these clashes for a quick lunch. But halfway through my ham sandwich, I heard screams from the street outside. I ran outside to see at least a thousand Catholic demonstrators come roaring past, singing and shouting anti-Khanh slogans. I grabbed a camera and followed, soaked almost instantly by a monsoon downpour. The mob was heading for the radio station, and this time they encountered resistance. An airborne battalion, bolstered by Civil Guardsmen, was waiting. After a long, inconclusive shouting match, the mob pulled back, clearly overmatched. Then, from down the block, came shouts that a Buddhist mob was approaching.

Instantly, the Catholic youngsters ran to meet them, hurling a barrage of bricks, rocks, bottles, and whatever else they could get their hands on. The approaching force replied in kind, then retreated. The group I was beginning to think of as "my" mob surged after the Buddhists, and one laggard was pounced on and brutally beaten. I moved in for a photograph. Suddenly, I found myself flat on my back, bleeding badly from the nose, and about to be trampled by retreating Catholics. I had been hit by a flying brick, and it seemed obvious that it was time to retreat: the Buddhist youngsters were charging back to rescue their bruised victim. (All I could think of, however, was the fact that my glasses had been knocked off. After a frantic minute of fumbling, I found them and ran.) Out of the line of fire, finally, I took stock. Covered with my own blood, scratched and bruised, glasses broken, I now felt I had the material I needed. Besides, my wife was arriving from Hong Kong. Saigon wasn't the nicest city in the world at the time, but it was, after all, our fourth anniversary.

The "radio riot," as it came to be called, was only one of several that day in Saigon and in Danang and Hue as well. And Khanh's decision to use troops resulted in precisely what he had feared: out at army headquarters, government troops fired on rioters at the gates, and six were killed. That, for Khanh, seemed to be it: late in the day, the junta announced that the Vung Thau charter was finished and that Khanh would be forced to share his power with Minh and Khiem. It pledged a return to civilian government within two months, and then dissolved itself.

Unimpressed, the rioters carried on for two more days. Finally, Khanh announced that he was stepping aside because of a "breakdown," and headed for Dalat. By the next day, Saigon was calm once more: Oanh was named to head a caretaker government, under the supervision of Minh and Khiem. On September 3, however, Khanh recovered sufficiently from his "breakdown" to return to Saigon and re-assume power.

It rapidly became apparent that this was a new Khanh. In the next few days, his old Dai Viet and pro-Catholic officials began to leave, to be replaced by men with Buddhist backing. First to go was Hoan. Khiem (regarded as pro-Catholic) resigned as defense minister, though he remained a triumvirate member. Two generals, Do Cao Tri and Nguyen Van Thieu, lost their commands, and the national police chief, Colonel Tran Thanh Ben, was fired. Interior Minister General Lam Van Phat quit. These men shared a common liability— they were on the Buddhist purge list. Khanh's shift of backers had become obvious: from then on, the Buddhists were calling his tune.

Until the previous spring, few observers took Vietnamese Buddhism—or Vietnamese Buddhists—very seriously. They existed primarily as "the others": if you weren't an army officer, a top government official, or a rich merchant, you were probably a Buddhist. And with the exception of the bonzes, not many Vietnamese Buddhists really had much of a clue as to Buddhism's real meaning. But the series of self-immolations in 1963 and Nhu's savage repression turned what had been largely a formless, faceless mass into a genuine political force. And for the time being at least, the Buddhists backed Khanh.

The strength of his support, which now included Minh and his fans as well as the Americans and the Buddhists, was demonstrated in mid-September, when Lam Van Phat, bitter over his ouster as interior minister, attempted a coup against Khanh. It failed after a confusing twenty-four hours, and Khanh seemed more firmly in control than ever. A few days later, there was another incident in the Tonkin Gulf: U.S. Navy vessels fired on four evidently hostile craft—which were never fully identified. Khanh profited again as attention switched back to the war. By the end of September, Khanh was secure enough to force the ouster of Khiem from the triumvirate, and Do Mau was eased out as well. Shortly afterward, the Buddhist leadership issued a firmly anti-communist communique. All seemed to be going well.

In late October, Khanh kept his promise, made in August, to establish a civilian government. Phan Khac Suu, a veteran of Diem's prisons, was elected chief of state by the High National Council, which just previously had issued a new constitutional charter. Suu named Tran Van Huong, another Diem foe, as premier. But Khanh retained a significant power: he kept his post as commander-in-chief of the armed forces.

Almost immediately, the outlook turned black. The Viet Cong, who had been relatively quiet for the past several months, staged a surprise raid on the huge American base at Bien Hoa, just outside Saigon, and destroyed an estimated $25 million worth of aircraft. On the central coast, massive floods devastated cities and hamlets, and a huge relief operation got under way.

In Saigon, Huong suddenly found himself in trouble. He had been criticized for not consulting religious leaders on his cabinet choices in early November, and on November 22, an estimated three thousand demonstrators took to the streets in protest. Huong reacted with much more determination than Khanh had shown in August: he ordered police and paratroopers to use teargas to disperse the crowds. The Buddhists, charging that Huong was discriminating against them, called for his overthrow. Tri Quang and a fellow Buddhist leader, Thich Tam Chau, staged a forty-eight-hour hunger strike to protest Huong's policies. There were sad parallels to the August demonstrations against Khanh: the same riots and the same rioters, the same aimless student militancy, the same drifting on the part of the regime. The Viet Cong, understandably, moved to capitalize on the dissension. Several hundred cadres moved into operation in Saigon, infiltrating both the student and the Buddhist movements. And just as it had during the late summer, the U.S. Embassy did everything in its power to keep Huong in place. Militarily, Viet Cong victories continued to occur; and in mid-December government troops were driven completely out of the An Lao valley.

On December 20, Huong's shaky government received a fatal blow. A group of younger generals, led by Nguyen Chanh Thi, a tough former paratroop colonel who had been involved in the abortive 1960 coup against Diem, and Air Vice Marshal Nguyen Cao Ky, dissolved Huong's de facto legislature, the High National Council. At least fifty leading politicians were arrested, and it was obvious that Huong was on his way out. Ambassador Taylor tried his best to stave off Huong's removal, but his protests had little effect. Behind the latest crisis was Khanh, and by this time the always-cool Khanh-Taylor relationship had almost completely dissolved.

By the end of the year, most of my American friends in Saigon were buried in gloom. The civilian government, which had been greeted with at least a degree of enthusiasm, had failed, and Huong's formal exit was only a matter of time. Forty miles from Saigon, the Viet Cong had overrun the town of Binh Gia and held it for twenty-four hours before pulling back. Four ARVN battalions were cut to ribbons: total South Vietnamese casualties came to more than five hundred, plus four American advisers, and three American choppers were shot down. Anti-Huong riots exploded in nearly every South Vietnamese city. In a year-end statement, the Liberation Front claimed it controlled more than three-quarters of the country and more than half of the population. Military intelligence sources estimated total VC strength at about 120,000 and found no evidence that the guerrillas were having any trouble replacing their losses. American losses had risen sharply: during 1964, 136 had been killed in action and 1,022 wounded. Khanh's ambitious pacification plan, launched in February, had been scrapped by late summer; in its place was a much more restricted plan involving only the five provinces nearest to Saigon—and that plan was deep in difficulty. It had been a disastrous year, and 1965's prospects were grim.

Huong and Taylor, in early January, did their best to try to hold the government together. Nothing seemed to work. Taylor met Tri Quang, to no avail, and the Buddhist protests continued. Taylor met the "young turks"—the junior generals who by now were allied with Khanh, again to no avail—and in the process gave the "turks" what amounted to a dressing-down in the best West Point style. That did nothing to strengthen relations between the Americans and the Vietnamese military. And the Buddhists, by this time, had turned strongly anti-American.

At the Vien Hoa Dao, political headquarters for the Buddhists, denunciations of Huong intensified. "He is backed only by foreigners," charged Tam Chau. A few days later, Tam Chau accused Huong of trying to split the Buddhist movement, and five bonzes began a "fast unto death" aimed at forcing Huong to quit. In Saigon, Buddhist demonstrators battled with troops and police.

By this time, however, the army was beginning to assert its power. After a reshuffle of Huong's cabinet, four generals popped up with posts. Among them was Marshal Ky, who retained his air force command. Four days later, the Buddhists began a series of viciously anti-American demonstrations: they stoned the embassy and USIS headquarters in Saigon, and, on January 23, the Hue office of USIS was sacked. In obedience to the Vien Hoa Dao's call for sacrifice, a seventeen-year-old girl burned herself to death in Nha Trang. Huong was unable to restrain the rioters, and on January 27 he was ousted by the military: Khanh took power once more.

For a month, political bickering continued, and finally, on February 15, Khanh succeeded in pulling a premier out of the hat. He was Dr. Phan Huy Quat, a northerner who had served Khanh the previous year as foreign minister. Mindful of Huong's mistakes, Quat chose his cabinet with great care: the military won three seats; the Catholics, four; the Buddhists, twelve; and the Cao Dai and Hoa Hao religious sects, one apiece. Whatever else the cabinet lacked (only four ministers were southerners, for example), it accurately reflected the current balance of power. Quat's accession, however, marked the end of the line for Khanh. Characteristically, it came about as the result of a coup.

This time, the master plotter was Colonel Pham Ngoc Thao, one of the original anti-Diem plotters, who had been shipped off to the United States after Diem's fall and, after a brief return, then assigned to Washington as press officer. In December, 1964, Thao was ordered home once more, but it became obvious that he suspected

Khanh of setting a trap. I ran across him at Tan Son Nhut on the day of his return, and made an appointment for a chat a day later. Thao, however, promptly went underground and began work on a coup against Khanh. It flared on February 19: for nearly twenty-four hours Thao's men controlled Saigon. But Khanh slipped away, and by the next day, Thao was on the run, defeated by the "young turks" supposedly still loyal to Khanh. As it turned out, the younger generals had finally had enough: led by Marshal Ky and General Thi, they voted Khanh out of office. Three days later, Khanh departed for the United States to serve as South Vietnam's "ambassador at large." Thao's coup thus wound up a success, but not for Thao: he was underground once more.

For nearly four months Quat held on to his job. On the whole, he was an effective premier. He had persuaded the army, which remained the major source of power, to go along with his plans, took advantage of frictions among the Buddhist leadership to keep the Vien Hoa Dao off balance, and convinced the Catholics that he would protect their interests in the bargain. In May, however, at the urging of pro-Buddhist General Thi, the army sentenced the still-hidden Thao, a Catholic, to death. Thao, in response, mounted another coup, but it died aborning, and he went back into seclusion. (Thao was captured in July near Saigon by army intelligence agents. He was killed immediately.) Despite the turning-back of the coup threat, Quat's days now were numbered. And in early June, after a series of angry Catholic demonstrations, the army ousted him.

After a period of wrangling within the army leadership, Ky emerged as premier, backed up by Thieu as chief of state. At the time, his chances of survival were estimated at something like one in a hundred. The embassy had its doubts about Ky, based on his youth and inexperience, and Taylor in particular was known to be skeptical. But Ky had several positive virtues: admired as a war hero, he had strong backing from the students. The Buddhists felt that Thi, who at that time was close to Ky, would protect *their* interests. And Thieu, a Catholic, held an important job as well.

For Ambassador Taylor, Ky's accession to power was the end of the line. Their relationship had started out badly the previous December when Ky and the other "young turks" received a stiff talking-to from Taylor. In July, he was replaced by Lodge, back for another round. And beyond the fact that Lodge would start out with Ky minus any past disagreements, it was apparent that Taylor's policies were simply not making rapid progress—and these policies had been in effect largely since his 1961 recommendations to President Kennedy. "If there is one thing certain in this world," a Saigon diplomat told me, "it's that if Taylor felt victory was at hand within a year, he would have stayed on."

For the balance of the year, South Vietnam's seemingly endemic political upsets sputtered out. In August, there were brief Buddhist demonstrations in Central Vietnam, but they were directed against Thieu, and had no effect. From politics, attention was turning to concentrate on the war: 1965 was a year of drastic military decisions.

And it started badly. As 1964 drew to a close, a major battle began in the Central Highlands: the Viet Cong were mounting an all-out effort to cut South Vietnam in half. And VC strength was rising steadily. An estimated 10,000 troopers had infiltrated the south from North Vietnam during 1964; and VC main force (*chu-luc*) units now totaled about 35,000 men. With district forces, but excluding part-time guerrillas, the VC had at least 120,000 men under arms. Facing them were 615,000 ARVN regulars and national police: the ratio was about 5 to 1. (In 1960, the ratio had been 200 to 1.) If British experience in the twelve-year Malayan "Emergency" was to be believed, a 10-to-1 ratio was the minimum for success. Saigon's troops were not succeeding in their efforts to whittle down VC strength. Obviously, it was becoming a new sort of war.

For several years, both Americans and Vietnamese in Saigon had maintained that the war would be won or lost in the rice-rich Mekong Delta. Until late 1964, the point had seemed uncontestable, and the swelling VC concentrations in the paddies and fetid swamps of the delta had forced the southward shift of the ARVN 25th Division from Binh Dinh, in then-quiet II Corps. This corps area includes 49 percent of the land area of South Vietnam, but it is thinly populated. Most of its two and one-half million people are concentrated in the coastal areas, notably Binh Dinh Province itself. With the departure of the 25th for the south, only two divisions remained in II Corps. They were the 23d, in Banmethuot, and the 22d, which in midwinter sent part of its strength east from Kontum to Bongson, in Binh Dinh, in an attempt to give the province at least a partial shield.

It was not enough. Down from North Vietnam, across the 17th Parallel's western end and then southeast along the spine of the thickly jungled Do Xa range into northern Binh Dinh, came the North Vietnamese 801st Regiment. "We picked up their trail in early December," a United States adviser in Pleiku told me, "when ARVN troops captured a Chinese-made SK automatic carbine in a fight north of Kontum." In scattered fights in Kontum Province over the next month, prisoners were taken. All were wearing tan combat fatigues—a change from the usual *chu-luc* black pajamas—they were in excellent physical condition and, even more interesting, were ethnically North Vietnamese.

On February 7, 1965, the war escalated one more step. Using captured American mortars, Viet Cong raked II Corps headquarters and an American helicopter base at Pleiku, in the western highlands, killing eight Americans, wounding 108, and destroying five choppers. In retaliation, U.S. carrier jets bombed Dong Hai, in the north, and on February 8, American and South Vietnam aircraft bombed northern targets once again. President Johnson ordered the evacuation of U.S. dependents from South Vietnam as China, North Vietnam, and the Soviet Union issued a series of fiery protests against the new American raids. On February 10, Viet Cong terrorists blew up an American barracks hotel at Quinhon, in Binh Dinh, killing twenty-three Americans and wounding twenty-two. And forty miles south, five ARVN units were almost wiped out in a VC ambush on Route 1, the major north-south highway.

"By mid-February," a senior U.S. adviser told me later, "South Vietnam was effectively cut in two. We were in desperate shape. Everything we had was committed, but the Viet Cong still were winning." Route 1 was completely cut, and the vital highway between Pleiku, near the western border, and the port of Quinhon, was in Viet Cong hands. There was an ominous historic parallel: in 1954, just before the battle of Dienbienphu, the Viet Minh had successfully isolated the highlands and in the process destroyed French Mobile Group 100, an elite armored unit with an excellent record of performance in Korea.

American advisers saw the danger clearly; in early March, more then thirty-five hundred U.S. Marines began flowing ashore at Danang to provide security for the enormous air base complex. No officials would say they feared Danang was slated to become a second Dienbienphu—but off the record, their concern was clearly expressed. It was apparent, in addition, that the Marines were only a spearhead; by fall, one source predicted, American troops would be bearing a major share of the fighting. (The arrival of the Marines brought the total of U.S. forces in Vietnam in mid-March to slightly more than twenty-seven thousand, but proportionately few were in combat units.)

At almost the same time, Binh Dinh's bleak outlook began to clear slightly. On March 8, Viet Cong regulars smashed at a Special Forces camp at Kannack, in the heart of the province. Their attack had been thoroughly planned—even to the extent of bringing along battery-powered searchlights. In wave after wave, the VC flung themselves on the post's barbed wire. They were unable to break through: next day, one American counted 129 bodies hanging on the wire, and total casualties were put at about seven hundred. It was a major failure for the VC. For the moment, at least, the battle for Binh Dinh had ended. Within a few days, the highway was open between Quinhon and Pleiku, and convoys were trucking much needed supplies into the highland headquarters. (But in early 1967, Binh Dinh remained a major battleground.)

The improvement in Binh Dinh, important as it was, was almost ignored. A year before, it would have been hailed as a watershed— but now it was far overshadowed by the fact that the post-Pleiku retaliation raids had become institutionalized. North Vietnam was being bombed almost daily, and the tempo of airstrikes in the south had stepped up sharply as well. On March 30, the Viet Cong retaliated: terrorists triggered five hundred pounds of explosive in the street outside the U.S. Embassy in Saigon, killing two Americans and wounding forty-five. Eighteen Vietnamese also died in the blast. But the lines were clearly drawn: from then on, the Vietnam war was to become largely a conflict between the Viet Cong and the Americans.

For the moment, American troop units were not involved. But American advisers very definitely were in the thick of the ground fighting, as were helicopter pilots and crewmen. The advisers, by this time, had become a distinct minority among the masses of Americans in Vietnam. In late April, after thousands more American marines had arrived, the total of American troops in Vietnam came to forty-two thousand—but only four thousand were advisers.

It was a strange role. Exact definitions were elusive: "An adviser," one captain said, "is an officer with a counterpart." That counterpart was a South Vietnamese officer, a veteran of long years of fighting, and moreover a man with a deep concern about "face." Perhaps the best definition was offered by a senior U.S. general: "He gives expert advice on modern military technology. He acts, in a military sense, as the conscience of his counterpart." There were two

types of advisers in Vietnam at the time: the tactical adviser, who
worked directly with ARVN troops, and the sector adviser, who
worked with the province chief on both civil and military matters.

The typical tactical adviser was a captain, in his late twenties or
early thirties, in Vietnam for a year of duty. One man I remember
clearly was Francis "Mo" Lynch, a thirty-one-year-old Newark, New
Jersey, native, who had graduated from Seton Hall University in
1955. He was a stocky, serious man, with a wife and son back in the
States, and in March, 1965, he was senior adviser to the ARVN
Twenty-first Ranger Battalion, based at Pleiku. On March 29, the
Twenty-first was winding up a four-day patrol northwest of Kontum.
It was not a terribly lucky day.

"We'd had our first contact that morning," Lynch told me later.
"They hit us in force in mid-afternoon, while we were moving
through a bamboo thicket. We were reasonably secure on three sides,
but the Viet Cong held the tree-line above us. Muntner (Sergeant
First Class Milton Muntner, Jr., part of the three-man U.S. adviser
team) was hit twice in the foot by the first burst. We tried to get
assaults moving, but the VC was beautifully dug in. No progress. We
called in air strikes and artillery and dug in for the night."

That night, they stood off four VC attacks, helped by flares
dropped by a C-47 circling overhead. Lynch and Captain Sach, his
Vietnamese counterpart, planned an attack the next morning to try to
break the VC grip. But the fighting that night was rough. First
Lieutenant Alanson D. Bartholomew, of Tok, Alaska, recalled being
with a BAR team on the flank when they heard someone crawling
toward them. "We waited until he grabbed the barrel," Alanson
recalled, "and then we opened up. That morning, we found him
sprawled in front of the position. He was carrying a Chicom sub-
machinegun, was wearing tan fatigues; a healthy, well-muscled guy."
That was when Lynch and his team began to realize they had run into
North Vietnamese, not Viet Cong. "They were well-disciplined, well-
trained," Lynch said. They were, in fact, part of the North Vietnamese 801st Regiment.

The ARVN Ranger attack, next morning, was turned back, and
infantry units nearby were unable to link up with the Twenty-first.
Painfully, a helicopter landing area was hacked out: the battalion had
suffered fourteen killed and nineteen wounded by this time. But the
first chopper to arrive was shot down; its four U.S. crewmen unhurt.

No more came in. The battalion was ordered to hold on for another night.

As night closed in, so did the VC. "By 2000 there'd been four strong attacks," Lynch said. "Headquarters told us to pull out at midnight, taking our wounded along, leaving our dead. But at 2245, the VC hit us hard. They rolled back our east flank. Sach left the headquarters trench to try to stop the retreat, but they continued to fall back. We decided to get the hell out."

Slowed by the wounded Muntner, the Americans were left behind. At 0100 on March 31, the VC attacked. "They charged down the hill," said Lynch, "weapons blazing. They knew somebody was there, but they couldn't spot us. We hit the dirt and played dead. For two hours, the VC prowled around us—they came within four or five meters—but they missed us."

For the next twelve hours, Lynch and the other Americans crawled toward what they hoped would be safety. Finally, they reached a clear area, and the VC seemed to have left. Lynch started waving a T-shirt and, in an awfully lucky break, they were spotted by a chopper. Within a few hours, they were back with their battalion. "Captain Sach was very withdrawn," Lynch recalled. "Later he wept in front of the general."

It was not a particularly happy experience. Lynch and his fellow advisers had clearly been abandoned by the retreating battalion, though some effort evidently was made to find them. Despite it, Lynch said he was ready to sign on again: "I think we're making great progress out here," he said. "Training a young army is exciting, and you get to love these people."

There was, in fact, a great diversity of opinion on the advisers, expressed by the advisers themselves, the Vietnamese, and American brass as well. In most cases, a genuine rapport was established between Americans and Vietnamese, particularly at lower levels. But the arrival of American combat units, in a sense, pointed up the failure of the effort: despite enormous quantities of training, arms, and other supplies, the South Vietnamese could not stand up alone to the increasing pressure being put on them by the Viet Cong and Hanoi.

More American troops arrived in April: thirty-five hundred paratroops went into Bien Hoa and Vung Thau to guard base installations, and at Chu Lai, south of Danang, nine thousand Marines landed to provide security for a huge new airbase. Australia announced it was sending an eight-hundred-man battalion, and a few weeks later, New Zealand followed. But despite the continuing troop buildup, the next several months brought a series of military disasters.

The first came on May 11 at Song Be, a provincial capital fifty miles northeast of Saigon. Neither the Viet Cong nor the ARVN and their American advisers came out of the battle with any great glory: the VC had planned to hold Song Be for at least two days but were driven out in less than twenty-four hours by airstrikes that produced heavy casualties. Saigon's forces, however, had been alerted to the attack forty-eight hours before, and should have been able to inflict a solid flogging. They didn't. When *Newsweek*'s Mert Perry and I arrived in Song Be, on the morning after the battle, the little town was a shambles: nearly every building had been badly shot up and morale was at rock bottom. Five Americans had died, at least partly because the American compound's defenses were less than totally secure, and South Vietnamese military and civilian casualties came to more than two hundred. Viet Cong losses, officials claimed, were about the same, although Perry and I saw just one body. Perhaps the most trenchant comment on Song Be was one U.S. intelligence officer's appraisal: "Our information is getting better and better," he said. "But here's a situation where we had all the intelligence we needed before the attack—and we blew it."

The killing continued. In a series of vicious battles in central Vietnam, notably at Ba Gia, government troops took at least one thousand casualties in late May and early June. On June 10, the VC overran the district capital of Dong Xoai, held it for twenty-four hours and, before withdrawing, killed hundreds of ARVN soldiers as well as inflicting heavy casualties on American advisers and Special Forces troopers. On June 25 in the highlands, the district capital of Toumorong was overrun. On the same day terrorists exploded two home-made antipersonnel mines at Saigon's My Canh floating restaurant. They went off in sequence; the second blast caught terrified diners fleeing the scene. When I arrived fifteen minutes later, large puddles of blood were everywhere; chunks of flesh were scattered for fifty feet. The death toll came to forty-two, including twelve Americans, and at least eighty were injured. And still the killing continued: Ba Gia erupted again in early July, and the district capital of Dak To fell to the Viet Cong about the same time.

On August 18, however, the string of Viet Cong victories came to a halt. Near Chu Lai, more than five thousand Marines trapped two thousand Viet Cong on the Van Tuong peninsula. It was the first major engagement for American troops in Vietnam, and it was a successful one: against the light Marine casualties, the VC lost six hundred killed and more than one thousand wounded. In late August, despite the loss of the district capital of Dak Sut, the grave situation in the highlands began to improve. Highways were reopened, and supplies began to move more rapidly.

Coincident with the movement of American troops into the South—there were seventy-five thousand Americans in Vietnam by mid-1965—there was a marked increase in the number of North Vietnamese regulars. In October and November, two large-scale battles erupted in the highlands, at Plei Me and in the Ia Drang Valley. Plei Me was described as an American victory, but U.S. losses were heavy. And the Ia Drang clash was equally bloody: again, it was described as an American victory, but reporters on the scene differed with the official descriptions. Whatever the outcome, however, it was clear that the war had become a major confrontation: to misquote Mao, politics were no longer in command. It was still a political war, but the emphasis in South Vietnam itself was clearly on war, not politics.

Outside South Vietnam, however, the early-1965 escalation of the war was matched by an increasingly determined search for peace. At the time, it seemed an almost impossible quest: Hanoi, backed firmly by Peking, had publicly adopted the hardest possible line; South Vietnam's fledgling civilian government (later ousted by the military), was obsessed by the question of its own survival, and the United States, concerned about morale in Saigon and clearly in an uncompromising mood, showed little interest in negotiations. But in Moscow and the United Nations, efforts were under way. And though word didn't trickle out until much later, there had been several efforts to get negotiations moving as early as 1963, though in some cases the validity of the efforts seemed dubious.

At least one, however, might well have been pursued. In September, 1964, U Thant returned to the United States after talks in Moscow, Paris, and Cairo. In a meeting with Johnson and Rusk shortly thereafter, Thant said he believed that any peace conference would have to be prefaced by highly secret and informal conversations. Next step was a Thant message, via Moscow, to Ho Chi Minh, asking him to agree to such talks. He agreed. Rangoon was picked as a tentative site: Thant passed the message along to then-U.N. Ambassador Adlai Stevenson. All that happened, Thant later told *Newsweek* columnist Emmet John Hughes, was "a long silence." Some three months later, Thant asked what had happened to his suggestion, this time proposing that the talks be held on an ambassadorial level in Rangoon. Washington rejected the idea, saying that independent checks, made by the Canadians in Hanoi, had indicated the North Vietnamese were not sincerely interested in talks. Later in the month, Washington rejected another Thant suggestion, this one to the effect that the U.S. and North Vietnamese ambassadors in Rangoon meet. This time, the rejection, transmitted in January, 1965, reportedly was based on American fear that the Saigon government might collapse if it became known that peace talks were under way.

There had been earlier turndowns as well. In November, 1963, Rusk told a press conference that the United States had spiked a French proposal for a neutralized South Vietnam—a proposal that Hanoi evidently had been willing to discuss. During 1964, at least two other proposals also drew rejections: in July, U Thant's suggestion to reconvene the Geneva Conference that produced the 1954 accords, and in December, a Ho offer of talks passed along by the French. Two months later, in February, 1965, France's Charles de Gaulle, at Ho's suggestion, called for a Geneva conference on Southeast Asia, a proposal echoed by the Soviet Union. Again, the answer from Washington was negative.

The Soviet Union, by this time, had sharply increased its efforts to bring about a settlement. There were ample reasons: before the Vietnam escalation, a Soviet–U.N. detente had been in the wind, and in view of the steadily eroding Soviet-China relations, an improvement in Moscow-Washington links appeared even more desirable than before. Accordingly, Soviet Premier Aleksei Kosygin visited Peking and Hanoi in early February: his arrival in North Vietnam all but coincided with the VC attack on Pleiku. On Kosygin's return, the Soviet decided to add its influence to De Gaulle's move, mentioned earlier.

But in the aftermath of Pleiku, and the followup VC blast in Quinhon, the United States expanded its bombing of the north. Clearly, the American aim was twofold: to bolster the morale of the sagging government in the south, and to punish the North Vietnamese until they agreed to come to the conference table without preconditions. In Hanoi, however, the bombings had the opposite effect: talk of negotiation stopped abruptly and Hanoi braced for a long war.

Then, on April 7, President Johnson told an audience at Johns Hopkins University that the United States was willing to enter into discussions without preconditions. It seemed a major advance toward talks—but despite the President's disavowal, it seemed clear that some conditions *did* exist. The NLF, for instance, was cut out of any meeting by Johnson's statement that the United States was willing to talk with the *governments* concerned—it seemed clear that the NLF was not regarded as a government. Hanoi was quick to reply: next day, Premier Pham Van Dong laid out the now-famed Four Points. Summarized, they were as follows: 1) Withdrawal of all U.S. troops and weapons and dismantling of all U.S. bases; 2) reactivation of the military provisions of the Geneva Accords; 3) settlement of South Vietnam's internal affairs by the South Vietnamese themselves, in line with the NLF program; and 4) reunification, to be arranged by the Vietnamese people without foreign interference. These were, in essence, Hanoi's preconditions to any conference, and they met a stony response from the United States. The bombings continued.

A little more than a month later, however, Washington ordered a bombing pause. Reportedly, Rusk simultaneously told Hanoi through the North Vietnamese ambassador in Moscow, that the suspension would be continued if the pace of the war in the south slowed markedly. Five days later, after no response had been received, the bombings of North Vietnam resumed. This action was criticized on the ground that five days was scarcely enough time for a discussion between hard and soft liners in Hanoi. And in fact, just after the attacks began again, Hanoi contacted Washington via the French to say that it was prepared to negotiate *before* the withdrawal of American forces—a significant modification of the original Four Points. From May onward, other "peace feelers" arrived in the United States through several channels. Nothing came of them.

Late in the year, however, Washington's position began to shift. Peking, in fact, took a distinctly alarmed view of the prospect of peace: "Does this mean the Johnson Administration will lay down its butcher's knife in Vietnam?" asked a December *People's Daily* editorial? "No, no. The word 'peace' from the lips of Johnson and his like is but an overture to a further escalation of the war."²⁹ Later in the month, the NLF seemed to ignore Peking's warning: it offered a twelve-hour Christmas cease-fire. Pope Paul VI and U Thant supported the idea, and in Saigon, the Americans and the South Vietnamese countered with their own offer: a thirty-hour cease-fire, effective both on the ground in the south and in the air over the north. Evidently, the VC decided to ignore both offers: Christmas Day was marred by eighty-four VC-initiated incidents; four Americans and fifty-four South Vietnamese were killed, and on December 26 the war got under way once more.

The airstrikes against the north, however, did not resume: this time, the pause lasted thirty-seven days. And the VC, on December 28, offered a second cease-fire, this time for Vietnamese New Year (*Tet*). It was to last from January 20 to January 23. Westmoreland accepted, and over the four days, there were only eighty incidents initiated by the VC—a marked percentage fall-off from the previous period.

On the diplomatic front, there was a major burst of American activity. Early in January, Johnson dispatched a galaxy of top-level officials to world capitals. W. Averell Harriman jetted off to Warsaw, then on to Belgrade, New Delhi, and points east. Arthur Goldberg called on Pope Paul and Italian leaders, then flew on to Paris and London for meetings with Charles de Gaulle and Harold Wilson. In Moscow, Ambassador Foy Kohler spent a busy hour with Soviet President Nikolai Podgorny, and a day before, leading party official Aleksandr Shelepin had headed for Hanoi. Vice President Hubert Humphrey visited Tokyo for a talk with Prime Minister Eisaku Sato, then visited South Korea, Taiwan, and the Philippines as well. And McGeorge Bundy left Washington for Ottawa to see Prime Minister Lester Pearson. Johnson had carefully touched all the bases: the Canadians, Poles, and Indians were members of the tri-nation International Control Commission, which in 1954 was set up to police the Geneva Accords. And just about every national leader visited had been involved, at one time or another, in the transmission of what came to be called "peace feelers." It was a spectacular effort, perhaps too spectacular for Hanoi. At any rate, there was no response, and this time, clearly, the blame was Hanoi's.

Over the next several months, the search continued. In July, for example, India's Prime Minister Indira Gandhi visited President Tito in his summer home at Brioni, then flew on to Moscow for what turned out to be inconclusive talks on the subject of Vietnam. China, staunchly urging Hanoi to carry the war through to the end, saw "a new Munich plot" in the making: Premier Chou En-lai said that unless American troops were withdrawn from Vietnam, a reconvening of the Geneva conference was "entirely out of the question."[30]

Then, in October, Johnson flew to Asia. At the Manila conference, the Vietnam allies announced that within six months after North Vietnam had disengaged itself from the war, Allied forces would be removed from the south. There were indications, moreover, that the pullout would begin almost immediately. (As several sources pointed out, the sheer logistics of transporting the more-than-370,000 U.S. and Allied troops from Saigon to their home countries would be staggering.) Just as significant, however, was a distinct moderation of the previous hostile stand of the Saigon government. In February, Premier Ky and fellow leaders had insisted on "total defeat" of the aggressors, but at Manila they insisted only that aggression be halted, and accepted the idea of continued partition pending nationwide free elections. Predictably, U.S. military officials—and others—developed a severe case of misgivings, pointing out that a mass evacuation would mean enormous waste and would force a closing-down of several potentially valuable construction programs such as the new port for Saigon as well as several new airfields. More important, however, was the fact that unless both North Vietnamese and Viet Cong main-force troops pulled back, the ARVN would be left to cope with a foe that had given them enormous difficulties in the past. There was some doubt, in fact, that the ARVN could effectively handle the VC on its own.

The next great burst of activity on the peace front came in January, 1967. *New York Times* correspondent Harrison Salisbury managed to obtain a Hanoi visa, and from there cabled a series of stories indicating the North Vietnamese attitude might well be becoming more flexible. U Thant and British Foreign Minister George Brown were actively probing Hanoi's sentiments, and in Washington, Harriman and his team of "peace feeler feelers" sat with antennae twitching. Another Christmas truce had broken down in a wave of incidents, and few officials radiated any particular confidence about the *Tet* pause. In South Vietnam, however, Ky tried to pretend that he'd become something of a dove: in a speech at Hue in early January, he announced he was "ready to go anywhere, any time to talk to them, but I want an answer from Ho Chi Minh."[31]

In February, two distinct peace signals arrowed into Washington. One came from Cairo, where intensely secret talks were continuing between North Vietnamese and American officials. The second arrived via Senator Robert Kennedy, who, as it turned out, didn't quite know what it was. But U.S. Embassy official John Dean, who interpreted for Kennedy in the Paris interview with French Asian affairs official Etienne Manac'h, understood immediately. In effect, it was a three-stage bid. First, Hanoi said, would come a discussion of U.S.– North Vietnamese relations. (The United States has never accorded diplomatic recognition to Hanoi.) The second stage would be a discussion of the American role in South Vietnam. The third—and most important—segment would consider a settlement. There were a few preliminary indications the move was being taken seriously—but almost immediately, the peace effort died.

Through the spring of 1967, in fact, it seemed that communications between East and West on the question of a settlement in Vietnam had all but stopped. No more was there a continuing probing of each other's ideas; attitudes, on the surface at least, seemed to freeze. There were no new approaches, no new ideas: in both Washington and Hanoi, there seemed to be no interest in movement. It was true enough to say that North Vietnam had failed to produce a single responsible emissary for Washington to meet with; it was equally true that Washington had produced no fresh initiatives worthy of attention in Hanoi. There was always the possibility that discussions were being carried on in deep secrecy—but no reporter had managed to ferret it out.

And neither the Soviet Union, France, Britain, or Communist China had really contributed much to the search for a solution, despite their pledges to aid. Charles de Gaulle clung stolidly to his theories of neutralization for Southeast Asia, without offering concrete advice on how this solution was to be brought about—save by the unilateral withdrawal of American forces from Vietnam. Britain's George Brown met only rebuffs in his attempts to bring about talks. And the Soviet Union, still rigidly committed to the outmoded idea that it was the leader of world communism, continued stonily to condemn the U.S. for its stand in the South, continued to ship war material to North Vietnam—and seemed absolutely unwilling to put any effective pressure on Hanoi for talks lest it sully its image as the self-appointed savior of the underdeveloped world. China itself, caught up in the turmoil of the Great Proletarian Cultural Revolution, continued to proclaim its unswerving support for the Liberation Front and North Vietnam, but there was little prospect of immediate Chinese intervention in the spring of 1967. Instead, the Peking government seemed almost totally absorbed by the problems of ruling China itself, rather than extending China's influence abroad. On this point, Hanoi was less than pleased: in the May issue of the authoritative party journal *Hoc Tap,* for instance, the lead editorial made several pointed remarks about what it called the "deification" of a leader. In what was a clear reference to Mao, *Hoc Tap* noted: "We respect and love our leader, but we do not deify him." And later it added: "If a leader commits errors, yet refuses to correct them and insistently maintains them, he cannot keep his leadership role forever." But despite this clear unhappiness with the trend of affairs in China, there was little likelihood that Ho could split completely with the Chinese—for sheer geographical reasons if none other—and a move toward the status of an Asian Tito seemed even more remote.

In South Vietnam, the war became even bloodier. American and South Vietnamese forces continued to report huge opposition casualties in the ceaseless chain of operations across the country, but no officers in Saigon were predicting victory soon. On the contrary, there were clear signs that still more American troops were soon to be assigned to Saigon. Over the long run, however, the purely military side of the war was obviously far less important than the pacification program, and there was no great progress here. In May, the military was given full responsibility for pacification, which previously had been in civilian hands—a move that severely upset civilian staffers. It was argued, by the military, that until an area had been totally secured by force of arms, any efforts at political reconstruction were bound to be futile. Extended, however, this argument meant that until every town, village, and hamlet was garrisoned by American or ARVN troops, political reform could not be begun. And this in turn seemed ridiculous.

How was the war going? In the spring of 1967, no one really knew. The usual measurements of a war's progress meant little in Vietnam: kill ratios, captured weapons, and defections were only part of the story. It was indeed a war of attrition, but while part of the attrition could be measured, the key area remained dimensionless; how could Saigon measure the depth and persistence of Hanoi's commitment, or vice versa? To many American officials, South Vietnamese sentiments seemed to be unfathomable, but *Washington Post* reporter Ward Just summed up the feelings of many in Saigon when he wrote: "To Vietnamese, it seems a case of killing a man in an auto accident to save him from cancer."[32]

It was true enough to say that given the firepower of the American presence in South Vietnam, it was no longer possible to lose the war militarily. But that was only part of the story: the war that must be won is political, not military, and by mid-1967 there was still little indication that much realistic attention was being paid to this point. In 1961, I reported that "the South Vietnamese themselves must win this war; the United States can only help them. And if they cannot win it with U.S. help, however dedicated their nationalist elite may be, then the United States must seriously reconsider its position." Five years later, that statement still stood up.

1. An interesting analysis of France's tenure in Vietnam is carried in Bernard Fall's *The Two Vietnams,* Praeger, New York, 1963, Chapter 3.
2. For a detailed account, see, among others, Fall's *The Two Vietnams.*
3. Fall, *op. cit.,* pp. 99–100.
4. See bibliography.
5. More than $12 million in bribes was handed out—mostly by the United States.
6. Douglas Pike, *Viet Cong,* MIT Press, Cambridge, 1966, p. 76.
7. *Ibid.,* p. 137.
8. *Hoc Tap,* January, 1960, quoted in Pike, *op. cit.,* p. 78.
9. Pike, *op. cit.,* p. 79.
10. Viet Cong is an abbreviation for *Viet-nam Cong-san* (Vietnamese Communist), a name publicized by Ngo Dinh Diem and which supposedly has derogatory connotations.
11. Quoted in Arthur Dommen, *Conflict in Laos,* Praeger, New York, 1964, p. 133.
12. Air America is a subsidiary of Nationalist China's Civil Air Transport, and operates under charter to the U.S. Government. It is generally conceded to be under the CIA's direction.
13. Wolfkill was released August 17, 1962. He tells the story of his imprisonment in *Reported To Be Alive,* written with Jerry A. Rose, published by Simon and Schuster, New York, 1965.
14. AP dispatch, *South China Morning Post,* Hong Kong, May 21, 1963.
15. Thailand had supported the right-wingers in this coup, supposedly on the theory that the United States would be much more likely to come to this faction's aid should the military situation show signs of imminent collapse.
16. Martin A. Herz, *A Short History of Cambodia,* Atlantic Book Publishing Co., London, 1958, p. 65.
17. Seymour Topping, Hong Kong bureau chief for *The New York Times* 1964–66, became foreign editor of the paper in late 1966.
18. Seymour Topping, in a *New York Times* article reprinted in the Hong Kong *Tiger Standard,* October 20, 1965.
19. *Hsin Hua* (New China News Agency) dispatch, December 26, 1960.
20. *Jen-min Jih-pao* (*People's Daily*), Peking, December 22, 1960.

21. *Hsin Hua,* May 21, 1965.
22. Article by Klaus Mehnert, *Far Eastern Economic Review,* Hong Kong, April 8, 1965.
23. UPI/AP dispatch, *South China Morning Post,* Hong Kong, December 14, 1963.
24. Sihanouk never quite understood that the American press was not completely controlled by the U.S. Government. Other Asian leaders made the same error.
25. *Agence Khmere Presse,* May 4, 1965.
26. Four months later, in April, I flew over Ap Bac en route to an operation further south. The APC tracks looping away from the treeline still were clearly visible.
27. See David Halberstam, *The Making of a Quagmire,* Random House, New York, 1965, and John Mecklin, *Mission in Torment,* Doubleday, New York, 1965.
28. For detailed accounts of events during the coup of 1963, see David Halberstam's reconstruction of events in *The New York Times,* November 7, 1963, and Robert Shaplen, *The Lost Revolution,* Harper and Row, New York, 1965, Chapter VI.
29. *Jen-min Jih-pao,* December 14, 1965.
30. Quoted in *The New York Times,* July 12, 1966.
31. Reuters dispatch, *The New York Times,* January 8, 1967.
32. Ward Just, "This War May Be Unwinnable," the *Washington Post,* June 4, 1967.

two

A PROBLEM
OF POSTURE

Thailand

As the sun balloons over the horizon, Bangkok's roar begins. Hundreds of boats, from sampans to small freighters, churn and clatter into life on the Chao Phraya River, Thailand's major waterway, which coils like a huge amiable python through the capital's heart. The streets of Bangkok, somnolent until now, come awake as well: shop shutters rattle up, the three-wheeled *samlors* (scooter-taxis), trucks, and cars cough, rattle, and spit as they get under way. And that din is only the overture. This was the Bangkok of the sixties, a boom town whose boom could be seen as well as heard.

Shops were crammed with luxuries for Bangkok's growing middle class: from imported candies and prophylactics right up to enormously expensive jewels, nubbly Thai silks, and flashy English and Japanese sports cars. New luxury hotels, capitalizing on the tourist boom, seemed to open every day. From noisy, bouncing Patpong Road, capital of the fun belt, to the city's outskirts were bars and nightclubs boasting names like Amor, Bali, Blue Eden, Cherry, Julie's Heart, 007, The Red Door, Siamese Doll, and Why Not? Down in the docks area, the Venus Room advertised "Don't Bring Your Wife." Luxurious bathhouses euphemistically offered "tension-relieving massages," and if the visitor asked firmly enough, he might even have gotten a bath. Just about everything was available, at a price. And the price was high. But the economic indicators pointed up, foreign investment continued to flow in, and the prosperity was evident. The Thais of Bangkok were prospering mightily.

"Look at the map," a confident Thai foreign ministry official instructed me in 1964. "There is no peace in the countries around us.

And then look at Bangkok." He had a point. Compared to Malaysia, Cambodia, Laos, and Burma, Thailand's immediate neighbors, Bangkok indeed provided a wondrous contrast. And not only the capital alone. Outside the city thousands of acres of rice paddies[1] surround the city like a sparkling green net. Far up into the fertile central plains north of Bangkok, and south as well, the neat lush checkerboard of fields stretches on and on. Thailand is one of the world's great rice exporters, and the reason is obvious to the eye. Further north, in the mountains of northern Thailand, the tribal peoples and the central government have come to a reasonable agreement: until Bangkok's experts turn up a cash crop as easy to raise—and as profitable—as opium, nobody's rice bowl is going to be broken. And far to the south, in the Kra Peninsula, the threat of subversion from the remnants of Malaya's CTs (Communist Terrorists) had ebbed sharply by late 1966. Thailand, so the casual visitor might surmise, is a land at peace, a nation progressing. And so it is.

Except for the Northeast.

Since the late 1950's, this remote and poverty-ridden area has been the scene of an increasingly desperate struggle. In 1959, Bangkok committed itself firmly to an effort to raise the area's living standards and productivity. The purpose: to tighten the Northeast's links to Bangkok, which had long ignored it. In the mid-sixties the harshening tone of China's propaganda attacks on Thailand, including Foreign Minister Chen Yi's offhand 1965 remark to a visiting Westerner that "we hope to have a guerrilla war going in Thailand before the year is out," accelerated the Thai drive in the Northeast. And the effort was vital. As a senior American diplomat put it to me in 1966: "For Peking, Thailand is by far the most attractive target— once South Vietnam is finished."

Comparisons to South Vietnam are all but irresistible, even to the Thais, who should know better. For example, Deputy Defense Minister Dawee Chullasapya told me that "Thailand today (1966) is in the position of South Vietnam in 1959."[2] Because the problems are different, comparisons such as Dawee's are not totally relevant. But the threat remained the same.

"I'm not worried about the Thais," a leading American officer told me, "they have so much going for them." And they do. The Thai monarchy, for example, is a genuine plus. Young King Bhumiphol Adulayej and his lovely Queen Sirikit are broadly revered as being the next thing to divine. Attractive both physically and intellectually, they command a following in Thailand no political leader can hope to approach.[3]

Combined with the Thai attachment to the monarchy is a long-standing tradition of national independence. The Thais, in stark contrast to every other Southeast Asian nation, were never colonialized. World War II was a watershed for Southeast Asia. In more or less rapid succession, Indonesia, Malaysia, Burma, Laos, Cambodia, Vietnam, and the Philippines shed their Western rulers: Holland, Britain, France, and the United States. Over the centuries the Thais played off one Western nation against another so skillfully that they maintained a significant degree of freedom.

Beyond this, Thai unity has been promoted by a genuine religious commonality. Buddhism has been, and remains, a strong unifying force, in contrast to the Catholic-Buddhist schism that threatened to tear South Vietnam apart in 1963 and still is an important divisive factor. Coupled to this is the fact that Thailand's population is much more homogeneous than that of South Vietnam's, although the Thai Malays, in the four southernmost provinces, have their differences with Bangkok. So—and this is much more important—do the Thais of the Northeast. Also worth mentioning, though it will be detailed later, is the almost complete absence of a domestic revolutionary organization comparable to the Viet Minh or Viet Cong of South Vietnam.

There are, of course, real weaknesses as well. And no one discounts the potential of these defects. Most important is the fact that Thailand traditionally means simply Bangkok and the Central Plains. "The government only now is beginning to fill out its frontiers," said an American diplomat. Because Bangkok is a magnet for young Thais, Thailand's intellectual resources congregate there, and national wealth accordingly tends to accumulate primarily in the capital. "It's a one-way street," said a Thai professor. "Bangkok soaks up most of the country's talent and resources and gives little back."

Accordingly, the links between Bangkok and the provinces suffer. Officials in the capital admit that Bangkok has paid far too little attention to outlying areas in the past, but insist the links are now being tightened. But the Thai bureaucracy, knotted in its own red tape and corrupt in the bargain, will in all probability slow progress for some time to come.

Beyond these shortcomings is an army well below its authorized numerical strength. Reasonably well-armed in proportion to its size, "it pales in comparison to South Vietnam's forces," to quote a source who has seen both in action, "both in terms of manpower and efficiency."

These points, in brief, represent the strength and weakness of Thailand today. "If the Thais were left alone," said a British diplomat, "they would be able to make considerable progress." But because of the country's important geographical position and its natural wealth, it is a wholly attractive target for Communist China. For centuries, Thailand has been afflicted in varying degree by pressures from its huge northern neighbor. Today, as the threat grows larger, Thailand is resorting to its well-tried strategy of seeking a counterbalance. This time around, that force is the United States. But America is a relatively new element in Thai politics, while the Thais and the Chinese have dealt with each other for centuries.

The Thais, in fact, sprang from Chinese soil. As far back as the sixth century B.C., Chinese historians made reference to the "barbarians south of the Yangtze," who are now thought to be the ancestors of the present-day Thais. There are close physical and linguistic resemblances between Thais and the Han Chinese, and several sources believe the two races share a common stock. Early in the Christian era, these "barbarians" fell under Chinese control, but the sketchy records available indicate they were never completely pacified. By the middle of the seventh century A.D., the Thais had coalesced into the Kingdom of Nanchao, which controlled most of present-day Yunnan. For the next hundred years, the warriors of Nanchao battled the Chinese, both in China itself and in the tributary states of Tonkin and Annam. But the Chinese prevailed: Nanchao became a Chinese vassal state by the end of the ninth century.

For the next three hundred years the Thais drifted south into what is now Thailand and Burma. Small Thai kingdoms were formed in the present-day Shan states, as well as in northern Thailand. In 1253, Nanchao lost the last vestiges of its independence when Kublai Khan swept down from the north to capture its capital, Ta-Li. During those three centuries, there was frequent contact between Nanchao and China in trade, diplomacy, and war, and these contacts led to the growth of striking likenesses. "Chinese chroniclers of the Tang Dynasty, and Marco Polo as well, recorded the similarities in customs, dress, and administration between China and the Thai kingdom."⁴ And Chinese conquest failed to change the pattern. "The Thai have always shown a striking ability to recover from adversity and to assimilate the ways of other peoples,"⁵ an ability still evident today.

Nanchao's defeat, then, merely accelerated the southward movement of the Thais. There were three currents in the migration: the first into Burma, the second into Laos, and the third into the upper reaches of the Chao Phraya, where the Thais defeated the Khmer commander of Sukhothai and laid the foundation for what was to become what many historians call "the cradle of Thai civilization," the first important Thai kingdom within the borders of present-day Thailand. The Sukhothai era's fourth king, Rama Khamheng, is generally regarded as its greatest ruler. During his reign (1275–1317), he supervised the spread of Thai domination over an area stretching from northern Laos to the Bay of Bengal and down into the Malay Peninsula. "The linchpin of Rama Khamheng's policy," says a current historian, "was the maintenance of the most cordial relations with China."⁶ He paid two state visits to the Chinese emperor during his reign, and brought back Chinese experts, even including porcelainmakers. (Sukhothai, to the Chinese, was known as Sien, and it seems reasonable to assume that this is the root word for Thailand's historic name, Siam.) With the death of Rama Khamheng, however, Sukhothai spun into a decline that ended with its fall and the establishment in 1351 of the Kingdom of Ayutthaya, with a capital only about thirty miles north of present-day Bangkok. Ayutthaya lasted until 1765, when Burmese armies seized and destroyed the capital.

During its early years, the new kingdom flourished, at least partly due to the sharp decline of Chinese influence in the area as a result of the decay of the Mongol Yuan Dynasty. But the ascension of the Mings to the Dragon Throne saw Chinese influence rise again. By 1371, the Ayutthaya Thais were among several smaller Asian kingdoms recorded as having sent tribute missions to the new rulers of the north, and they did their best to cultivate the friendliest of relations. But the later Ming emperors were less interested in overseas contacts than their predecessors, and during Ayutthaya's four-hundred-odd years its major foreign relations problems took the form of wars with the neighboring Khmers (Cambodians) and Burmese. Trade with China, of course, continued, both by caravan over the mountains of Yunnan and, later on, by sea. Beyond this, the first wave in what was eventually to become a tide of overseas Chinese began to arrive in Thailand. "For the seven hundred years of Siam's history," one source asserts, "the Chinese have been bound up with the life and trade of the country."[7]

Testimony to the closeness of this association is the fact that after the final Burmese conquest of Ayutthaya in 1765, it was a Thai Chinese who pulled Thailand together again. He was King Taksin, son of an immigrant Chinese farmer and a Thai woman, who set up his capital in Thonburi, across the river from Bangkok, and ruled for five years. Taksin was overthrown in 1782, and mistrust of his Chinese blood was said to have been one reason for his fall. His successor, Chao Phya Chakri (1782–1809), was the founder of the Chakri dynasty, which still rules Thailand. He was a son-in-law of Taksin, and one source reports the Chakri family itself is of partly Chinese descent.[8]

Under the Chakris, the history of Thai-Chinese relations became one largely of the Chinese in Thailand. China, in the later years of the Ming Dynasty (1368–1662) and the Chings (1662–1911), turned in upon itself and fell increasingly under foreign domination. By the early nineteenth century, however, tribute was still being sent annually to China, and at least one Thai king formally acknowledged his subservience to the Dragon Throne. (It seems fair, however, to ascribe this to a desire to share in the prospering China trade rather than to fear of Chinese power.) During the first half of the nineteenth century, the numbers of emigrant Chinese increased markedly and, perhaps uncoincidentally, these years were marked also by a series of Chinese rebellions, starting in 1733 and continuing in 1824, 1842, 1847, and 1848. None of these, however, was serious enough to shake the Thai regime, or even to damage permanently the status of the Chinese in Thailand.

To put it bluntly, the Chinese prospered mightily. Only indirectly involved in politics, they concentrated their efforts on trade, and during the latter half of the nineteenth century many of the more enterprising immigrants built up sizable fortunes. Today, the descendants of these men play an important role in the economic boom that characterizes Thailand in the 1960's. Thai policy toward the Chinese immigrants has varied widely, from outright persecution to all-out efforts toward assimilation. Today, the emphasis is on assimilation: one Bangkok authority estimated that 90 percent of Thailand's estimated three million Chinese are, for all intents and purposes, Thai.

"Many Chinese," he told me, "have gone completely over the fence . . . they can't even trace their Chinese background."⁹

As China's influence abroad dwindled, its place was taken by the Western powers. Thailand, long wary of the *farang* (foreigners), began to open its doors to traders from the West under King Mongkut, the fourth Chakri king, who attained a somewhat dubious notoriety in our time as "the king" of *The King and I*. In 1855, Mongkut signed a treaty with the British that cleared the way for other foreigners as well. Under heavy pressure from the British and French, both of whom had hopes of turning Thailand into a colony, Mongkut succeeded in playing off one against the other and thus carved out what amounts to Thailand's foreign policy of today. He and his son, King Chulalungkorn or Rama V, deserve much of the credit for Thailand's success in remaining largely free of outside control. And the tradition of independence gained in the process is, as mentioned earlier, one of Thailand's great assets in its resistance to Chinese Communist pressure today.

The Chakris themselves, however, lost their absolute power in 1932, when a typically bloodless revolution established the constitutional monarchy that still exists—in degree—today. The leader of that revolution was a brilliant, French-educated lawyer named Pridi Phanomyong, who now lives in exile in Communist China. The first years of Pridi's stewardship were rocky: a series of coups and counter-coups rocked Thailand almost without pause. In 1935, King Prajadhipok (Rama VII) abdicated after ten years on the job, and his ten-year-old nephew, Prince Ananda, became Rama VIII, guided by a three-man regency council. Pridi's mildly leftist ideas, meanwhile, angered those who led a trend toward military dictatorship, and in 1938 an extreme nationalist, Pibul Songgram, took over as prime minister on what amounted to a pro-Japanese platform. After the Japanese landings in Indochina in 1940, Pibul signed a treaty with Japan which, after a certain amount of Japanese pressure on the Vichy French leaders in Hanoi, resulted in Thailand's acquisition of about twenty-one thousand square miles in Laos and Cambodia.¹⁰ When Japanese troops landed in Thailand on December 8, 1941, Thai troops put up a five-hour token resistance before the Bangkok government agreed to allow the Japanese transit rights to Burma and Malaya.¹¹ Shortly thereafter, Pibul's government declared war on the United States and Britain.

The United States, however, did not reciprocate. Thailand's

ambassador in Washington conveniently "forgot" to deliver the message and set to work organizing a Free Thai movement. With close cooperation from the Office of Strategic Services (OSS), the Free Thais under Pridi's leadership succeeded by 1944 in organizing a widespread and efficient intelligence network which paved the way for a projected large-scale Allied invasion of Thailand. The invasion proved unnecessary. But Pridi and his Free Thais established Thailand's bonafides with the Allied powers. Once again the Thai genius for survival was evident: Thailand had covered its bets.

In the postwar years, despite a succession of the endemic but bloodless coups-d'etat, of which the Thais are masters, Bangkok's foreign policy remained consistent: increasingly closer links with the United States in the face of Communist China's growing power. Thailand joined the United Nations in 1947, and in 1950 was one of the first Asian nations to send troops to Korea under the U.N. banner. Four years later, Thailand was one of the founding members of the Southeast Asia Treaty Organization (SEATO), and has benefited perhaps more than any other Asian member, both militarily and economically. (SEATO headquarters is in Bangkok, and SEATO has concentrated much of its attention on Thailand—perhaps uncoincidentally.)

Internationally, the contest for political power between Pibul and Pridi ended in 1949, when Pridi was forced into exile for what now seems the last time. He had swept the elections of 1946, but his right-wing enemies linked him to the mysterious death of young King Ananda in June of that year, labeled him pro-communist in the bargain, and the slide began. A year later, Pibul swept Pridi aside, and Pridi's attempt to regain power in 1949 was smashed.

Pibul, now a field marshal and solidly backed by the Thai army, led Thailand into the period of economic expansion and grim anti-communism which still characterizes the government's policies. In 1949, when the communist triumph in China aroused a great deal of pro-Peking sentiment on the part of the Thai Chinese community, Pibul cracked down hard. And as communist pressure increased in other Southeast Asian nations (such as Vietnam, Malaysia, Burma, and Laos), Pibul redoubled his efforts against domestic Chinese in the not-altogether-unrealistic belief that they constituted a very real potential threat. Though this pressure relaxed slightly, beginning in 1954, Pibul continued to be deeply suspicious of the Chinese.

The parliamentary election of February, 1957, was the beginning of the end for Pibul. In an attempt to ensure victory, his followers perpetrated a series of vote-buying scandals that caused even the normally passive Thai electorate to erupt in protest. Pibul was forced to declare a national emergency, the constitution was suspended, and democratic government was replaced by overt military dictatorship.

In September, Pibul was forced to flee. His two main props, Police General Pao Sriyanon and Army General Sarit Thanarat, had become violently hostile to each other, mostly because of a severe difference of opinion on the division of profits from corruption, and Sarit won out. Pao was allowed to go into Swiss exile. Pote Sarasin, and later General Thanom Kittikachorn, spent brief terms as prime minister, with the blessings of Sarit. But in 1958, Sarit took full control and governed harshly but effectively until his death in 1963.

He was, by all accounts, an unusually effective leader, for all his wenching, graft, and drinking. (Though he died, officially, of heart and kidney disease, there is good reason to believe that cirrhosis of the liver was a major factor.) He left behind, for example, an estimated seventy concubines, or "minor wives," as the Thais call such blossoms. And he amassed a personal fortune estimated as high as $140 million during his six years as prime minister. But despite this unusually spectacular record, Thailand under Sarit made significant progress economically. And, more important, Sarit played an important role in gearing up his country's efforts to cope with the threat of communist subversion in the Northeast. A Northeasterner himself, Sarit was quick to realize the dangerous potential this deprived area represented. His successor as prime minister, Marshal Thanom, carried Sarit's programs forward.

The Northeast's problem can be summed up in one word— poverty. Long neglected by the central government, populated mainly by ethnic Lao (there are more Lao in Thailand than in Laos), and desperately short of natural resources, the Northeast provinces were, and are, an obvious target for communist propagandists.

To the eye, the Northeast is a vastly unpromising land. Its terrain resembles that of Wisconsin or Minnesota, with gently rolling hills and thick scrub forests. But the lushness of the American Midwest has no counterpart in the Northeast: for six months of the year, it is bone-dry, while during the rainy season its streams and rivers overflow, turning the surrounding lands into swamps. The soil is poor; rice yields per acre average about a third lower than in the rich central plains. And the people of the Northeast are equally poor:

barely educated, poorly fed, generally impoverished, they are ripe for communist subversion.

And the mechanism for that subversion is at hand, in the form of the Patriotic Front of Thailand (PFT), organized in Peking in 1965. The roots of the PFT stretch back to the late months of World War II, when the Free Thai movement organized by Pridi had largely taken over control of the Northeast. Before the Free Thais' existence, the people of the Northeast had no concept of themselves as Thais, or indeed much of anything else. Their world was their village. But the Free Thais taught them they were in fact part of something called Thailand. And, more important, the Free Thais taught Northeasterners the concept of resistance.

In these years, of course, the resistance was directed against the Japanese. But by 1946, a former Free Thai named Tiang Serikhan emerged as the leader of a small but well-organized group advocating separatism from Thailand and annexation to Laos. Tiang was one of the many communists who infiltrated the Free Thai movement: his Marxist orientation reportedly was obvious. By 1952, Tiang had about a thousand followers, and his increasing influence was beginning to trouble Bangkok. But he was assassinated that year, and his killer was never found.

By this time, however, a new leader had appeared. He was Krong Jantawong, another Free Thai leader, whose Marxism reportedly was much deeper than Tiang's, who was much better organized, and who evidently was a genuinely charismatic leader. He built, on Tiang's base, what was first called the "Solidarity Movement" and later became the "Thai Exiles' Association." Krong established links with the Lao Issarak movement of Prince Souphanouvong, as well as with the Vietnamese communists, who had cells in the Northeast as far back as 1927. By 1960, the Thai Exiles' Association included an estimated four thousand members, among them many Free Thais and some former leftist members of parliament as well.

Krong himself, in 1955, had been sentenced to thirteen years in prison for conspiracy against the government. But he was pardoned and released in 1957, and resumed his work. In 1961, Sarit decided Krong had gone too far; he was arrested, along with 134 followers, and executed on May 31.

Over the next two years, on evidence supplied by several of the arrested men, Thai intelligence units broke up six major subversive networks in the Northeast, seizing 473 more communists in the process. A clandestine party newsletter, *The Patriot,* was suppressed, but a clandestine radio station called "The Voice of the Thai People" continued to broadcast communist themes from Laos to the Northeast.

In the late fifties, as Krong's movement was expanding, Thais of both Chinese and Thai origin were undergoing training in China for eventual return to Thailand. By 1962, a series of quiet killings in the Northeast aroused the interest of intelligence officials in Bangkok—though there was no direct political link, it seemed strange that so many of the murdered men were known police informers. More were slain in 1963. But the first eight months of 1964 were quiet, a mood broken abruptly by five carefully planned slayings of community leaders and police sources in Nakorn Phanom, one of the three "hot" areas of the Northeast. (The other two delicate provinces are Kallasin and Sakol Nakhon.) Then, on November 1, 1964, the Thailand Independence Movement was formed in Peking.

Abruptly, propaganda themes changed from advocacy of separatism from Thailand, to internal revolution against the "Thanom-Prapas clique." And in early 1965, the target area of the subversives expanded: men in Thai uniform began to draw sniper fire. In July, a well-organized camp site was found, and in August there were three brief firefights between subversives and provincial police patrols. These clashes occurred in Nakorn Phanom and Ubon. In November, three or four more were recorded in the same area, and in addition a Mobile Development Unit was attacked. Hub of the activity was Nakorn Phanom, where the subversives were strong enough to risk clashes.

By 1964, an increasing amount of propaganda from Peking was being directed against Thailand. Representatives of the now-defunct "Thailand Independence Movement" were showing up at Chinese-sponsored international conferences. And in 1965 the PFT began to be mentioned. Its leader, according to Radio Peking, was Lieutenant Colonel Phayum Chulanont. On November 1, 1965, Phayum's PFT swallowed TIM and its leader, Mon Kon Nanakon. Mon Kon was still mentioned in Peking dispatches, but in what seemed to be a subsidiary role. Also linked to the front was author Kularb Saipradit.

Intelligence sources in Bangkok, both Thais and Americans, seem to know little about these men. "They weren't interesting while they were in the country," complained one. The little that's known about them is summed up as follows:

Phayum Chulanont: An army lieutenant colonel whose commission was revoked by the Thai government in 1964, he was in parliament from 1948 to 1950 and at the same time continued to work for the army's public relations department. Defeated in 1950 for re-election, he ran in later elections and failed each time. In 1958 he left the country, reportedly first to Burma then to China. One source called him a long-time follower of Pridi, but others disagreed.

Mon Kon Nanakon: A southerner from Trang, he was arrested in 1952 (in connection with the plot in which Krong was also involved) and released in March, 1955. He was a member of Trang's provincial council and owned a sawmill there. In 1964 he left his wife and family behind and went to China. Reportedly, he was helped to escape by Malayan Communist leader Chin Peng, who sailed him from Thailand to Cambodia. Mon Kon was fifty-four in 1966.

Kularb Saipradit: Once one of Thailand's most popular authors, he served with the Free Thais, was sentenced in 1955 to twenty years in prison for complicity in the 1952 plot, but was pardoned in 1957 because of his Free Thai record. Later that year he led a group of Thai writers on a visit to the Soviet Union, returned, and the next year took another group of artists to the Soviet Union and Communist China. The others returned from that trip, but Kularb stayed behind in China. By 1961 he was an announcer for the Thai-language broadcasts of Radio Peking. (Kularb, it should be added, studied in Australia in 1948–49, and was seen publicly with Australian communists during this time.) A Bangkok professor, who knows his writings well, told me that his novels and short stories display no Marxist orientation. During a stint with a Bangkok newspaper, however, he made a reputation with his anti-American analyses. Kularb, though he is mentioned in connection with most PFT gatherings in China, evidently hasn't yet an official job with the Front.

Perhaps the most interesting Thai in China is Pridi himself. The fact that he lives in Canton, far from the intrigues of Peking, is believed to indicate that he plays no active role in the intensified Chinese activity against Thailand. He has not been mentioned in any Peking story so far about the PFT, or TIM, for that matter. Though he did see Mao in October, 1965, no communique resulted, which also can be regarded as unusual. Kularb, Phayum, and Mon Kon are generally believed to be Pridi disciples in that all were influenced by him to some degree, but as General Prapas Charasuthien pointed out to me, "I studied under Pridi myself."[12] A Western intelligence source summed it up this way: "Either the Chinese are holding Pridi in reserve, or else he's holding himself in reserve. And on balance, I'm inclined to think the latter is the best bet."[13]

The three Thais most closely connected with PFT, however, aren't highly regarded in Bangkok. "The Chinese had to use whatever front men were available," Foreign Minister Thanat Khoman told me in 1966, "and there wasn't much to choose from."[14]

The PFT, through most of 1966, had not been notably successful in Bangkok. A few leaflets and handbills that popped up in the mail from time to time was about the sum of overt activity. But most of the transistor radios that infest Thailand can pick up the broadcasts of Radio Peking as well as the Voice of the Thai People without much trouble, and the tone of these broadcasts has sharpened considerably, almost precisely in tune with the increased American presence. In early 1966, Radio Peking was devoting twenty-one hours a week to broadcasts toward Thailand, in Thai—the highest total ever. Content of the broadcasts, however, showed a certain lack of imagination. Typical was this report: "Under the oppression by U.S. imperialism and the corrupt, avaricious, calamitous, and anti-popular rule of the traitorous, dictatorial Thanom Kittikachorn government, the Thai people are suffering tremendous hardships, and life for them is a continuing series of impoverishments."

Carefully avoided, in propaganda of every sort, is any hint of Chinese involvement. This, of course, is highly intelligent politics as far as Thailand is concerned. And most analysts in Bangkok are convinced that the PFT is intrinsically less important than the Chinese Communist net in Thailand. "I'm not worried by the operation we know about," said a senior Western intelligence official. "It's the net we don't know about that really bothers us." And most sources in the Thai capital are convinced that any really effective subversive operation must inevitably be directed by Chinese Communist agents, if only because communism and its attendant intrigues in the past have had little appeal for most Thais.

A more concrete indication of Peking's intentions toward Thailand is the steadily expanding network of roads constructed in South China beginning in the early part of the decade. These roads link up the communist-controlled portions of Laos with China, and North Vietnam and Burma are connected as well. Thai officials are most directly concerned by the road that runs from southern Yunnan Province across the Laos border at Muong Sing, then swings south to

Nam Tha and Ban Houei Sai on the Thai frontier. Another road branches off inside China from the previously mentioned route and swings east into the northern Lao city of Phong Saly. Further south, more links connect central and southern Laos with North Vietnam, including the so-called Ho Chi Minh Trail—which is something less than a superhighway. There are reports that the trail has been made usable by trucks for part of the run south from North Vietnam. But for the most part, the "Hochi" trail isn't much more than a complex of jungle paths.

Still, the Thai Northeast remains the focal point. The wide, coppery Mekong serves as a border between Laos and the Northeast, but it is more a link than a barrier. And across the Mekong every day float little boats carrying cadres and weapons from Pathet Lao territory into the Northeast. Their primary target is the Vietnamese refugees who fled to Thailand during the Indochina war. In their homes, the infiltrators receive food and shelter. And there are an estimated forty thousand Vietnamese still in the area, though about fifteen thousand were repatriated to North Vietnam in the early sixties after an agreement between the Thai and North Vietnamese Red Cross organizations. "There's no question but that the Vietnamese support the infiltrators," a senior American official told me in 1966. "But they're not 'expansible'—the Vietnamese stand out in the countryside," he added. "Not until Thais begin joining the movement in real quantity will there be serious insurgency problems."

When the Western position in Laos began to crumble in 1959 and 1960, Thais and Americans in Bangkok suddenly awoke to the threat of Pathet Lao infiltration into the Northeast. By 1961, Sarit was accelerating plans for a sudden injection of economic and social assistance. Only a minimum of pressure was needed from Americans: "It's simple," an American official in Bangkok told me in 1962. "Nobody here wants another South Vietnam."

No one, so far, claims any majestic accomplishments. "We've made a solid start," said an American official, "but there's always a long way to go." Despite the endemic modesty, it seems apparent that at least some progress has been made. Basic to this effort have been two interrelated methods of approach: the so-called Mobile Information Teams (MITS) which are indeed mobile; and the Mobile Development Units (MDUS) which are anything but.

Both MITS and MDUS have concentrated their efforts in the provinces which lie roughly between Ubon (in the southeast corner) and Nongkhay, just opposite Vientiane. In addition, MITS have penetrated North Thailand on several occasions, and MDUS are also at work in Thailand's Deep South, on the Malaysian border.

The information team plan went into operation in January, 1962. Its purpose is to solidify links between the Thai government and its people in the remotest areas of the Northeast and North. In addition, MITS gather information on what is politely called "conditions and attitudes"—in other words, subversive currents.

The teams are small—eight to ten men, usually—and are headed by an Interior Ministry official. Also included are a doctor from the Ministry of Health, an information officer, a district officer, and an official American observer. As of September, 1964, provincial MITS took up the job, thus decentralizing the effort. The United States supports the trips to the tune of 50 percent, or $400 a journey, though these efforts are out of the main stream of the usual USIS effort to boost the American image.

MITS average a village a night on their two-week trips. The pattern: Thai films, a few informal speeches, plenty of talks with individuals in the villages. "We try to find out what they need," said a U.S. observer, "and though we can't promise to fulfill all their requests, we can help more often than not." The doctor, of course, is kept steadily busy: he is "the action arm," as one observer said. The films cover a variety of subjects: reconstruction and construction, the King and Queen, and even an occasional American Western. Almost all the films are dubbed in the Lao dialect, which is spoken by most peasants in these areas.

In addition, portraits of Buddha and the King are handed out at every stop. "We made a mistake with the first portraits of the King," said an American information official who has made many trips. "These showed the King talking informally with an old village woman . . . but they weren't kingly enough. Now we distribute pictures of him in royal regalia. That seems to be what's wanted."

A measure of the effectiveness of the MITS is the fact they are steadily and noisily denounced on the "Voice of the Thai People."

The MDUS grew out of the MITS, a product of the demonstrated need for fast and effective action, which emerged from the first MIT trips. Essentially, the MDUS are intended to produce immediate effects, to fill in the gaps between long-range government planning and urgent necessity. In 1966, there were fourteen MDUS in operation, ten in the Northeast and North, and four in the far South. These units are supposed to spend at least a year in the area they've been assigned to help. Realistically, their stay is at least two years and in several areas probably must be much longer. In other words, the mobile development units are, in reality, static.

Before a team (usually about 150 men, headed by a Thai Psywar colonel and including representatives of thirteen government agencies) goes into the field, it receives a month's briefing in Bangkok, based on information produced by Thai military intelligence and MITS. The first field phase lasts about forty-five days, and includes careful investigation of the four hundred or so villages within a team area, as well as long talks with Buddhist abbots and headmen, before planning is solidified. In Phase Two, actual construction begins: roads, schools, dispensaries, dams, and wells go in. Phase Three, in theory, means phasing-out MDU officials and phasing-in local representatives. So far, no MDU has reached this stage and it's fair to say this isn't likely in the immediate future.

Though most American officials are enthusiastic about both programs, results are difficult to assess. In specific areas, it seems reasonably accurate to say that some progress has been made. In others, the opposite is clearly true. Thai participation seems reasonably enthusiastic, and those officials who do well on the MDUs are assured their careers will prosper: double promotions and sizable salary boosts, though unpublicized, make their isolation from Bangkok more attractive. By 1966, government work in the Northeast had all but become chic. "The younger men," says an American official, "now realize that they'll advance their career faster in the Northeast than in Bangkok."

To the south, in the skinny, steamy Kra Isthmus that links Thailand and Malaysia, MDUs are also at work. Though the threat of serious subversion ebbed sharply after the Indonesian anti-communist coup of 1965, there were accurate reports in 1965 that the Chinese terrorists on the Thai-Malaysia border had managed to recruit, train, and equip the equivalent of three battalions of insurgents. Historically, the Bangkok government had ignored Thailand's Malays almost as effortlessly as it forgot about the Northeast. In early 1965, however, the government began efforts in the south which, while lower-keyed than those further north, were able to make at least a dent in the problems. A program of university scholarships was under way, a huge mosque was built with government funds in the South, and though the CTs had by no means been wiped out, the threat had eased.

Inevitably, problems arose in connection with the MDUs. In 1965, it became obvious that provincial officials did not have resources sufficient to pick up effectively where the MDUs left off. To fill this gap, the Thais, with American assistance, that year started the Accelerated Rural Development program (ARD). Despite the un-doubted progress, the Northeast's problems cannot be simply solved. In 1964, reporting for *Newsweek* on the situation, I wrote that "MDUs and MITs can help, but they are essentially first aid. A complete cure remains somewhere off in the middle distance." As this book was written, the middle distance remained exactly that.

For the Thailand of the mid-sixties, one of the single most important assets in its efforts to resist Communist China's pressure was the steady flow of American aid. From fiscal 1946 through fiscal 1964, American assistance to Thailand totaled $836.5 million—$463.7 million in military aid and $372.8 million in economic programs. In fiscal 1965, economic and military assistance totaled just under $80 million, split fifty-fifty. And beyond this was a growing American military presence, important to both partners for both similar and individual reasons.

The Thais, of course, believe with excellent reason that the U.S. presence is physical proof of American earnestness about the future of Thailand in particular and Southeast Asia in general. About a third of the twelve thousand American troops are army, whose specific task it is to help build up the Thai road system, which is another solid benefit. American soldiers also help train the Thai army. There are also U.S. advisers for the navy, air force, marines, and special forces.

But two-thirds of the American military men in Thailand in 1966 were from the air force, and the Thais rapidly became ultra-sensitive to any publicity over their strikes on North Vietnam.

For centuries, Thailand endured by means of a foreign policy of non-alignment. Early in the sixties, Thailand made its decision: the Chinese Communist threat was too strong to be resisted alone, and the eternal Thai pragmatism had come into play. The U.S. military buildup began, with Thai approval. There were problems, however. First, the Thais are intensely jealous of their sovereignty. Second, there were conservative elements in the government that disliked the trend and believed Thailand could solve the problem of insurgency on its own. For these reasons, press reports on the American presence created difficulties not only for the U.S. military and diplomatic leadership, but also for the more forward-looking elements of the Thai government itself.

One of the few Thais willing to discuss some of the differences of opinion was Air Chief Marshal Dawee Chullasapya, deputy defense minister and chief of staff of the supreme command. An engaging and articulate man of fifty-one, Marshal Dawee was a key figure in the drive to transform the Northeast. Asked about the changing nature of the Thai commitment, he said: "You must realize there are pros and cons, because this is a free country. There are three categories of Thais on this question. The first group feels it's very good to have the United States involved, that we haven't the re-sources to fight Peking and Hanoi. The second feels: 'No, we are independent. We do not want foreign troops on our soil.' And the third? All they want to do is to be left alone to make money. Sooner or later the second group will change their minds."[15]

Despite Thai reluctance to admit publicly that U.S. airmen were present in quantity, the fact was that the bases were essential. At least 80 percent of the strikes—every ground-based raid—against North Vietnam were flown from bases in Thailand. Every strike against Viet Cong and Pathet Lao targets in Laos was flown from Thailand. "If we lose these bases, we lose the air war," said a well-qualified source.

In charge of the U.S. military effort in Thailand was Major General Richard G. Stilwell, commander of the Military Assistance Command—Thailand (MACTHAI), and until mid-1965 General William C. Westmoreland's chief of staff in Saigon. Stilwell, a tough, balding man who served a CIA tour in the early 1950's, has a deserved reputation as one of the army's few intellectuals. And he is an enormously hard worker with a habit of wearing young and pre-sumably resilient aides into the ground. His twelve thousand–man establishment was scheduled to level off at about sixteen to seventeen thousand men, up from ninety-five hundred in July, 1964, and from fifty-five hundred in July, 1963. MACTHAI was made independent in mid-1965; previously, U.S. forces in Thailand were under overall con-trol of Westmoreland.

The USAF units were not, obviously, in Thailand on a training mission. They bombed North Vietnam, and their mission was to defend Thailand by striking at the base areas of the infiltrators. At Takhli, there were three squadrons of F105s; at Korat, two squad-rons of F105s and one squadron of F4C Phantoms; at Ubon, two squadrons of F4Cs, and at Udorn an "Air Force stew" of RF-101 Voodoo recon jets, T-28s, and perhaps a few A-1-Es. In addition, an air force air-sea rescue squadron operated out of Nakorn Phanom, on the Thai-Lao border, and Bangkok's Don Muang airport was headquarters for a detachment of the Eighth Aerial Port Squadron, as well as a half dozen jets for security purposes.

The bulk of the U.S. Army contingent in Thailand was assigned to the Ninth Logistical Command, with headquarters at Korat. This included two engineer battalions working on road projects, in addition to support units including a signals battalion, ordnance battalion, and the Thirty-first Mobile Hospital Group. Base security was provided by the Thais, and U.S. forces worked unarmed unless detailed as couriers.

South and west of Korat, on the Gulf of Thailand, is the Thai naval base of Sattahip. Linking the two cities is the "Bangkok Bypass," a wide, all-weather highway that will help to open up the Northeast. At Sattahip, a $12 million construction program was scheduled for completion by 1967.

In 1966, Bangkok was the sole deepwater port of any significance in the entire country. But it had drawbacks: because of a huge sandbar at the port's mouth, plus the winding Chao Phraya River itself, the largest ship that could enter the port at maximum tide was a vessel with a 27-foot draft and a length of 500 feet overall. Sattahip's expansion was intended to ease the burden. Beyond port expansion, other projects are under way or at least in the planning stage: a 10,000-foot runaway, an ammunition cargo pier and a separate petroleum and oil dock facility, and an ammunition depot.

For the Thais, the increase in external pressure meant a consequent lessening of efforts to move away from a benign military dictatorship into a constitutional phase. When Thanom assumed power after Sarit's death, he promised the nation that work would begin soon on drafting of a new constitution. And drafting in fact did begin: by 1965, primary work had been completed, and a document was under study by a review board.

"Lacking the threat in the Northeast," said a diplomat long resident in Bangkok, "Thanom might well have approved the change by now." Another diplomat added: "There's a general desire to move into a constitutional situation, but there are many problems involved, such as creating new political parties, as well as the basic question of literacy." (The literacy rate, according to official statistics, is about

70 percent, compared to 95 percent in Japan and 45 percent in South Vietnam.) In addition, the enormous political confusion created by Thailand's 1957 experiment with democracy is reason for a generally cautious approach.

Thanom, it should be added, did not have the same absolute power Sarit wielded. A kind and dedicated man without much of a reputation for fast thinking, Thanom essentially shared power with General Prapas, deputy prime minister and minister of the interior. And while Thanom's reputation is excellent (a Thai called him "the only reasonably honest soldier in government"), Prapas has had what might politely be called image trouble for years. He's profited heavily in office: "If there's a richer man in Thailand," said a cynical foreigner, "Prapas better not find out about him." Despite differences in their outlook, Thanom and Prapas reportedly worked well together. "They need each other," said a Western source.

Though the government was at base a military dictatorship, civilian ministers hold several key posts and command a large degree of influence. "You must be very careful about calling Thailand a military dictatorship," said one top-ranking Thai official. "Our foreign minister has the rank of colonel but he doesn't even know how to do about-face."

Despite what appeared to be a reasonably sound governmental approach to the problems of the Northeast, as well as action on the general proposition of improving Thailand's social and economic infrastructure, there were articulate Thais who felt the pace was too slow. "Too many officials still think of themselves as mandarins," said a teacher. "They are more concerned with their relations with Bangkok than their relations with the people they govern."

And foreign observers agreed to some extent. "I think they're moving," said one Western diplomat. "The question is whether they're moving fast enough." And in part, said another foreigner, "it's a question of cross-cultural communication; we ask Aristotelian questions and get Confucian answers."

There are genuine problems. "We know," said Marshal Dawee, "the communists are trying to lure young Chinese back from Bangkok, and that they are training them and sending them back here as agents." And despite Thailand's efforts to galvanize the economy, there were serious complaints about the unbalanced distribution of national wealth. "The rich get richer," said the teacher quoted earlier, "and the poor stay poor." Labor laws barely existed; there was no minimum wage law, and the average ditch-digger was lucky to make 5 baht (25 cents) a day. Efforts to broaden the educational base were often stalled by the elite's feeling that education "is a privilege, not a right," as a Thai said. "Again, bureaucracy is the reason. And many teachers are even more bureaucratic than civil servants themselves." Corruption, on the other hand, is grounds for only mild complaint by the Thais themselves. "Our officials are no more and no less corrupt than others in Asia," says a Bangkok Thai, "and the problem is much less here than in the Philippines or Indonesia."

The government's emphasis on economic development created a striking anomaly: though its base was essentially military, the regime devoted roughly 70 percent of its annual national income to building the nation's infrastructure. Accordingly, Thai armed forces, totaling about 130,000 men, were well under the authorized strength of 200,000.

The army is organized into three divisions, a regimental combat team and, of all things, a horse cavalry division. (That cavalry division has thirty thousand "horses," which actually are Thai ponies that can carry only about the load a Thai trooper can manage by himself. And each pony must have an individual handler.) Soldiers of the First Division (Bangkok) and the Cavalry Division were described as "coup troops," elite but at only about half strength.

Most foreign military sources agreed that the army suffers from a top-heavy officer structure, but added that it was a reasonably effective force. Its top-heaviness is traced to the fact that the army traditionally is the route to power: since the revolution of 1932, military men have directed the nation's course with only a few exceptions. Most of the enlisted ranks are filled by conscription, while officers and NCOs are career men. The Thai draftee spends two years in uniform, then is discharged to a large but not too-well-organized reserve. Each year, there is a turnover of about thirty thousand men.

It's worth noting that the major tactical reason for this relatively small army is that the Thais have traditionally believed that counter-insurgency is a police rather than a military task. Thus the army is considered adequate to counter potential threats from Burma, Cambodia, and Laos, while a large-scale invasion would activate foreign assistance under the SEATO treaty.

The Thai navy and air force totaled about twenty-five thousand men apiece. The air force was scheduled to receive a squadron (eighteen planes) of F-5 counter-insurgency fighters from the United

States, and in addition flies F86s, T28s, T6s, C123s and C47s, and H34 helicopters. These aircraft are organized into four composite squadrons, based at bases also utilized by American aircraft.

The navy's job was coast patrol; its biggest ship was a destroyer escort. There were six battalions of Thai marines; three excellent and three substandard.

Counter-insurgency, as noted, so far has been a task alloted to the police. And that force was being rapidly expanded as the result of Thai-U.S. decisions formalized in mid-1965. The two forces most directly involved in counter-insurgency, the provincial and border police, were both affected. The provincial police force, for example, is scheduled to grow from twenty-eight thousand to thirty-two thousand men, while border forces will go from six thousand two hundred to six thousand seven hundred.

This expanding security force was backed by an economy that continued to blossom. Economic policy continued to be what might be described as "old-school Thai": credit for this goes to Dr. Puey Ungpakorn, the conservative governor of the Bank of Thailand. Over the Thai fiscal year of October 1, 1964, to September 30, 1965, foreign currency reserves of $639 million were roughly equal to annual import totals. Exports stayed almost level in 1965 as compared to 1964, but the 1964 increase was 23 percent over the previous year. As the *Bangkok World* commented: "Even by maintaining the figure for two years, we have registered an annual increase of almost 12 percent, which should be considered commendable from any point of view."[16] Rice exports of an estimated 1.7 million tons were a shade below 1964 figures, and rubber exports, which increased by about 26 percent, increased in value by only 3 percent because of a fall in world prices. Balancing this was an increase in world tin prices, which boosted value of tin sales abroad by 29 percent, though the quantity of exports remained the same, at about 22,000 tons.

Imports rose by 8 percent, continuing an increase that was kicked off by an 18 percent jump in 1964 over 1963. The resultant trade deficit of 2.5 billion baht was shocking, but "invisible" factors such as tourism, insurance, and spending by foreign military and diplomatic personnel, plus official transfer payments, shaved the deficit to 700 million baht ($35 million).

The differences between South Vietnam and Thailand, on balance, seemed greater than the similarities . . . "a world of difference," as Thanat said. "The South Vietnamese situation is the legacy of a long history of colonial rule, of a long series of errors by colonial rulers—not least of which was the French effort to apply the principles of desert warfare to the jungle."

"We hope and expect," he added, "that the counter-insurgency effort will be successful. We will do everything we can. Without boasting, I believe we can cope with the threat."[17]

But the Thais realized the dangers ahead. "Much depends on what happens in Vietnam and Laos," said Dawee. "Our problems will not be ended until that struggle is ended."[18]

Other sources worried about a lack of urgency at high levels. "In the thirty to forty-five age group," a Western technician said, "there's real passion, real urgency. But there's not so much at the top. Too few people have too many assignments—there's just not enough time to think."

Thailand's move toward increasingly closer relations with the United States since World War II had its bumpy periods, for both internal and external reasons. Broadly speaking, the Thais feel that their backing for American policy entitles them to special consideration, over and above the other nations of Southeast Asia. The strained relations between Washington and Bangkok in late 1965 and early 1966, described earlier, provide one example. Most of the tensions, however, stem from Thailand's problems with Laos and Cambodia, and there is little prospect of change in this area.

For Prince Sihanouk, Cambodia's chief of state, Thai leaders have nothing but contempt, and they make no effort to conceal it. Sihanouk, as far as the Thais are concerned, sold out to the Chinese long ago, and he is regarded in Bangkok now as a will-less puppet. During the early sixties, as the United States tried fruitlessly to bring about changes in Sihanouk's orientation, the Thais were enormously resentful, professing total failure to understand why American aid and weapons were being given to a nation they regarded as pro-communist at best.

But the reasons for Thai-Cambodian hostility go back to the founding of Thailand's Kingdom of Sukhothai, in 1238 A.D. In the deciding battle, the Thais smashed the defending Khmer forces and forced them back eventually on the great capital of Angkor Wat. By the fourteenth century, the Khmer Empire had collapsed, and Angkor was left to molder in the Cambodian jungle for almost five hundred years.

For most of those five centuries, the Khmers were dominated by the Thais. Their relationship was comparable to that of the Greeks to the Romans: Khmer artisans and scholars—and slaves—served their Thai rulers in many ways and contributed significantly to what the Thais see today as strictly Thai law and custom.

When Sihanouk's swing toward China became obvious in 1961, relations soured rapidly. A Sihanouk press conference in Tokyo early in November, 1961, triggered a harsh response from Sarit in which allusions were made to "a pig who dares to challenge a lion," as well as charges that Sihanouk was allowing Cambodia to be used as a base for communist subversion of neighboring countries. The latter charge just barely might have been allowed to pass without drastic response, but references to Sihanouk's chubbiness were unforgivable. Cambodia broke relations, and in retaliation Thailand closed the border. For the second time since 1958, the split was in the open, and now it was destined to endure for a long time.

A year later the dispute worsened, and this time the United States was directly involved. Since 1958, the two nations had been engaged in a dispute over the ownership of the ancient temple of Preah Vihear, located smack on the border between them. In 1959, Cambodia took the case to the International Court of Justice at the Hague, and the Thais, after a *pro forma* protest, agreed to rest their case pending the Hague's decision. Relations were resumed in 1960.

But on June 15, 1962, the court ruled in favor of Cambodia. Thailand immediately erupted in anger, both against the decision and against the United States. Bangkok was particularly bitter about the fact that Dean Acheson, at that time President Kennedy's adviser for NATO affairs, had served as Cambodia's counsel in the temple affair, and hinted darkly that they had been sold down the Mekong by Washington. On June 20, 1962, Thailand announced a boycott of all SEATO meetings as well as the fourteen-nation Geneva conference on Laos. (A month later, however, the boycott was lifted without explanation.) And in September, 1962, when Cambodia took delivery on a half-dozen U.S. basic training aircraft, Thailand grew even angrier. "Thailand will change her policy," said General Prapas, "if the United States government is willing to please pro-communist neutral countries like Cambodia at the expense of allies like Thailand." That fuss lasted at least a month, and there was a great deal of muttering among Americans in Bangkok at the time who pointed out that in May of that year, the United States rushed four thousand

Marines to Thailand as a shield against possible further collapse in Laos. This move had been made primarily in the context of a Rusk-Thanat agreement in Washington that spring, though three other SEATO members eventually sent token detachments of troops. Thai thinking in times of stress, however, can be summed up in one line: "But what have you done for us *lately?*"

Stripped of diplomatic niceties, the Rusk-Thanat understanding was a simple piece of horse-trading: in exchange for going along with the Geneva decisions on Laos, the Thais won what amounted to a bilateral military agreement. And Thai insistence on it reflected Bangkok's genuine anxiety about the haphazard kingdom to the north. Laos, of course, had been under Thai control twice in the recent past. After the Geneva Accords on Indochina, signed in 1954, the steady deterioration of affairs in Laos caused many Thais to believe the idea of Lao viability was only a dream—and that Laos should be made part of Thailand once more.

Sarit himself, in a desperate attempt to prop up the Vientiane government, paid millions of dollars over to his cousin, Lao General Phoumi Nosavan. Sarit's concern was a solid example of Bangkok's policy principle of preserving a pro-Thai government in Vientiane. And Thai anger about the anti-Phoumi coup in Vientiane in April, 1964, strained Bangkok's links with Americans to the utmost. Phoumi, as indicated in Chapter I, had become superfluous to United States policy in Laos. And Sarit's death in late 1963 cost Phoumi much of his leverage in Thailand. But it was no coincidence that Phoumi was granted asylum in Thailand after he was finally forced into exile.

To many Thai leaders, events in both Cambodia and Laos are part of a wide-ranging Chinese Communist plan of aggression against their country. In January, 1966, in the midst of another of the periodic border squabbles between his nation and Cambodia, Thanat told me: "Cambodia's attacks are carried out in close concert with Communist China and North Vietnam. There is no sign that they will stop."

In a broader sense, Thanat's statement is even more to the point. If Peking's tactics versus Thailand follow the pattern laid down earlier in Vietnam, pressure will increase exponentially over the coming years. Historically, China has dominated Thailand in varying degree for centuries. And to Peking, Thailand's natural wealth and strategic location make it a highly attractive target.

As the pressure from the North increases, Thailand in turn can be expected to lean hard on the United States for additional backing, and over the postwar years the Thais have become terribly proficient at such leaning. If they fail to obtain what they consider adequate support, as an Australian historian noted, "they will try to reinsure with China."[19]

For Bangkok, the key to future policy lies in the outcome of the war in South Vietnam. If the United States and South Vietnam prevail, the Thais can be counted on. But failure will see the Thais first in line at Peking's reinsurance counter. "If we get foxed at the conference table," warned a high-ranking American officer in Bangkok in early 1966, "if communist-siding regimes appear in Laos and South Vietnam, then for Thailand the pressure will be unbearable. If the U.S. welches on the Thais, they almost certainly won't fight on by themselves."

1. Admittedly, "rice paddies" is a tautology. "Padi" is the Malay word for rice, and other Asian languages use variations of it. In my defense, I cite common usage, a devastating point.
2. Air Marshal Dawee Chullasapya, Bangkok interview with author, January, 1966.
3. The King as jazz buff has transcended his stereotype. Though Thai officials profess unhappiness at references in print to his abilities on clarinet and saxophone, the King himself doesn't seem to mind. In late 1965, for example, his public rendition of a current Thai hit (Pu-Yai Lee) had his audience at a charity affair shouting for more.
4. Wendell Blanchard and others, *Thailand,* Human Relations Area Files Press, New Haven, 1958, p. 24.
5. *Ibid.,* p. 22.
6. D. G. E. Hall, *A History of Southeast Asia,* London, Macmillan, 1955 and 1964, p. 163.
7. Victor Purcell, *The Chinese in Southeast Asia,* London, Oxford, 1965, p. 86.
8. *Ibid.,* p. 91.
9. Private conversation with author, Bangkok, January, 1966.
10. In 1943, the Japanese turned over to Thailand two of the Shan States of Burma and the four northernmost provinces of Malaya. This "gift" territory, as well as that in Indochina, was returned in 1945.
11. Those five hours of hostilities are commemorated today in Bangkok by a huge concrete Victory Monument in the shape of a sword. The Thais are terribly proud of it.
12. General Prapas Charasuthien, interview, Bangkok, 1966.
13. In May, 1967, Pridi reportedly asked the Peking government for an exit permit, to take up residence in Europe.

14. Foreign Minister Thanat Khoman, interview, Bangkok, 1966.
15. Same as 2.
16. *Annual Review, Bangkok World,* Bangkok, 1965.
17. Same as 13.
18. Same as 2.
19. D. E. Kennedy, *The Security of Southern Asia,* London, Chatto and Windus, 1965, p. 89.

three

THE
HERMETIC HERMIT:

Burma

One winter evening, at Rangoon's huge Shwe Dagon Pagoda, a group of Burmese[1] milled uncertainly. It was past midnight, and as a rule Rangoon's streets are empty at this time. We stopped our car, and the driver asked several men in the crowd just what was going on. "There is a white mist around the spire," one man finally answered, "and it may be a bad omen." Sure enough, there were a few cloudy wisps atop the pagoda. But as my host pointed out, just about *every* cool night in Rangoon drapes mist around the pagoda.

Now the Burmese are an inordinately superstitious lot, even in the eyes of other Southeast Asians who rush to their friendly neighborhood astrologer on any pretext. But to me, the little event pointed up the enormous, all-pervasive uncertainty of the country. "We don't worry so much about arrests any more," a Rangoon friend told me. "But we worry much more about our future. What will happen to our children? We don't know. We are afraid because so much is unknown."

He was, of course, speaking of his personal problems. But in fact the word *unknown* sums up Burma these days to both resident and outsider. Since the military coup of 1962, when General Ne Win seized power from U Nu's floundering civilian government, Rangoon has slowly but surely tightened the seals on Burma's privacy. Today no country in the world is so chary with visas, not even Communist China. Aside from official visitors and their entourages, a twenty-four-hour stay is the usual limit. And getting full mileage out of so brief a period is difficult: airline schedules arrange themselves so that a twenty-four-hour stay shrinks to eighteen, or even ten. (The last time a tourist arranged to "miss" a flight, he was picked up at his hotel, taken to the airport, and left to wait in the transit lounge for the next day's plane.) Tourism is not encouraged. Foreign correspondents are usually banned.[2] Even businessmen, who might help provide foreign exchange, must do their best in 1,440—or fewer—busy minutes. It is impossible, in so brief a time, to visit the ancient capital of Mandalay, or the beautiful hill states. For the few foreigners who manage to lay on a transit visa, Rangoon and only Rangoon must stand for Burma. Which is a pity.

For Rangoon is not the loveliest of cities. Developed from a small town by the British, who ruled Burma from the nineteenth century until independence in 1948, it is a city of broad streets, squat Victorian buildings mixed with a few dog-eared edifices in semi-modern style, and wooden homes on stilts. In comparison to Bangkok, Singapore, and Hong Kong, there is no traffic problem: cars are prohibitively expensive. By day, the city is crowded and lively. Sidewalk salesmen offering snacks are everywhere, bicycle taxis jostle for position in the streets, men and women in the ubiquitous Burmese *longyi* (the local version of the sarong) crowd the pavements. But at night, the city dies. On a two-mile walk through the center of the city just after dusk one evening, I saw only a handful of people—except on Sule Pagoda Road, where a half-dozen theaters offered aging American films such as "Aladdin and the Magic Lamp" and "The Adventures of a Young Man." The crowds were cheerful, and obviously fascinated by the sight of a stray European—*walking* of all things— through the city. But they weren't interested in conversation: talking to foreigners in public was not considered discreet.

In a larger sense, however, foreigners have never been more than politely tolerated in Burma. Rangoon, to be sure, looks outward to the sea. But it was a creation of the colonial rulers, not the Burmese, whose ancient capital was in landlocked Mandalay. "The Burmese have always looked inward," said a former British resident, "and the twentieth century hasn't changed them." Over the centuries, a tradition of xenophobia was built up; only a very few foreigners ever managed to become accepted in the truest sense.

If this deep-seated remoteness is generally characteristic of the Burmese, then Ne Win himself is the archetype. A trim, well-built officer in his middle fifties, he runs Burma as he sees fit, and one of the things he sees fittest is that practically nobody sees him. Foreign ambassadors meet him on the average of once a tour, to present their credentials. To most other foreign residents, he exists in name only.

Ne Win rules harshly and directly through the Revolutionary Council, the group of officers he led to power in 1962. "He runs the council like a meeting of the general staff," said an Englishman who worked in Rangoon in the sixties. "He chews out underlings regularly." As far as can be determined, the only person with direct and immediate access to the Bogyoke (General)[3] is Colonel Kyit Khin, chief of the Military Intelligence Service (MIS). Other council members must await Ne Win's pleasure, and they often wait for days. He is described as remote, aloof, almost humorless. Friends? "He's cut himself off from everyone since 1962," said a Western diplomat.

The change in Ne Win, most observers agreed, was remarkable. Before taking over that year, he seemed a different man: sociable, convivial, approachable. If after 1962 he became the stereotype of the military dictator, little in his background suggested such was inevitable. Born in Prome, on May 14, 1911, the son of a minor government official, he attended high school there and went on to university in Rangoon. Next came a stint in the government's post and telegraph department; his enemies still sneer at him as "the postal clerk." During the thirties, he became increasingly involved in the clandestine independence movement, and as the Pacific War drew nearer he and twenty-nine friends were invited to Japan for military training.

This group of men carved out an important place in Burma's recent history. Known variously as the "Thirty Comrades" or the "Thirty Heroes," they adopted the style of "Thakin" (Master) to demonstrate their equality with the British colonialists. And about this time the Bogyoke changed his name from Shu Maung to Ne Win, which means Radiant Sun and seemingly indicated a certain attraction toward things Japanese.

When the Japanese marched into Burma in 1942, Ne Win was a colonel of the Japanese-sponsored Burma Independence Army. With him were the other "Heroes," and for a time they fought well for the Japanese against the British forces in Burma. But as the occupation took shape, they became less and less enchanted by the Japanese, whose clumsy efforts to incorporate Burma into the Greater East Asia Co-Prosperity Sphere had little success. By 1945, Ne Win was one of the leaders of the anti-Japanese resistance, and was commissioned a major in the Burmese army shortly after the war ended.

Four years later, in 1949, Ne Win became army commander-in-chief. And in the same year, he had his first taste of political power.

He assumed the portfolios of home and defense minister and held them until late 1950. To some degree, his step down from the cabinet posts was due to a genuine lack of enthusiasm for government work. But one historian says he resigned because he refused orders to use regular troops against illegal rubber and tin operations in Tenasserim —after the government rejected his suggestion that these industries be nationalized.[4]

During the next several years, Ne Win continued as army commander-in-chief. Politically, he was relatively inactive, following what at that time was army custom. Sources who lived in Burma during the fifties described him as a gregarious man, fond of sailing, gambling, and billiards, who gave lavish parties in his ornate residence on Rangoon's Inya Lake. Those parties, however, did not soften his character: in 1955, during a post-football-game riot in Rangoon Stadium, he reportedly rescued a batch of besieged policemen almost singlehandedly, after responsible officials shrugged off the problem.[5] He traveled abroad during these years to the United States (1952), Indonesia (1953), and Communist China (1955) and revisited China in 1960 and 1961.

Before those return visits to China, however, Ne Win had spent eighteen months as premier. In 1958, as the always-shaky Union of Burma seemed about to collapse, then-Premier U Nu (Mr. Tender, in translation) asked Ne Win to take over as premier for six months on an emergency basis.

Almost at once, the strains began to disappear. Ne Win named a small, non-political, civilian cabinet, and proceeded to impose a judicious degree of military order on the restless populace. Political rebels, as well as bandits, were rounded up and jailed; several threatening strikes abruptly ceased to threaten, and a broad program of economic reforms was begun. To most Burmese, the return of relative order was more than welcome. His six months up, Rangoon politicians approved his desire to stay on another year, and progress continued. By early 1960, however, Ne Win decided to move aside in favor of a civilian government, and in April of that year, after nationwide elections, he was succeeded by U Nu.

Promptly, Burma began to disintegrate once more. Minority nationalities again began to agitate for federal autonomy, and communist terrorism began to rise. Economic problems mounted, and U Nu's cabinet ministers seemed unable to cope. So, for that matter, did U Nu, who seemed increasingly obsessed exclusively by the idea of turning Burma into a Buddhist theocracy. Before dawn, on March 2, 1962, Ne Win seized control of the government once more, arresting U Nu and other cabinet ministers and suspending the constitution. "Under the present circumstances," Ne Win told a gathering of Rangoon politicians in early May, "parliamentary democracy is not suited for Burma." And he made no promises for the return of civilian rule.

Since then, the path has not been smooth. In early 1963, for example, Ne Win and his number two man, Brigadier Aung Gyi, parted ways in the climax to an estrangement that began just after the coup. Basis for the disagreement was what Aung Gyi politely called a "difference of opinion" on carrying out the socialization of Burma; more accurately, Aung Gyi lost out in a struggle for power with far-out leftist Brigadier Tin Pe. After his resignation, Aung Gyi entered a Buddhist monastery in the Kachin Hills of Burma's "far north," ostensibly for a period of meditation. But Aung Gyi (described as a "determined power-seeker" by sources who have met him) returned to Rangoon in the spring of 1963, and the rise in anti-government agitation on the part of the Buddhist leadership that followed seemed something less than coincidental.

Ne Win, acting in accordance with established principles, jailed Aung Gyi in 1965, and imprisoned about a hundred leading monks as well. With that, the Buddhist protest faded rapidly, though its latent strength remains considerable. The Bogyoke dealt with an outbreak of student unrest in 1963 in exactly the same fashion; when students unhappy with the government staged demonstrations in late November of 1963, he simply closed the universities and arrested student leaders. Eventually, the universities were allowed to reopen—purged, of course, of all agitators.

It was obvious, by the mid-sixties, that Ne Win the party-loving general had become Ne Win the stern and remote autocrat. Little was known of his personal life beyond the facts of his marriage and his two children. Through Rangoon, recurrent rumors ran saying he was ailing, that he had imported foreign doctors, or that he was going abroad for treatment, as he did in the first years of his reign.

But nothing could be verified, and a foreign resident of Rangoon shrugged the stories off: "He's perfectly healthy. Trouble is, he tends toward hypochondria." There was also, obviously, a strong streak of vanity. Burmese in general are unusually sensitive to criticism, from whatever source, and if Ne Win sums up Burmese xenophobia within himself, he's equally representative along this line.

As his regime continued in power, there was more and more to criticize. Ne Win himself, in a December, 1965, speech to the first congress of the ruling Burma Socialist Program Party (BSPP), summed it up crisply: "The state of affairs in the country is very bad now." Rangoon's usually subservient press was even more outspoken: "Our economy is in a mess," noted the *Guardian*.

And so it was. The usual economic indicators simply do not exist in Burma. During the BSPP meeting, Ne Win complained about the lack of accurate figures to work with: "It is all very bewildering," he said. "We asked the students to gather statistics during their school holidays, but the figures are not correct . . . we therefore find difficulties in drawing up plans."[6] The all-out nationalization begun when he seized power in 1962 had caused many problems, he admitted, but "anyhow, since we had started, we had to proceed. It was as if we had caught hold of a tiger's tail." (This was followed by "applause and laughter," according to the *Working Peoples' Daily*.)

Foreign observers, Ne Win, and the average Burmese all agreed on one point: the center of the mess was commodity distribution. Basic necessities such as razor blades, toothbrushes, toilet paper, and soap were usually purchasable only on the black market—at twice their official cost in the nationalized shops and on the extremely rare occasions these items were obtainable. And in early 1966, the government cracked down hard on black marketeers. *Ngyapi* and *ngapuiye,* the paste and liquid versions of the foul-smelling fish sauce without which no bowl of Burmese rice is complete, were difficult to find. "Without these," complained a Burmese, "rice isn't worth eating." Ration cards entitled each Rangoon adult to one-half ounce per month, although the average man is used to consuming ten ounces every four weeks. The balance was purchased on the black market, at four times the official price of 4.2 cents a quarter-ounce. The Burmese paid.

Even rice was rationed in Rangoon, though Burma is one of Southeast Asia's major rice exporters. At the government shops, four cups of rationed rice cost about seventeen cents. The top-quality rice most Burmese preferred cost four cents more and was available only on the black market. The government stores offered only low-grade rice: the best was supposedly reserved for export. Equally annoying was the shortage of cloth. "If I want to buy a new *longyi*," said a Rangoon resident, "I have to line up in front of the store at midnight." By dawn, when the clerk arrived to check ration books, there were often as many as three hundred in line. But only 10 percent had a chance to buy: there simply wasn't enough to go around. "There's not much choice of color or pattern," he noted, "and my wife hates this."

And if a wife was unhappy, she had plenty of time to complain. Night life, except for the movies, was almost non-existent. Rangoon's sole nightclub, the Mayfair, was patronized mostly by foreign residents desperate for a break in the monotony, by smugglers who had plenty of *kyats* to chuck around, and by the few tourists who turned up. At the black market rate for the *kyat* (16 to $1), prices were reasonable: 8 *kyats* for a scotch and soda, 4 *kyats* for a beer, and 5 *kyats* an hour for a hostess. But most outsiders exchanged their money at the official rate of slightly less than 4 to $1, which made for a sober evening.

Few in Rangoon had that sort of money to toss around. A civil servant with ten years on the job, for instance, made about 300 *kyats* a month. An army captain, however, made twice as much, plus free housing and certain ration privileges. And the editor of the *Guardian*, it was reported, made 1,000 *kyats* a month, plus privileges which included a car. These men, and others like them, were loyal to Ne Win. But increasing numbers of others were not, though this manifested itself more in apathy and private grumbling than in outspoken criticism.

Behind the economic troubles was a flabby, mystical economic policy called "The Burmese Way to Socialism" and masterminded by Tin Pe. No one yet has offered me an adequate definition, beyond labeling it "Marxist Buddhism." Perhaps the closest was a statement by a still-bemused foreigner in Rangoon: "It uses Marxist terminology, and it aims at a centrally controlled economy. But the 'Burmeseness' is just as important—there's no slavish adherence to alien philosophies. It will be defined by what happens, not by strict dogma. The government displays a certain amount of trial-and-error pragmatism as to means, *but* not to ends."

The "BWS" aims at "Burmanizing" the nation's economy, and to carry this through, the government has employed a process of all-out nationalization that has surprised, and distressed, Soviet and even Chinese Communist observers in Rangoon. Since 1962, Burma has nationalized banks, schools, all foreign firms, domestic and foreign trade, transportation, and industry. Land rent was abolished in 1964, but land itself had not been nationalized two years later. Despite Ne Win's publicly announced unhappiness with economic affairs, however, there was no sign either he or Tin Pe were about to slow down the BWS express. "Tin Pe," a Rangoon friend told me, "has managed to totally ignore all the lessons of East Europe since 1945." It seemed reasonably certain these lessons would continue to be overlooked.

Despite the mess, however, there was reason for feeling things *could* have been worse. Foreign exchange reserves, for example, were being held at about $200 million: government officials kept imports down to the level necessary to produce a slight annual trade surplus. And rice exports, which produce an annual 70 percent of foreign exchange earnings, were holding steady at about 7.5 million tons.

In 1962, Ne Win explained his reassumption of power by citing his fear that the dissident minority nationalities were about to break away from the Union of Burma. Even now, it is difficult to determine how much justice there was in this statement, though the belief was probably sincere. But whatever the situation in 1962, it was becoming clear in 1966 that separatist feelings were on the rise again. "The government," said a Rangoon diplomat, "controls about two-thirds of the country by day, only half by night." In the heartland—the Irrawaddy Valley—government authority was reasonably firm. But even near Rangoon, in the Irrawaddy Delta, dissident elements controlled some areas. In the hill states, Rangoon's troops held sway only as long as they were physically present. Once they moved on, rebels took over again.

To the Northeast, the Shan tribesmen largely run their own show. Shans are Burma's single largest minority (about 2.8 million of an estimated total population of 24 million), and they have never been terribly fond of the ruling Burmese, feeling closer to the Thais with whom they have cultural, historic, and linguistic affinities.[7] In the spring of 1965, a British television team hiked into the Shan States from Northwest Thailand, attached themselves to the Shan National Army, and wandered through the area for five months without being bothered either by Burmese soldiers or government officials. But the Shan tribes are united only in their dislike for Rangoon: at the moment, as in the past, they are badly split among themselves and lack any ability to take concerted action.

Further north, the Kachins (about 2 million) constitute a much more potent anti-government force. They share the Shan distaste for the central government, and since 1945 have to a large degree controlled their own affairs, just as they were left to do under British rule. During World War II, the Kachins fought extremely well, under the leadership of the American oss and the British Force 136, against the Japanese. A British visitor to the Kachin areas in the early sixties reported a substantial amount of hope still remaining that the Americans and British would some day return. Needless to say, the Burmese resent this sort of sentiment.

To the Southeast, along the Thailand border, are the Karens, who in the past have posed the most serious threat to Burmese authority. Largely Christianized as the result of over a century of work by American Baptist missionaries, the Karens more than once have rebelled against the central power: shortly after Burma's independence in 1948, the Karen National Defense Organization (KNDO) triggered a rebellion that still has not been totally crushed. Because the Karens are at once more sophisticated than the Kachins and more united than the Shans, they are regarded today as the most explosive national minority in Burma.

North and west of the capital are the Arakanese, Chins, and Nagas, all ethnically apart from the Burmese and at times as restive as the larger minority blocs. The Burmese themselves live in the central valleys of the Irrawaddy and the Salween; there is some truth to the saying that the Burmese control their "own" territory and not much more.

Complicating Ne Win's domestic policies still further is the question of the domestic communists, split (as everything else in Burma seems to be) but still capable of causing serious difficulty. The largest grouping is the Communist Party of Burma (CPB) rebels, known as the White Flags and led by Thakin Than Tun. The White Flags have about two thousand men under arms in the Prome-Toungoo area, plus perhaps five thousand sympathizers, but in the past several years they have been almost totally quiescent. Ideologically pro-Peking, the White Flags are known to have received limited supplies and arms from China over the past several years.

In 1963, when Ne Win made his sole effort so far to bring the minorities under central government control, he promised immunity to their leaders for talks in Rangoon. About thirty White Flag negotiators popped up on the next flight from Peking, and presented a series of uncompromising demands which led off with a request that Ne Win resign. He declined, and at least twenty-eight of the thirty promptly went off into the jungle. If nothing else, Ne Win's offer allowed the White Flag leaders an easy return to the homeland.

A year later, the White Flags provided a sadly amusing sequel. Pledging their loyalty to Peking on China's National Day (October 1), they referred to their continuing struggle "for the establishment of a new Burma of real independence, politically and economically, and of peace, democracy, unity, and happiness."[8] Communist China broadcast the text back to Burma, stirring up a hornet's nest of angry comment in the government-controlled Rangoon press. Typical was the *Guardian* of October 7, 1964: "The only conclusion to be drawn is that the loyalty of the CPB is not to the Burmese way of revolution, but to something alien." Unpublicized but obvious was the strain put on state relations between Burma and China: the countries pretend to be the best of friends.

In definite opposition to the White Flags, and just about everything else, is the Burma Communist Party (BCP), known as the Red Flags. They have an estimated five hundred armed men in Arakan, and are commanded by Thakin Soe, a veteran revolutionary. Ideologically, the Red Flags are best described as wildly Trotskyite, and they have been even silenter than the White Flags over the past years. There have been recurring reports since the 1963 amnesty that Soe had been slain by rivals, but nothing has been proved. His daughter, Nini, surrendered to government officials in October, 1964, saying she "could not endure the hardship of guerrilla life any longer." Of Thakin Soe, little more has been heard.

In the spring of 1965, a new opposition group arose and, unsurprisingly, it was formed by Karens. This group, which calls itself the Council for National Liberation (CNL), is now regarded by Burmese intelligence officials as perhaps the single most dangerous present threat to the regime. A major reason for this preoccupation is that by the fall of 1965, the CNL Karens had been joined by Burmese and Mons (a smaller tribal group) as well—one of the few times in Burma's eighteen-year history of independence that Burmese and Karens ever found it possible to make common cause. Their headquarters was on the Thai-Burma border.

Chairman of the council is former Brigadier Saw Kya Doe, an older (fifty-eight in 1966) Delta Karen who reportedly commands general respect in Rangoon. Deputy chairman and leader of the CNL Burmese is former Brigadier Bo Yan Naing, once the army's deputy chief of staff and a hero in the fighting against the Japanese late in World War II. His opposite number among the Karens is Saw Tha Din, another influential Karen; the council's leading military leader is Bo Mya, a non-commissioned officer in the British army during World War II.

A high-ranking council official, interviewed in 1965 outside Burma, admitted his forces numbered only about three hundred men under arms, but added that with sufficient funds ten times that many could be armed. "We have to turn away recruits," he added. "We haven't enough money to take care of them."

Non-Burmese sources confirmed the CNL statements that they have support within Rangoon's army, as well as in the Buddhist hierarchy, but no one knew just how much. Their potential obviously was much greater than their actual position in 1966. At least one intelligence source confirms that Ne Win's officials are concerned about the council. "The danger," he said, "lies not only in Karen strength but in the fact they've been able to link up with the Burmese themselves." And council emissaries are now in contact with the Kachins. "If the Shans ever manage to pull themselves together," a CNL leader told me, "we're willing to work with them. Otherwise no."

There were reports of army defections to the council, so far not completely substantiated. Representatives claimed, for example, that in December, 1965, a company of Burmese troops joined them in south Burma. It was also reported, and this seemed reasonably well substantiated, that an entire elite battalion of Chins—the 101st Special Battalion—came over to the council in November, 1965. Other government units have gained a reputation for being willing to sell weapons, and to the limits of their funds, the Council men have made purchases.

The council seemed in 1965 to be slowly but surely gaining a reputation in Burma as the sole effective non-communist force then organized. Their handbills popped up in Rangoon with enough frequency to spur government intelligence agencies to concentrate efforts against them. And their platform had a strong appeal inside Burma.

The council's manifesto cites its determination to "liberate Burma and all its people from the clutches of the Ne Win clique which

. . . established a dictatorship in this country." Asserting that Ne Win had locked up more than five thousand men and women, murdered students, and raided monasteries (all of which is more or less true), the manifesto charges that "the Ne Win regime is moving ahead relentlessly toward communism, and that its indoctrination and programme has progressed so far that communism is bound to be entrenched."

And the council completely rejects Burma's current absolute neutralism: "We don't want to be fence-sitters; we want to be part of the free world bloc," as a council agent told me. "Even if we have to die, our children will benefit. The Karens and Kachins are not afraid of communists. Why should the Burmese be afraid?"

Legal and organized political opposition, of course, does not exist. Ne Win, on his assumption of power, neatly solved that problem by immediately jailing both actual and potential foes. Still more arrests followed, and all were held in "protective custody" without trial. Former Prime Minister U Nu, perhaps the best-known political prisoner, had a list of distinguished cellmates.[9] Among them were Edward Law Yone, former publisher of Rangoon's best-respected newspaper (the *Nation*) and a Magsaysay Award winner; U Kyaw Nein and U Ba Swe, leading political opponents of U Nu before 1962, and U Raschid, a naturalized Indian and cabinet minister who is considered one of Burma's few top-ranking economists.

Though U Nu is the best-known of Ne Win's political prisoners, much more dangerous to him is Aung Gyi, jailed in 1965. Some foreigners tout Aung Gyi as the only person who could possibly lead Burma out of the economic mess. But he is, by all accounts, a proud and arrogant man who would have difficulty recruiting a mass following.

So, of course, would Ne Win, whose performance in 1958–60 earned him broad and sincere respect which has since dissipated. Despite this unpopularity, of which he seems well aware, Ne Win remains convinced that socialism is the answer. And he backs his associates to the hilt, at least outwardly. At the December, 1965, BSPP conference, for example, he went out of his way to reject allegations that Tin Pe was solely responsible for Burma's economic chaos. "He carried on because he had our consent," he said. "It is no use singling out one culprit. We sink or swim together and we are together through thick and thin."

There are foreign diplomats in Rangoon today who still shudder slightly about that statement. The prospects for any change in Burma's currently chaotic course "shrank about 80 percent," said one observer. By assuming full responsibility for the country's economic troubles, another source said, he threw away any chance to dump Tin Pe and try something new. (Though, it must be noted, Ne Win has shown no lack of resource along these lines in the past.) But the Burmese Way to Socialism is Ne Win's way. Tin Pe follows it to the letter.

There are traces, in official Burma government publications on the Burmese Way to Socialism, of Peking's influence. Though the wording is peculiarly Burman, the rapid pace of nationalization, for instance, mirrors Chinese efforts to achieve the transformation to true communism in a year by means of the Great Leap Forward. This effort, of course, was something less than successful in China. But the lesson may have been lost on the Rangoon government: at the least, the frenetic pace of attempts at the transformation of Burma is all too reminiscent of Peking's pattern. Whatever the results, the influences are obvious—and have been obvious for centuries.

From the beginnings of recorded history, China has influenced and at times dominated the area we know today as Burma. Chang Chien, the great Chinese historian of the years before Christ, wrote of the great caravan route between China and India that led through Burma. In 69 A.D., China established the prefecture of Yungchang in northern Burma to protect this route, and governed the area for three hundred years. By 342 A.D., however, the route had been abandoned, and Yungchang passed into history as well. Toward the end of the eighth century, however, the Thais of the Kingdom of Nanchao (see Chapter II), reopened the great caravan route, and the Pyu people of northern Burma used the route to send missions and tribute to the Tang Dynasty emperors.

Unlike the Thais, however, the various races that first settled in Burma seem to have drifted down from northeast Tibet instead of China proper. Their recorded history is scanty at best, and through the first thousand years of the Christian era little is known of the area. The first great date in Burmese history is 1044, when the Kingdom of Pagan was founded by Anawrahta. Not only was he the first to unite the greater part of the area comprising today's Burma, but he imposed on the country the matrix of Buddhism, which today is still a key element in Burma's makeup.

Pagan lasted, under Anawrahta and his successors, until 1287.

During that period, at least two important missions went to China; perhaps, as some have suggested, to facilitate trade between Yunnan and Pagan. But the last Pagan king, Narathihapate, made the fatal mistake of overestimating his power. In 1271, after the Mongols had completed their conquest of China, Kublai Khan sent emissaries to Pagan to demand tribute. Narathihapate refused to receive them, and in 1273 murdered Kublai Khan's follow-up ambassador, as well as his entourage.

Still not content with his defiance, he ordered his troops to push north into areas dominated by the Chinese. This was too much. Kublai Khan's forces smashed south in 1277 and 1283, routed Narathihapate's armies and forced the king to flee. Five years later he was slain, ironically *after* he had tried to mend his ways and submit to China. Kublai transformed Pagan into a provincial capital, ruled for about a decade by a puppet king. (Narathihapate has gone down in Burmese history as Tarokpyemin, or the "king who fled from the Chinese.")

The destruction of Pagan's influence led to a Thai invasion of Burma, and in 1301, Chinese forces marched south again, to end the unrest on their border. This time they were repulsed by the Thais, who immediately moved to make amends by sending tribute to Peking. It was accepted, and for the next three centuries Thais ruled much of Burma, enduring at various times both Chinese support and Chinese meddling. Tribute was sent, but evidently on a somewhat spotty basis: when the Chinese emperor was strong, tribute had a way of turning up much more frequently.

Late in the fifteenth century, a new center of power arose at Toungoo, where Burmese leaders opposed to the Thais took refuge. By this time the first Europeans had reached Burma, led by the Portuguese, and Portuguese advisers played their part in the rise of the Toungoo kings. But in 1644, trouble with China began once more. The Manchus had succeeded in crushing the declining Ming Dynasty, and the last of the latter, Yung-Li, holed up in Yunnan Province, on Burma's northern border. His troops raided areas under control of the current Toungoo king, Pindale, conscripting troops and seizing supplies. In 1658, Yung-Li was driven out of Yunnan by the Mongols and fled to Bhamo, where he was disarmed and allowed to reside. Six years later, a Mongol emissary demanded Yung-Li be surrendered, and the Burmese gave in. The last of the Mings was strangled with a bowstring in Yunnanfu in 1664.

One hundred years later, the Toungoo Dynasty had been replaced by the Alaungpaya Dynasty (1752–1885), which drove the Thais out of Burma and reestablished Burmese hegemony. Almost at the beginning of the period, the Chinese once again became a problem. This time, Burmese success against the Thais led to the difficulty: with its southern border in an uproar, China sent "pacification" units southward into Thailand and Burma, weakening the Burmese hold on Thailand to an extent that allowed the half-Chinese leader Tak Sin to establish the Thai Dynasty that still rules the land today.

The first Chinese invasion began in 1766, and was repulsed. A second invasion that year was also thrown back, almost at the border, and a third, in 1767, penetrated only slightly further into Burma before being crushed. Two years later, the Chinese made a final attempt at invasion, but they failed once more. For the next two centuries relations between the fast-weakening Ching Dynasty and the Burmese remained reasonably cordial. Trade blossomed after the 1770 defeat of the Chinese, and continued at mutually profitable levels. But not until the rise of Communist China did relationships change measurably.

To be sure, newly independent Burma's relations with the China of Chiang Kai-shek had been reasonably cordial. The governing factor in 1958, as it had been through history, was that 1,358-mile boundary. Though agreements had been reached between the Chinese and the British (who then governed Burma) in 1886, 1897, 1914, and 1941, each agreement was later repudiated by China's rulers.

In 1957, then-Premier U Nu summed up relations between Burma and Kuomintang China in a speech before Burma's parliament: "When we regained our independence, the Kuomintang government was still in control of China, though they were fast losing ground to the communists. In accordance with our policy of establishing friendly relations with all countries, we made necessary arrangements in Nanking (the KMT capital), even before Independence, for setting up our embassy there. In fact the Kuomintang government was one of the governments which sponsored Burma's admission to the United Nations. But things moved fast in the Chinese Civil War and by the end of 1949 the Chinese Communists had obtained control over the whole of China except the island of Formosa on which Chiang Kai-shek took refuge. Faced with this reality, we recognized the new government of China at the end of 1949 and immediately took steps to establish our embassy there."

In that speech, perhaps the frankest ever concerning Burma's worry about its northern neighbor, U Nu went on to describe the ups and downs of Burma's relationship with China. He spoke of Burma's efforts on Communist China's behalf at the United Nations: "Our relations with the new Chinese regime remained uncertain for a number of years . . . the new Chinese government seemed inclined to give our communists their moral support, apparently regarding us as stooges of the West." Judged by Chinese treatment of Burma, that suspicion still exists, though in recent years the Chinese have become more and more uncertain about Burma's exact posture—in parallel with the emotions of Western diplomats. To put Chinese—and Western—confusion into perspective, it would be helpful to examine briefly the Chinese-Soviet line toward Southeast Asia during the early fifties.

From the end of World War II until 1955, both Peking and Moscow ostensibly believed the emerging nations of Southeast Asia were not truly independent, that their destinies were in fact controlled by puppets of the various colonialist regimes that had ruled previously. This belief, of course, was a governing factor in the spate of communist-led rebellions that broke out across Southeast Asia in the postwar years. But by about 1955, it became apparent to even the most fervent exporters of revolution in Peking that these insurrections were going badly. Accordingly, China switched its policy stress to developing friendly relations with the nations around its borders. At the first Afro-Asian Conference, staged at Bandung in 1955, Chou En-lai's skilled enunciation of this policy caused an enormous impression, the "Five Principles of Peaceful Coexistence" (or Panchsheela) became a foundation of foreign policies of several South and Southeast Asian countries, and in that area China assumed a leadership role that, though since questioned, has never been seriously challenged.

For the first few years after independence in 1948, Burma worked hard to develop a coherent and effective China policy. Uppermost in the minds of Burman officials was the thought that large-scale Chinese Communist encouragement of the White Flag rebels might well bring down the shaky new Rangoon government. Accordingly, they took steps to bring about what U Nu euphemistically called a "correct relationship" with Peking. The Chinese invasion of Tibet in late 1950 gave Rangoon some anxious moments:

and the government made its unhappiness clear. But when Chinese troops marched into Korea in early 1951, Burma hedged, justifying its refusal to join in United Nations condemnation of China by saying it felt such action would not contribute much toward a solution. In 1952, U Nu made a point of saying that "no nation can always be right or wrong" and paid tribute to the good things he had found in countries across the political spectrum, citing China, the United States, the Soviet Union, and Britain.

In essence, Burma has followed this policy of balance ever since, trying its best to demonstrate an absolute neutrality. Implicit in this view was a rejection of Western belief that China constituted a danger to Southeast Asia. And contributing to the idea was the annoying presence of remnant KMT troops in northern Burma.

These forces filtered south from Yunnan as the KMT government fell apart on the mainland. They comprised most of the KMT Eighth Army, under command of General Li Mi, and their occupation of several areas in the Shan States caused deep concern in Rangoon, not only because of the threat to internal security but because their presence offered Communist China a convenient pretext for invasion, just as the Manchus had entered Burma in the fifteenth and seventeenth centuries. Rangoon's efforts in 1950 and 1951 to drive them out were unsuccessful and caused a diversion of forces from attempts to cope with other domestic rebellions. Complicating affairs still further was the fact that the KMT remnants by this time were receiving substantial quantities of aid, both from Taiwan and the Central Intelligence Agency offices in Bangkok. In 1953, Burma took the KMT question to the United Nations, and cut off American aid in the bargain. Taiwan finally agreed to an evacuation in 1954, but only about half the forces were finally removed. Another evacuation took place in 1961, however, and the few KMT troops remaining no longer constitute a serious problem. Intelligence sources in Bangkok and Vientiane report most have settled down to opium farming, which provides a steady income and keeps them out of political mischief.

Through the middle fifties, Sino-Burmese ties gradually tightened. U Nu and Chou En-lai exchanged visits, trade agreements were signed, and in June, 1954, U Nu joined Chou and Indian Prime Minister Jawaharlal Nehru in subscribing to the Panchsheela. During U Nu's visit to the United States in June, 1955, he defended Burma's decision to maintain close relations with China, telling American audiences that China wanted peace, that its leaders were sincere and primarily concerned with internal rather than external problems. "It is the Burmans who have much more to lose in the event I am wrong," he said, "and it was in full realization of this that I sincerely believe that the present government of China truly wants peace."

Shortly after his return to Burma, however, Rangoon began receiving reports of clashes between Chinese Communist and Burman troops in the Northeast. In July, 1956, the Rangoon daily *Nation* charged that Peking troops had occupied more than a thousand square miles of Burmese territory. This, of course, was denied by the Burman government, but as border negotiations continued, there were more and more reports of continuing Chinese infiltration. By 1959, some sources claimed there were more than ten thousand illegal immigrants from Yunnan in the Wa and Shan states of the Northern border. Most of the infiltrators seemed to be members of tribal groups in existence on both sides of the border, but there were also refugees from Chinese Communist oppression among them. Peking's agents were specifically linked to a band of Kachins led by the outlawed Naw Seng, who fled Burma in 1950 and lived for a time with Kachin tribesmen on the Chinese side of the border. (It should be pointed out, however, that little has been heard of Naw Seng and his men since about 1960.) Beyond this, there are persistent reports that Chinese Communist troops in Burman army uniforms have been active in Rangoon's operations against the KMT remnants.

Burma's long and careful cultivation of relations with the Peking regime paid off in 1960, when U Nu and Chou En-lai signed the Sino-Burma Border Treaty. Four years of negotiation lay behind the final approval, and there were times the Chinese gave the impression of both being in no particular hurry to reach agreement, and of intending to bite off huge chunks of north Burma as its price for a treaty. Chinese claims to certain areas had been of long standing, and maps published in Peking in the early fifties showed large areas of Burma as being under Chinese control.

In 1956, shortly after Rangoon newspapers published the reports of Communist Chinese troop incursions into Burma, U Nu visited Peking and returned to report that China had agreed in principle to a settlement. But during 1957 and 1958, little more was accomplished: the Chinese showed little intention to hurry things along, and the Rangoon government was split seriously as a result of continuing domestic political agitation. In 1959, however, after Ne Win took over the leadership for the first time, he reopened negotiations with China on the border question, and on January 28 signed a Friendship and Non-Aggression Treaty as well as an agreement on the border question. Though the Border Treaty as such was not signed for another year, the Ne Win–Chou agreement set out the guidelines and these remained unchanged.

After a joint border survey, China and Burma finally signed the treaty in Peking, on October 1, 1960, China's National Day. U Nu, who had resumed power, was signatory for Burma. In essence, both sides accepted the lines agreed upon by the British and the Chinese in prewar years. Burma gained 90 square miles in return for ceding 134 square miles, picked up four villages and lost four others.

On balance, there were gains for both sides. For China, the bait of a border settlement had brought about a non-aggression treaty that brought Burma more closely within the Chinese sphere of influence. The peaceful resolution of the border problem was used as a major propaganda point by China two years later, in the Sino-India conflict. Why, Peking seemed to ask Delhi, can't you be as reasonable as Rangoon? Burma lost little territory by the agreement, and in return succeeded in stabilizing a problem that had concerned Rangoon for years. Though some argue that the treaty did in fact link Burma closer to China, the fact was that it simply ratified a de facto situation.

Since that time, Sino-Burmese relations have flowed reasonably evenly; U Nu, Ne Win, Chou En-lai, Liu Shao-chi, and Chen Yi have turned up in each other's capitals with great regularity, and on the surface all seems well. But the very frequency of these visits offers grounds for speculation: Burma probably has received more top-level Chinese since 1960 than any other Southeast Asian country, including North Vietnam. To some degree, this is because Burma is China's back door to the world, and with the worsening of the Sino-Soviet dispute, Chinese leaders have found it more convenient to fly via Rangoon on visits to Asia and Africa.

There is good reason to believe, however, that in Burman eyes the much proclaimed *paukphaw* (deep friendship) relationship of Burma to China is very much that of the smallest kid on the block to the local bully. Despite the fact mutual visiting continues, the results are un-startling. The communiques issued after each meeting, whether in

Rangoon or Peking, have an oddly metallic ring—the sound of the mass-produced message in which only the names of the nations involved must be filled in. Typical was the communique that followed Ne Win's Peking journey in late July/early August, 1965: both sides proclaimed their intimate friendship, the cordiality and sincerity of the talks, the further implementation of the trade and aid agreements, and reaffirmed their faith in the Five Principles. Curiously absent, however, was a direct condemnation of the beastly U.S. imperialists in South Vietnam, though both sides expressed their "deep concern" over the situation and added the usual ambiguous statement that a settlement could come only if the "Vietnamese people were free to settle their own problems and determine their own future without any foreign interference." This could be taken as a reference to the United States; it also could mean North Vietnam.

The communique, in sum, was far from the usual noisy trumpeting aimed at the United States. It is reasonable to believe Peking wanted much more along this line than it got. (The contrast to Sihanouk's usual statements in Peking, for example, is startling.) It seems reasonable to agree, however, with the historian who estimated several years ago that the Burmese foreign office spends more than 50 percent of its time on the China problem. A Burmese put it more sharply: "When China spits, we swim." Accordingly, Peking can exert considerable leverage in Rangoon, if Peking wishes to employ it. Repeated often in Rangoon is the story that Chen Yi and Chou En-lai in 1964–65 all but wore out their welcome on their many trips to Asia and Africa. Burmese officials, including Ne Win, understandably became more than somewhat bored by having to rush out to the airport to greet the Chinese leaders en route elsewhere.

Chinese aid to Burma is second only to that offered by the United States. And while the $85 million in American aid has been largely drawn down, China's $84 million has barely been touched, though the original loans were ratified almost five years ago. Chinese survey teams started work in 1961 just after the agreements were signed, but through mid-'65 only about $18 million had actually been drawn. The Chinese-aided projects include a 750-foot suspension bridge over the Salween River at Kunlung, three hydroelectric projects, two plywood plants, two sugar mills, a paper mill, and a tire factory. Sino-Burman trade produces an annual balance heavily in China's favor: exports to Burma came to $29 million in 1962, $26 million in 1963, and $39 million in 1964. In contrast, imports from Burma totaled

$19 million in 1962, $12 million in 1963, and only $5 million in 1964.

But Peking's trade profits have little effect on Burma's Chinese community, which might ordinarily be expected to profit from it as middlemen. In fact, Peking's efforts to enlist the support of Burma's Chinese residents were described by one Rangoon diplomat as "very low-level, very low-key." The Chinese Communists over the years have established an agent network in Rangoon. But despite the government-to-government friendship, Burman officials remain highly suspicious of their Chinese residents. And they make a point of applying the onerous restrictions on all foreigners to the Chinese aliens as well. Peking's subversive activities in Burma suffered a severe blow when all banks, including the Bank of China, were nationalized in 1964: funds for clandestine activities had been distributed through this channel for years. In general, Burma's 300,000-odd Chinese are viewed as apolitical. Rangoon has made it reasonably easy for them to attain Burmese citizenship, and those who choose to do so are broadly accepted. Those who, on the other hand, elect to retain Chinese passports have a much more difficult time. And following Thai precedent, Burma has nationalized all Chinese schools (seven hundred run by pro-Peking organizations, two hundred by pro-KMT forces), so that much of the Chinese heritage will eventually be lost. Assimilation, of course, is the explanation for this decision, but security aspects inevitably played a part.

Because of the preoccupation of Burma's foreign office with Communist China, other problems, however large, inevitably become secondary. And it is perhaps a tribute to Burman diplomacy that relations with its other two neighbors, India and Thailand, are reasonably good.

Despite the historic Thai-Burman animosity, both Thailand and Burma in recent years have made a determined effort to get on well with each other. Ne Win has exchanged visits with Thai leaders, a border control agreement has been signed, and though Thailand has made less-than-wholly-determined efforts to roust out Burman rebels from its territory, on balance the rebels have been restrained to some degree. Perhaps the most sensitive area in Thai-Burman relations is the fact that SEATO headquarters is in Bangkok, and that the Thais are SEATO's staunchest Asian supporters. Burma, reluctant to enter any alliances and particularly suspicious of SEATO, views Thai backing for SEATO as a mistake at the very least.

Relations with India have remained reasonably stable despite Burma's drive to rid its economy of what amounted to an Indian stranglehold. Since 1962, an estimated 150,000 of Burma's 700,000 Indians have left. They had, with British encouragement, for decades maintained control over money-lending. Strict currency laws ensured they took little of their money along. In addition, the greater number of the small shops in Rangoon as well as other cities had been in Indian hands. Ne Win's policy of nationalization has largely deprived these Indians of their livelihoods. In 1965 and 1966, Ne Win and the late Indian prime minister, Lal Bahadur Shastri, exchanged visits to each other's capitals. The subject of compensation for nationalized Indian property was at the top of the agenda each time. Beyond this area of sensitivity, however, state relations have prospered reasonably well.

Burma's relations with the West rest at a much more formal level. The evident willingness of the British to grant independence after World War II cut sharply into the anti-colonialist sentiments of pre-war years. Until 1962, Burma's best students headed almost automatically toward Britain and the United States for graduate study. Now, only a few students travel abroad for graduate study, and while a few still go to Britain, more are sent to the Soviet Union and Europe. Only a very few continue their studies in the United States.

In general, the tone of relations with the United States was described in Rangoon as "correct but cool," though it seemed apparent that the United States was regarded more warmly on a personal basis than on governmental levels.[10] Since 1953, Burma's policy toward the United States has been one of steady withdrawal, beginning with the shutdown of American aid in 1953 (although projects already agreed upon were allowed to continue). In the early sixties non-governmental American operations such as the Ford and Asia Foundations were asked to leave, and contact today between Burmans and American diplomats is minimal. In 1966, only a handful of American missionaries remained, and those who left were not granted re-entry visas. Americans were subject to strict travel restrictions—but, it should be added, so were all other foreign nationals, including Communist Chinese.

Burma, in short, intends to follow its own way toward Burmese socialism. "They don't want any advice from anyone," said a high-ranking American source. "They'll rock along like this for the foreseeable future. It's an unhappy stability, but the Burmans are a

patient people." Though foreigners have reason to doubt that Ne Win
has a firm grasp of socialist principles, he is utterly committed to his
ideals. No one dares speak out against current trends: results or no
results, Ne Win seems to say, "I'm right and time will prove me
so."

Indeed, little change seems to be in the offing. The rebellious
minorities are disorganized, the CNL is in its infancy, and domestic
communists are quiet. (There is reason to believe, however, that if
Peking became unhappy about its relations with Burma, the White
Flags would be back on the warpath reasonably rapidly.) Ne Win,
isolated and intent on fulfilling his own ideas, sums up Burma's
current stance in himself. Southeast Asia being as unstable as it is,
there is *always* the possibility of radical change, or even of revolution,
in time. But leadership is at the bottom of too many of Burma's
problems, and no great man has appeared. "They need a leader like
Kennedy, with ten years in which to work, to pull them out of this
mess," a Western diplomat in Rangoon told me. But there are no
Kennedys in sight.

As far as the rest of Southeast Asia is concerned, Burma is largely
forgotten. "They're not giving anybody any trouble," as an American
official put it to me, and it's fair to say this sums up the feelings of the
great power blocs.

Perhaps the clearest impression one receives in Burma is one of
futility. There has been no attempt since 1963 to solve the vexing
question of the national minorities; if anything, hostility has
deepened. (As a Shan leader stated it recently, "The British sucked
our blood, but the Burmese eat our bones.") And Ne Win's efforts to
solve his country's second great problem have not amounted to much
more than admitting that the economic mess is a mess indeed.

In Burma these days, a story about the Lord Buddha is much
quoted. It seems that Buddha, in one of his many incarnations,
turned up as a fish. One day, swimming in the sea, he and another fish
were netted. His fellow victim struggled, and was clubbed to death by
the fisherman. But Buddha had observed the boat was leaking, and
lay still. A storm arose, the boat sank, and Buddha was free once
more.

The parallels are obvious. "We are a very patient people," a
Burmese friend told me, "and we believe today is not forever." Indeed, in the summer of 1967 significant changes seemed to be under

way. Severe anti-Chinese rioting swept the country for nearly a month, and Ne Win's government did little to stop it. Economic czar Tin Pe vanished from the scene in late spring, and there were reports that Ne Win was thinking of scrapping his disastrous economic policy. And Aung Gyi was freed from prison—there was one unverifiable report that he had been asked to rejoin the government. Just how far—and how fast—this change might move was impossible to predict. But it was clear that Burma, after years of immobility, faced a much more tumultuous future.

1. *Burmese* and *Burman* were used interchangeably by the academic sources consulted for this chapter. For my purposes, I have used *Burmese* to describe the race and *Burman* to describe a citizen of the Union of Burma, of whatever racial stock.
2. After three years of waiting, I finally applied for a visa as a businessman, instead of as a journalist. The application was granted within twenty-four hours.
3. *Bogyoke,* or General, was first popularly applied to Aung San, hero of Burma's independence, who was murdered in 1947 by a political rival. Ne Win inherited the sobriquet when he took power in 1958.
4. John F. Cady, *A History of Modern Burma,* Cornell University Press, Ithaca, N.Y., 1958, p. 610.
5. Cady, *Supplement to a History of Modern Burma,* Cornell, Ithaca, 1960, p. 7.
6. This unusual approach to the gathering of economic statistics has one counterpart, to the writer's knowledge. Following the collapse of the Great Leap Forward in 1958, with the consequent exposure of widespread statistical inaccuracy, Communist China tried the same system with similar results.
7. "Thailand," said a Rangoon resident, "is simply the largest Shan State."
8. NCNA broadcast to Burma, September 30, 1964.
9. U Nu was released in 1967, but was kept under house arrest.
10. Relations with China, on the other hand, were called "cool but correct" by a Rangoon official. The difference is subtle—if it exists at all.

four

OFF TO
THE RACES

Malaysia and Singapore

Tunku Abdul Rahman Putra Al-Haj ibni Almarhum Sultan Abdul
Hamid Halim Shah is a kindly, straightforward old Malay gentleman
who intends to go down in history as Bapa (Father) Malaysia. Lee
Kuan Yew is a brilliant, hard-driving, and unscrupulous politician
whose goal in life is to mold Malaysia in his own pattern. Both men
agree that the Malaysia concept is essentially workable, but they
differ widely on the steps to be taken toward making it viable. They
are, in themselves, men of totally different worlds despite the fact
both were born and raised only about five hundred miles apart. Lee
Kuan Yew today is prime minister of a Singapore split off from its
parent; the Tunku is prime minister of Malaysia. In their differences,
and in their similarities, is summed up the story of their embryo
nation.

To many of the two million Chinese of Singapore, Lee Kuan
Yew[1] is something of a hero. No overseas Chinese politician has
risen so far so fast. His brilliance is unquestioned, but he is not
wholly trusted save by his closest associates. Superb in debate, fluent
in Mandarin and Hakka, English and Malay, he is a wholly effective
speechmaker. And though he is a doctrinaire socialist, he has been
wise enough to keep his hands off the free-enterprising Singapore
economy. The island's communists have been trampled under foot.

There is no greater contrast than that of Lee with the Tunku,
whom I met at Alor Star, in northern Malaya, early in 1965. I had
driven up from Penang through a series of breathtakingly lovely
rubber plantations, jungles, and sleepy little Malay towns. The roads,
a legacy of the British, were superb, as they are all over Malaya. And

the Tunku himself was pleasingly substantial, precisely in accordance with the mood his country produced in me.

He has a face the color of oiled walnut, all his own teeth, a tiny gray moustache, and a great many virtues. Of the latter (I wrote after the interview), perhaps most attractive is a solid simplicity, uncharacteristic of the run of the Malay nobility, beguiling in itself and even more interesting in contrast to the complexity of Lee Kuan Yew. We talked at Bukit Chorat, his private retreat, which perches atop a hill eleven miles from Alor Star. In that city, which is the capital of Kedah Province in Malaysia's Far North, he has two homes, Merdeka House and Malaysia House, but Bukit Chorat is a favorite hideout. (Old friends in Alor Star have a habit of dropping around to ask for a government job, or perhaps a loan, or perhaps just a hand in getting little Abdul into a really good school. The Tunku deals with his visitors easily and warmly, then retreats to Bukit Chorat when life becomes too hectic.)

To a reporter who has viewed, with some awe, the various palaces of former President Sukarno that are scattered around Indonesia like dew in the morning, Bukit Chorat is a shock. I mistook it at once for the guard's shack.[2]

Outside, there's a straggling grapevine or two, a few flowers, a view over the wide irrigation canal, and the surrounding acres of rice paddy. The lodge itself consists of just one room, with a small bar, dining table, and chairs, as well as a sofa and two easy chairs facing the small picture window that overlooks the paddy. There's a small kitchen in the back, and a toilet. The outside walls are brown log slabs and inside, the walls are wallboard. A large green rug lies on the floor. A few pictures—one a sketch of the Tunku in full ceremonial garb—hang on the walls.

The Tunku himself wore a navy-blue terrycloth T-shirt, gold fountain pen clipped to a pocket, baggy brown-and-white cord trousers, and no shoes. On his wrist, a gold watch and band; on his right hand, a silver ring with a large jade stone; on his left hand a gold signet ring bearing the device of UMNO, the United Malay National Organization, which he heads.

Interviewing the Tunku was a reporter's dream, again in contrast to other Asian politicians. His English was excellent, he talked easily on any number of points, and he was remarkably frank. Once one fights his way through the screen of advisers and lesser officials, the Tunku is receptive to ideas, tough questions, and even jokes.

He looked tired, which is understandable, because we talked in the last week of the Moslem fast of Puasa (Ramadan), and the Tunku keeps it conscientiously. By early afternoon, he's often grumpy: I was lucky, or so I was told later, to catch him in a good mood.

We started off on the subject of Malaysia's assets.

"Economically, as you can see, we are strong," he stated. "We have been able to make the fullest use of all our natural resources. Our rubber yield, for instance, is triple that of Indonesia. And the market prices now are more than competitive with synthetic rubber. We are encouraging the growth of light and heavy industry; of all business, for that matter.

"And we are trying hard to ameliorate the condition of the poor in the villages. We are building roads, irrigation canals (pointing out the window), providing more land and cheap housing for workers.

"I think I can say there's no other country in the world that's doing so much for its people."

Malaysia's economic strength, as the Tunku pointed out, was obvious. About 15 percent of Malaysia's total revenue, for example, is plowed back into rural development. For the moment, the threat of synthetic rubber seems to have been met, but there's room for concern as far as the future is concerned. Diversification, as the Tunku knows, is the answer, and Malaysia is moving ahead on this front. The implied contrast with Sukarno's Indonesia, which the Tunku made throughout this interview, is worth attention:

"Politically, we are as sound as any country. We are the only country in Southeast Asia which carries out elections at all levels, and this means we are politically very stable. We encourage political expression at all levels. We are carrying out democracy quite well, considering that we are practicing British parliamentary democracy.

"Everybody always wants to know about racial problems. Well, these people (the Chinese) have been here for generations, and there's been no trouble. I worked for independence beside Chinese and Indians in order to make it go, so as not to cut our throats after independence. Our constitution ensures justice and equality of all. If the people of Malaysia will honor their constitution, will uphold it conscientiously, then I can't see any trouble.

"After we (the Alliance) won 90 percent of the seats in the last election, I could have smashed the constitution to smithereens. (The implication here was that he could have done this *if* he had been purely a Malay nationalist.) But the only changes I have advocated are administrative changes, to bring things up to date. And this despite the fact my party is a *Malay* party, I am a *Malay*.

"Once one of my ministers, a Malay, tried to please all the Malays by confiscating all rubber-purchasing licenses in two provinces from the Chinese holders. I said *no,* and gave all the licenses back, which was one of the most difficult things I ever had to do. But they (the Malays) understood why I did it.

"While we honor the constitution, there will be no trouble. But we have enemies outside—Indonesia—and enemies inside." He stopped to polish his heavy, dark-rimmed, slightly tinted glasses, then put them back on. "The enemies within are the CCOs (Clandestine Communist Organizations, the local version of Viet Cong) and those irresponsible dissident politicians who support Indonesia. The Indonesians are more dangerous to us than the others. But the people here want peace, nothing but peace."

The conversation turned to Sukarno, and the Indonesian problem. "What a mess he's made. From the moment he took power, he's done nothing but bring Indonesians misery and unhappiness. Even in sports: he withdrew from the Olympics. Politically, his mentality doesn't seem sound. He makes one mistake after another, then blames all his mistakes on the imperialists.

"He'll say anything, do anything, to impress his people. But Indonesia's reputation has gone down, while Malaysia has won the admiration of people all around the world." (When the Tunku talked about Sukarno, he remained calm, spoke quietly, tried to be objective.) "He knows that his people in Sumatra, in particular, look to Malaysia, and he thus will always worry about us. He must attack us because Sumatra admires us.

"But we don't intend to encircle him; we want to live at peace, developing our economy, our youth.

"That man has become such a nuisance, not only to us but to people everywhere. Now he's left the U.N., which has done so much for the people of the world. Does he want to start a new U.N., with China? What use is that? That man is wicked: he does harm the way other people do good. He is mad. He talks peace and plans war. And he takes no responsibility for anything.

"I will tell you a story about Sukarno. At our Manila conference, there was a pretty girl reporter from Radio Malaysia. Sukarno thought she was an Indonesian and asked for an introduction. When he learned she was Malaysian he redoubled his efforts, sent his aide to ask her for a date. I had to send her home, to Kuala Lumpur, to avoid an incident."

As for the future, the Tunku said he always has been politically minded, making it clear he will stay active in politics for some time to come. "Before the war, I was a provincial official in Kedah, popular with the poor people but not with the higher-ups. After the war, we started to work hard for independence. We took our time, to ensure stability. I've always been bitterly opposed to colonialism: this was hard on my family."

Small wonder. The Tunku's family was definitely one of the ruling class, which owed its ease and affluence to unflagging support from British colonial officials. He himself was born in the family palace in Alor Star, on February 8, 1903, the third son of his Thai mother, who was the eighth wife of the Sultan of Kedah. No scholar, the Tunku was pushed through school by his determined mother, and schoolmates remember him as a boy who paid little attention to princely privileges and mixed well with his fellow students. At Cambridge, the Tunku won his spurs as a playboy prince, neglecting his studies in favor of cultivating interests in fast cars, golf, and horse-racing. (The latter two interests continue to fascinate him. Until recently, he would not accept engagements until he had consulted the racing calendar.)

The Tunku picked up a bachelor of arts degree in the twenties, just scraping through after diligent coaching. Law school was tougher: after he failed his examinations at Cambridge three times, he returned home to join Kedah's civil service. At the urging of an elder brother, he decided to try again at Cambridge, but the war intervened. In 1945, however, the Tunku finally got back to Cambridge and after a long and intensive cram course finally succeeded in passing, twenty-five years after his first attempt. (Among his coaches for the second bout was Tun Abdul Razak, now Malaysia's deputy prime minister.)

The Tunku has been married three times: first to a Thai Chinese girl, by whom he fathered a son and daughter before she died in 1935; then to an Englishwoman whom he married in 1937 and separated from in 1939 (they were later divorced), and finally to his present wife, Puan Sharifiah Rodziah, in 1939. No children resulted from the second and third marriages, and from time to time the Tunku and his wife have adopted children from poor homes. These youngsters, his grandchildren, and the offspring of the Indian gardener romp through the Tunku's Kuala Lumpur residence at will, sometimes disrupting press conferences or chats with visiting dignitaries. The house, the former residence of the British governor of Selangor, is a large, rambling, unpretentious home on Swettenham Road, surrounded by flowers. Equally unassuming is his official car, a 1955 Chrysler Imperial.

Despite his Western education, the Tunku pays the usual Asian attention to soothsayers and astrologers. One and three are his pet numbers; any horse wearing 13 will be backed automatically. He chose August 31 as the date for Malaysia's formation at least partly for numerological reasons, and was distinctly unhappy when political troubles forced postponement to September 16. His astrologer reportedly told him, however, that though immediate auguries for this date were black, all would turn out well in the end.

Thus the Tunku: a straightforward Malay gentleman, very much of the old school, sincere, honest, but perhaps a little too naive for his own or his nation's good.

Lee Kuan Yew is, to put it mildly, different. Born in 1923 to a middle-class, third-generation Chinese family, Lee made himself conspicuous early on, both as a scholar and a debater. The Japanese conquest of Singapore forced him to break off his studies when he was nineteen, but in 1946 his father, at that time with Shell, borrowed from his firm to send Lee off to Cambridge.

Kuan Yew came home in 1950, engineered for his career like a bullet for a rifle. He had become anti-British, anti-colonialist, an admirer of Britain's Labour Party, a nationalist, and a polished orator. And his record showed an extraordinary double first in law at Cambridge. He was admitted to the Singapore Bar in 1951 and simultaneously launched a political career that shows no signs of slowing down. First step toward eventual political power was the trade unions: Lee served as adviser to several of the most important and built support for the future. In 1954, he and eight friends founded the People's Action Party (PAP), which dominates Singapore politics today. A year later he won a seat in the Legislative Assembly; PAP took three of the four seats it contested. It was an auspicious beginning, but for the next four years Lee fought bitterly with the communists and fellow travelers who infiltrated the party's ranks. In 1957, Lee was reelected to the assembly, and two years later, as Singapore waited on the threshold of self-government, a PAP largely purged of subversives swept forty-three of fifty-one assembly seats and seized leadership. On June 3, 1959, Lee became prime minister of an independent Singapore.[3]

Lee's political philosophy, by this time, was clear. Anticommunist and anti-colonialist, Lee's policies echoed those of Britain's Labourites. But his socialism was tempered with clear realism: Singapore's free-wheeling entrepreneurs—traders, manufacturers, merchants—would not flourish under pure socialism, and Lee knew it. And despite his anti-colonialism, Lee realized Singapore's heavy dependence on the revenue produced by Britain's enormous naval base on the island. More important, Lee knew that PAP could not prosper as a "Chinese" party, that PAP's future depended on its ability to attract support from Malays and Tamils as well as Chinese. And this, inevitably, became the basis of the Malay envy—and fear—of Singapore that doomed the Malaysia concept to endless bickering and led eventually to Singapore's expulsion from Malaysia in 1965.

In June, 1965, as the tensions between Kuala Lumpur and Singapore were building fast, I talked with Lee on several occasions —twice at his office, then (inevitably) on the golf course. It was the first time I had met him, and my notes reflect the impressions he made: "Lee Kuan Yew is a gambling man, a hard-driving, hard-playing, hard-fighting man. His arched eyebrows give him the look of a young and perpetually amazed teacher but his rangy body and muscled shoulders add an impression of a tall skinny welterweight who never got tagged." Perhaps the word that best describes the man is competitor. He plays golf as he plays politics, bets on every shot, every hole, every match. He makes silly bets and smart bets; he thrives on tough competition and does his best to psych his opponents, be they golf partners or Malay politicians.

Our talks took place just after a bitter parliamentary debate in Kuala Lumpur, during which both Lee and the rival Malay leaders lost their tempers more than once. Lee had been accused of advocating secession for Singapore, of seeking the Tunku's job (and head), of plotting to tear Malaysia apart by inciting Malay-Chinese riots— the charges went on and on. Lee, in turn, accused the Kuala Lumpur leadership of trying to create a purely Malay Malaysia, a nation dominated by Malays in which the Chinese, Tamils, and smaller minority groups would be second-class citizens at best. Denying charges of PAP "communalism" (a polite way of saying racialism), he in turn accused Kuala Lumpur's UMNO[4] of being precisely that, quoting from the vicious attacks on him by the Malay vernacular press.

Lee defined the problem to me this way: "The nub of the difference is this—we believe all Malaysian citizens, regardless of race, religion or culture, are equally co-owners of Malaysia. UMNO believes Malaysia is Malay country, that non-Malays hold citizenship only through the generosity and grace of the Malays. They believe non-Malays should behave themselves politely, as guests living in the guestroom of their home.

"Ideological differences," he continued, "accentuate this. We believe in an egalitarian, open society, in which a man's status is not dependent on his rank at birth or status or wealth but on his ability and his contribution to society. UMNO, on the other hand, is trying desperately to preserve an old feudal order, the form of which was frozen under one hundred years of British rule. But under the pressures of urbanization and industrialization, the economic basis for this old order has changed. Now, the old order itself must change. It's only a matter of time. A static society is one that dies."

Lee refused to single out any Malay as the leader of the anti-Lee sentiments. "There are a number who share these ideas. They are not prepared to integrate the community. According to their ideas, the Malay is to be kept a separate type, completely different from other Malaysians.

"But we've got to look ahead," he added, "to act before the dam bursts. If you postpone the problems five to ten years, the Alliance will use this time to feed Malay minds with the idea that Malays are the owners and all others are guests. To get them to change then will be even more difficult."

And he specifically denied UMNO charges he advocated a breakup of the federation: "I have never advocated secession. I do not believe that secession is going to be the result of what follows if there is no Malaysian Malaysia. There are three possible developments if there is no Malaysian Malaysia: disintegration and absorption by a larger third power, not necessarily Indonesia; attempted domination by force of one race over the others, which will be extremely difficult to maintain, or recurring communal riots leading to segregation of the various communities in Malaysia into more or less defined geographical areas leading ultimately to partition."

Next day, Lee spoke out impressively in public, along similar lines. Five thousand Singaporeans shoved their way into the open-air

National Theater to hear their leader say: "This is the beginning of a new tide in the affairs of the people of Malaysia. We shall make haste slowly and we shall win and this will be a nation that will survive for hundreds of years." Lee was addressing the first rally of the Malaysian Solidarity Convention, the vehicle chosen to push forward Lee's thesis that Malaysian integration must be shoved into high gear by the Kuala Lumpur government.

Behind him, as he spoke, were signs reading "Malaysian Solidarity Convention—First Solidarity Rally" in four languages (Malay, Chinese, Tamil, and English), and the listeners themselves made Singapore's racial salad ever more apparent. Lee's slim, brilliant Chinese wife sat knitting in the front row. Next to her was a Malay in the traditional black *Songkok* (black cap), and nearby were darkskinned Tamils and Indians. Unsurprisingly, however, most of the audience was Chinese, reflecting the fact the island is 85 percent Chinese. And Lee, very much aware of the interest UMNO leaders were taking in his efforts, gave a virtuoso performance, speaking first in fluent Malay, then repeating his speech in Mandarin and English. Despite the repetition, few listeners left: Lee on the podium is splendid entertainment.

But in Kuala Lumpur a few days later, I found government leaders considerably less entranced. Deputy Prime Minister Tun Abdul Razak, who during the parliamentary debate a week earlier had called Lee "a great expert in creating a situation which doesn't exist" and charged "PAP means Partition and Perish," told me earnestly that "if Lee can't get into control of Malaysia, he will wreck it." Equally earnestly, he added: "We want to play this down. Lee isn't important enough to make so much fuss about." Other government ministers were more outspoken. Finance Minister Tan Siew Sin, for instance, said: "Lee would lick the Tunku's ass to get the foreign ministry. But no one trusts him, all his old friends are now his bitterest enemies. I'd rather be his enemy than his friend . . . it's safer." Minister of Information Senu bin Abdul Rahman echoed Razak's charges: "He is prepared to destroy the country to satisfy his own ambitions." And an American teacher in Kuala Lumpur labeled Lee "a nascent Fascist."

Lee, in short, arouses violent emotions with extraordinary ease. He scorns middle-of-the-road positions; accordingly, both critics and backers tend toward similar extremes. Beyond the question of personality, however, Lee in himself sums up what Malays see as a

Chinese threat to their future, and this is a threat that has existed, in varying forms, for hundreds of years. If Thailand has produced the greatest degree of Chinese assimilation, Malaya ranks at the opposite end of the scale.

Ironically, though Malays and Chinese today seem intent on going their separate paths, historians[5] theorize that the Malays themselves came originally from China several centuries before the dawn of the Christian era. Linguistic and cultural evidence indicates the Malays moved south from western China through present-day Cambodia, Vietnam, and Thailand to the Malay peninsula and out to the islands of Indonesia. And contact between the Hans, who populate China today (and who forced other races, including the Thais, Burmese, and Vietnamese, to flee south centuries ago), and the Malays began as early as the fifth or seventh centuries—and perhaps even before. Chinese historians of the seventh century mention traders who visited Canton from what evidently was Malaya.

The first contacts on which detail is readily available took place in the fourteenth century, such as the 1349 report of Chinese trader Wang Ta-yuan that in Tumasek (now Singapore) "the people live mixed up with the Chinese."[6] He also noted that a Chinese fleet's arrival had saved Tumasek while it was under siege by the Siamese. Modern Malayan history begins around 1400, with the founding of the Malacca Sultanate, at about the time of the great Ming Dynasty expansionism. In 1403, Ming emissary Yin Ching visited Malacca, and Chinese records report the sultan duly sent a tribute mission to China that year, with a request for Chinese protection against the marauding Siamese.

This protection was largely provided by Admiral Cheng Ho, known as the Grand Eunuch, whose junk fleets undertook at least seven expeditions southward between 1405 and 1431. During these years, Malacca's tribute missions to the Ming emperor were almost annual and continued for many decades. In 1511, the Portuguese seized Malacca, and the size of the Chinese settlement there began to increase. Immigration continued to rise after the Dutch ousted the Portuguese from Malacca in 1641. (The Dutch remained entrenched there until the Anglo-Dutch Treaty of 1824 ended their occupation.) Under the Dutch, Malacca's Chinese population grew from about 400 in 1641 to 2,161 in 1750, and continued to increase after the British took over. Further north, the British founded Penang in 1786, and

Chinese from the traditional emigrant provinces of Kwangtung, Fukien, and Kwangsi began to settle there as well.

But the most important center for Chinese settlement was Singapore, established as a trading post by Sir Stanford Raffles in 1819. In February, 1821, the first emigrants direct from China (Amoy) arrived, and hundreds followed. For the first thirty years, though their numbers increased, they made little impression. Then, in the 1850's, the discovery of large tin deposits in Perak set the emigrant Chinese on the route to eventual economic domination of Malaya. The Malays themselves showed little interest in developing the tin areas, and Chinese entrepreneurs imported hordes of *sinkehs* (coolies) from China to work the mines. Estimated annual arrivals in what became known as the "pig trade" (because of the wretched condition of the workers) rose from two thousand in 1833 to twenty-three thousand by 1873. In that year, Singapore's population was 60 percent Chinese.

The enormous influx of Chinese brought with it equally impressive problems. Chinese secret societies grew rapidly, and their constant (and bloody) quarrels were complemented by increasing anarchy in the Malay sultanates. There was piracy, gang warfare, and rioting. Basic in the increasing lawlessness was the bitter rivalry between two major branches of the Chinese Triad Society (known to Chinese as the Tian Ti Hui, or Heaven and Earth Society), the Ghee Hin, and the Ghee Hock. In 1851, street fighting in Singapore between the two groups took five hundred lives, and there were continuing flareups over the next fifteen years. Finally the British, who had earlier been reluctant to interfere, took much firmer control over local affairs, and the troubles began to ebb. Another factor in promoting increased internal stability was an increasing degree of responsibility felt by the wealthier Chinese themselves, who realized that continued unrest was simply not good for business. And business was booming for the Chinese, primarily in rubber and tin.

During the last half of the nineteenth century, the Ching Dynasty in China slowly fell apart. The emigrant Chinese of Malaysia felt little attachment to the government in Peking; for all intents and purposes, they were cut off from their homeland, though family ties were not broken. But the accelerating revolution back home reversed the growing isolation of the overseas Chinese. Sun Yat-sen visited Malaya and Singapore several times between 1900 and 1910, and the response to his pleas for support was enthusiastic. Large amounts of funds were immediately forthcoming, and political refugees were given comfortable asylum. The revolution's success, in 1911, accelerated the rise of Chinese nationalism among the Malayan Chinese. A local branch of the Kuomintang came into existence almost immediately, though it was banned by the British in 1914. The ban had little effect; as one historian puts it: "a direct, strong, active Chinese political organization operated in Malaya, working on the emotions of one community only, and the forces tending toward the creation of a plural society, which separated the peoples of Malaya, were increased accordingly."[7] Economically, the Chinese were very much a part of Malaya; politically, they were not.

For that matter, nobody in Malaya at that time was displaying much interest in the country, aside from making money out of it. The Indians cared much more about India's struggle for independence than about any sort of emerging Malayan nations, and the Malays themselves remained apolitical, at least in a national sense. The Chinese progressed fastest, and the spearhead of this trend was education. After 1911, the number of Chinese schools increased rapidly. By 1920, there were more than forty large Chinese schools in Singapore alone, more than thirty in Penang, and at least one in every other town in the Malay states. In 1938, one historian estimates there were about a thousand Chinese schools with a total enrollment of about ninety thousand, vastly exceeding any other group. And the students learned only about China: their textbooks were imported, as were many of the teachers. As a result, they were inoculated with generous doses of Chinese nationalism—and later, Chinese communism.

The interest of the Malayan Chinese in China, of course, was not exactly one-sided. The KMT regime was doing its best to woo the overseas Chinese, even to the point of sending inspectors to give advice on how overseas schools could bring their teaching more into line with education on the mainland. In 1930, the official ban on the KMT was lifted, and China redoubled its efforts among the Malayan Chinese. When the Japanese invaded China, Malaya's Chinese contributed heavily to the homeland. They did the same for Britain when Germany declared war in 1939. And once Japan attacked Malaya, the Chinese lined up even more solidly with their British rulers.

However resolute the Chinese support, it wasn't enough. The

British forces in Malaya, small, poorly arrayed and inefficiently led, were overwhelmed by the Japanese. And the Chinese of Malaya and Singapore suffered much from the conquerors. Immediately after the occupation began, however, communist and KMT underground organizations sprang up. Of the two, the pro-communist Malayan Peoples Anti-Japanese Union (MPAJU) was by far the strongest: the KMT forces never managed to raise more than about five hundred armed men. World War II, in Malaya as well as in the homeland, was the end of the road for the KMT.

Communism, in contrast to KMT progress in the thirties, made no real headway in Malaya until after the Japanese occupation began. During the twenties, communists had functioned within the KMT rather than separately; the split between communists and KMT in 1927, after the Shanghai purges, marked the beginning of separate communist efforts. The Nanyang (South Sea) Communist Party came into existence in Singapore in 1928, and was assigned to promote the spread of communism throughout Southeast Asia. Two years later, the Malayan Communist Party (MCP) was founded. In 1931, after only a year of existence, Singapore police raids nearly wiped it out, but it regained its momentum by 1935, thriving on labor unrest created by the depression. From then until the onset of World War II, the MCP developed slowly. With the formation of the MPAJU along popular front lines, as well as the simultaneous creation of the Malayan Peoples Anti-Japanese Army (MPAJA), it at last came into its own.

As the only really effective fighting force in Malaya, MPAJA attracted significant British support, which was funneled through the agents of Britain's Force 136. Estimates of its total strength range from seven to ten thousand, the bulk supplied and paid by the British. MPAJA was supported by the British in the hope it would be of major effectiveness in harassing the Japanese once an invasion was under way. But the war ended before an invasion was mounted, and there is evidence indicating MPAJA's leaders planned to use it to seize control of Malaya in the inevitable confusion of battle.

Whatever the Malayan communists' intentions, they were in an unquestionably strong position in 1945. They were influential in the Chinese community, had infiltrated the demoralized local police forces, and had formed a number of large and effective youth groups, which headed its rallies and protest strikes.

Officially, the MPAJA was disbanded in 1945. Its leader, Chin

Peng, was flown to London to participate in victory celebrations, and came out of the junket with an O.B.E. Though Chin had agreed MPAJA members would surrender their arms (on payment of bonuses), much of the armament instead was tucked safely away in the jungle, in confident expectation of its future usefulness. And Old Comrades Associations kept MPAJA's spirit alive, as well as providing useful rallying points.

For the next three years, until 1948, the MCP's major weapon was the strike. Although several local efforts had reasonable success, two calls for a general, nationwide strike failed miserably. In 1948, tactics shifted abruptly: armed insurrection was decreed. Sources differ over reasons for the three-year delay. One authority, Frances Starner, cites "the lack of direction from the international communist movement, and indecisive leadership."[8] It also seems reasonable, however, to assume that MCP leaders believed their postwar position was so strong that armed insurrection was unnecessary, that Malaya would simply fall into their laps. Another authority, Anthony Short, cites sources who believe that the shift to revolt was ordered by Moscow, and was not the result of an MCP decision. He cites a general Soviet-inspired increase in revolutionary activity elsewhere in Southeast Asia, and notes that, coming as it did, the insurrection "neatly dovetailed into the Soviet scheme, and became part of a policy of revolt intended to embrace all countries of the Far East and Southeast Asia."[9]

Whatever the source of the orders, it seems reasonable to presuppose a predisposition for China on the part of the MCP. The guerrilla forces of World War II were largely Chinese, and though Moscow was at the time the sole center of international communism, the MCP "leaned to one side" long before Mao invented the phrase.

And during the Emergency (1948–60), the links with the Chinese Communist Party became even more obvious, at least in terms of moral support. Material backing was necessarily scanty, both because of sheer logistical difficulties and a shortage of supplies in China. The MCP itself went underground in 1948 after its banning on July 23 of that year. But China's influence was clear: the guerrillas relied heavily on Mao's "people's warfare" tactics and even put themselves through an ideological purge in October, 1951, in careful imitation of the progress of events in the "liberated" mainland. Peking's propaganda organs were unstinting in their support of Chin Peng's efforts. And despite the fact the insurrection was finally put down in 1960, China maintains it continues still, basing its claims on the three battalions of about 600 men who eke out a precarious living in the jungles of the Thai-Malaya border. Chin Peng himself is supposedly leading the group, but there has been little news from them since 1960.

The emergency itself, for the first several years, was a time of deep terror for Malaya. Just as in other Southeast Asian nations, the sole effective political group was the Communist Party. Save for this, there had been in prewar years no organized anti-colonial party or parties; indeed, neither Malaya's Chinese nor Malays had displayed any particular interest in independence. The MCP stood alone. The insurrection, in fact, was largely triggered by a clumsy British attempt in 1946 to create a "Union of Malaya," which in fact would have strengthened British control over the area. When this plan ran into heavy Malay elite opposition, a federal system was substituted that gave the Malays a marked primacy over the Indian and Chinese communities.

Riots broke out, backed heavily by the MCP, and the insurrection took shape. And the shape it took was racial, which was at once its great strength and a crippling weakness. The Chinese of Malaya split sharply: the rich supported the British, who had created the conditions in which they became wealthy; but the poorer masses and the intellectuals threw in their lot on the side of the MCP.

This division along largely racial lines at first provided advantages. The close ties between the poor Chinese squatter farmers and the rebels gave the latter a regular food supply and provided communication links as well. Money flowed regularly from the Chinese of the cities and towns to the rebels in the bush, first willingly, later only as a result of coercion. The communists, to be sure, tried their best to create an impression of interracial cooperation; the old MPAJA was renamed the Malayan Races Liberation Army (MRLA), for example, in an attempt to escape the "Chinese" label. But its huge supporting organization was known by its Chinese name, Min Yuen, a clear indication of its racial composition, and the MRLA members soon found themselves labeled simply as CTs (for communist terrorists). Exact figures for total Min Yuen and CT membership are difficult to pin down: Kuala Lumpur sources estimate there were about 5,000 CTs at the height of the emergency, supported by perhaps 250,000 to 300,000 Min Yuen collaborators. Of this total, at least 90 percent were Chinese.

The terror began in late 1948: small guerrilla units laid waste to plantations, set up road ambushes, raided police stations, robbed, murdered, and sabotaged. Small British patrols were ambushed, though attackers inevitably broke off contact if the odds proved to be against them. It was, in other words, a classic example of the first stage in Mao Tse-tung's theories of people's warfare. As far as it went, it was successful. But the racial composition of the CTs, coupled with their inability to attract a significantly large following, kept the CT effort frozen at a level of simple guerrilla terror.

Three years of terrorism reached their peak in 1951, when the CTs succeeded in assassinating the British high commissioner, Sir Henry Gurney. His successor, General Sir Gerald Templar, concentrated his efforts largely on a single, key point: the isolation of the CTs from the population in general. Before his arrival on the scene, Templar's predecessors laid the groundwork for his operations. In 1950, the key step was taken: resettlement of an estimated five hundred thousand Chinese squatters who were a key source of supplies and information for the CTs. The squatters were moved to "new villages," which were closely supervised enclaves. Contacts with the CTs were all but ended, and the men in the bush began to suffer. Templar put this effort into high gear. And beyond this, a mixed security force of British, Malay, Chinese, Tamil, Fijians, and native tribesmen went into the jungles in pursuit of the CTs. Though these jungle operations were not always successful in bringing the troops into direct contact with the enemy, they succeeded in denying the CTs the use of fixed bases. The guerrillas were kept on the run, short of supplies, and their effectiveness was sharply reduced. Terribly slowly —but terribly surely—the incident rate died down.

By 1955, an amnesty was offered to all CTs who surrendered with their arms. Defections, which had already begun to rise, were accelerated, nationwide elections were held, and by 1957 the Federation of Malaya became an independent member of the Commonwealth. Though terrorism continued, it gradually was reduced to the level of banditry.

The failure of the MCP to seize power in Malaya had several distinct effects. It indicated, for instance, that Mao's theories of revolutionary warfare were not inevitably successful. It brought both the peninsula's Malays and Chinese to the realization that they faced a severe threat, and in effect contributed heavily to the latent sentiments of nationalism; it made both races realize that they must stand on their own. And the Malayan Communists, for the time being at least, were reduced to the level of simple outlaws. Until the emergency, Malayan politics barely existed. Under the pressure of the undeclared war, Malaysia began to take shape, slowly and, alas, awkwardly.

When the Federation of Malaya came into existence in 1957, the key power resided in the United Malay National Organization (UMNO). Led by the Tunku, UMNO was the keystone of the ruling Alliance, a group of parties that hopefully was to represent the various races of Malaya. But UMNO, with well over half the 159 seats in the parliament, is in full control, and with the consent of MCA and MIC. There is, it would seem, an unspoken bargain, allowing political primacy to the Malays and leaving economic power to the Chinese and Indians.

Population figures explain much of Malaysia's racial problems. Overall, according to the 1961 Census, Malays made up 46.2 percent of the total, while the Chinese accounted for 42.2 percent and Indians and Pakistanis 9.4 percent. On the Malay peninsula itself, there were 3.6 million Malays, 2.7 million Chinese, 813,000 Indians and Pakistanis, and 129,000 others. Singapore counted 1.3 million Chinese, 238,000 Malays, 142,000 Indians and Pakistanis, and 41,000 others. In Sarawak there were 529,000 Malays and tribesmen, 243,000 Chinese, and 8,000 others; while in Sabah (North Borneo) there were 320,000 Malays and tribesmen, 110,000 Chinese, and 45,000 others, including in this case Malays born in Malaya or Singapore.

Islam is Malaysia's state religion, and Kuala Lumpur reflects its predominance. Mosques are everywhere: the National Mosque itself, completed in the mid-sixties, is an enormous, modernistic affair that is beautifully designed. And many other buildings in the capital reflect the Moslem influence: spires, minarets, Arabic curves. The Central Railroad Station, for instance, looks like the Alhambra—or rather as the Alhambra might have looked had it been built in Victorian England. The Ministry of External Affairs, built at about the same time (the mid-nineteenth century), is in the same pleasantly archaic style.

The opposition to the Alliance, such as it is, is headed by the Pan Malayan Islamic Party (PMIP), with nine seats in the house, and the Socialist Front, with two seats. This particular opposition, it should be added, exists in Malaya only. Though it has only eleven seats, the two parties won 13 percent of the votes in 1964's general elections.

PMIP is strongest on Malaya's East Coast, and controls Kelantan Province. The party's base is Malay nationalism, and it seems to feel UMNO has sold out the Malays. It opposed the Malaysia concept for several years, wants a secular state, and urges that all Chinese be expelled from Malaya. But in January, 1965, PMIP suffered a heavy blow: federal police arrested its president, Dr. Burhanuddin Aldashhemi, on charges of attempting to promote pro-Indonesian armed rebellion in Malaysia. PMIP's vice president was seized on similar charges. Several leftist politicians were also arrested in the sweep. Police charged that those arrested had planned to go to Indonesia and there form a Malaysian government in exile.

The Socialist Front, which also suffered in the 1965 roundups, is an alliance of three parties: the Labor Party (Chinese), the People's Party (Partai Rakjat), and the National Convention Party. In the past, Malaysia's intellectuals have been attracted to the Socialist Front. But the front reportedly has been infiltrated by communists and has lost some of its appeal. It is strongly anti-Malaysia.

In general, the Socialist Front seems to contain several unsavory elements: the People's Party president has been in prison on security grounds for several years, and a number of Socialist Front cadres are known to have gone to Indonesia for training, then returned to Malaysia with infiltrating guerrillas. Most have been arrested, or so the government claimed.

Also active in Malaya, on a small scale, were the following: United Democratic Party (one house seat), which resembles the Liberal Party in Britain in its philosophy; and the People's Progressive Party (PPP), two seats, which controls the tin-mining town of Ipoh, has an almost all-Chinese membership, is run by two Indian brothers, and basically is a Tammany-type show.

In Singapore, the dominant party is Lee Kuan Yew's People's Action Party (PAP), which had thirteen house seats in Kuala Lumpur, before the Singapore 1965 ouster in 1965. Opposition is provided by the Barisan Socialis (which means Socialist Front in translation but is *not* directly connected with the Socialist Front in Malaya), with three seats.

Malay nationalism, angry but formless, is a problem. "Now," a Chinese lawyer told me, "the Tunku must control the ultranationalist wing of UMNO and the Malay other parties as well. If the radicals seize control of UMNO from the Tunku and Razak, things will be very difficult." And there are signs of flaring Malay nationalism.

One focus of agitation is language: Malay will become the peninsula's official language in 1967. English will still be taught in schools, but Chinese schools are expected to be hit badly if current plans go ahead unaltered. To handle the problems created by today's wide technical vocabulary, a special committee has cooked up at least forty thousand new Malay words, and the bulk of them are wildly awkward. No decision has yet been made on Borneo, though technically Malay won't become official there until 1973.

In many parts of Malaysia today, however, signboards make an imperious demand: "Satu Negara, Satu Bahasa" (One nation, one language). Highway signs, which now are in both English and Malay, are defaced: a sign just outside Kuala Lumpur's airport, for instance, said "airport" in both English and Malay, and the English word was partially obliterated by red paint.

And in central Kuala Lumpur, two "imperialist" statues were quietly removed in 1964. One was of King Edward VII, the other was of Sir Frank Swettenham, a former governor. They were spirited off to the National Museum and installed in a place of honor, but had to be moved to the back of the museum after protests began.

This nationalism, in great part, is aimed directly at the Chinese. For many reasons, most of which can be lumped categorically under the heading of simple envy, the Malays fear the Chinese. To protect themselves, they have written certain privileges into the constitution. In the Civil Service, for example, the legal job ratio is four Malays to one Chinese. The individual states determine who can own land, and Malays are always favored. Malays get preference on taxi and bus licenses, and this situation has given rise to the "Ali Baba" bus and taxi fleets: a Malay ("Ali") holds the fleet license, but a Chinese ("Baba") runs it. In 1970, however, some of these special Malay privileges expire.

Though Chinese realize the privileges are temporary, many are bitter. "We are second-class citizens," said a brilliant young Chinese doctor in Kuala Lumpur, "and we know it. I studied abroad to come back and help my country, but if I took a government post now I'd never be more than an underling." Another Chinese cynically adds: "When the Malays need money, they must come to us. That's our hope for the future."

It must be added that there are many fair-minded Malays and Chinese, including the Tunku and Lee Kuan Yew, who are perfectly well aware of the frictions and determined to end them. In the efforts of these men lies the hope for eventual solution, and, in effect, for the salvation of Malaysia. If they fail, the results have already cast shadows before them: twice in 1964, violent Malay-Chinese riots caused what officially was admitted to be fifty deaths and unofficially was put at nearly two hundred. Blame for the rioting falls largely on the Malays, who comprise less than 15 percent of Singapore's population. But Indonesian agents, particularly in the second affray, played a role.

In contrast to the cloudy social situation, the Malaysian economy continued sparkling. In terms of per capita gross national product, Malaysia's $256 is second only to Japan's $600. (Other figures: Taiwan, $160; Philippines, $131; Thailand, $101; and Indonesia, $85.) Life expectancy figures reflect a similar picture: Japan, 68 years; Malaysia and the Philippines, 60; Thailand, 50; Indonesia, 32.

Deputy Prime Minister Tun Abdul Razak explained the outlook of Malaysian officials this way: "We put the people first," he told me, "our government's purpose is to serve the people. We intend to help the peasants across the entire spectrum of their lives—health, agriculture, education, food, markets and roads."

Malaysia's basic economic problem is its over-dependence on tin and rubber. The solution, as Kuala Lumpur sees it, is to add new products. "We are diversifying into palm oil, sugar cane, and cocoa," said Razak, who is also Minister of Rural Development, "but we need outside help if we are to expand our armed forces and continue the pace of rural development at the same time. If we get this help, we'll be all right."

For the moment, Malaysia is doing well. The GNP has increased an average of 5 percent a year since 1961 (in 1963/64, the increase was 7 percent). Foreign exchange reserves are about $1.2 billion.

Though Singapore has recorded a trade deficit of M$760.3 million (US$253.4 million) in 1964, down slightly from 1963's deficit of M$960 million (US$320 million), Britain's defense expenditures there have just about made up the gap.

Malaysia's rubber production set an all-time record in 1964, jumping to 819,006 tons from 1963's 784,713 tons, and rose steadily in later years. A large-scale tree replanting program, using higher-yield trees, was credited for the increase. Singapore sources believe Malaysia, which now produces a third of the world's natural rubber, will fill 60 percent of the world market demand by 1975.

Central concern to Malaysian planters is the threat of synthetic rubber, now being produced in quantity both in the United States and Europe. In Kuala Lumpur, however, one leading non-Malaysian source said that though natural rubber prices were now 26 cents a pound, the price could go as low as 18 cents without eliminating profits, while synthetic rubber as now produced can't market for less than 23 cents a pound. Nobody believes, however, that synthetic, over the long run, doesn't offer a serious danger to the Malaysian planters. In this connection, a reliable recent survey showed that U.S. imports of natural rubber have fallen for the past ten years: America now imports about 400,000 tons a year, off almost 50 percent from its requirements of just a few years ago. West European buying has dropped similarly, but not quite as sharply. On the other hand, communist bloc purchases have risen to nearly five times the amount purchased in 1953. If the trend continues, Malaysia may find the communist countries its best potential customers. (In 1965, bloc nation purchases jumped more than 50 percent, to 154,225 tons.)

The other pillar of Malaysian prosperity, tin, enjoyed another profitable year in 1964. Production totaled about 60,000 tons, an industry record, and rose to 73,000 tons in 1965. Rising tin prices are attributable, at least in part, to drop in Congo and Bolivian production: the trend will probably continue. And Vietnam war demands helped measurably.

Foreign trade, reflecting the increasing demand for Malaysia's tin and rubber, improved markedly in 1965. A year previously, Malaysia's trade balance was $44 million in the red, but in 1965 a surplus of $59 million was recorded.

During the mid-sixties, Malaysia continued to advance despite definite problems at home and abroad. But there was little indication that the Kuala Lumpur leadership was paying sufficient attention to the two Borneo states of Sabah and Sarawak. Sabah, it could be argued, was doing fairly well. But in Sarawak, there were serious problems, and on balance they seemed to be getting more severe.

Physically, Sarawak is something less than pleasant. In itself nearly as large as Malaya (47,500 square miles, compared to Malaya's 50,700 square miles), it is severely underdeveloped. Three-quarters of the state is covered by jungle; it is a combination of swamp and rugged hill country, and much of it is uninhabited. Only 6 percent of the land area is under cultivation. Sarawak's economy is based on a combination of agriculture, forestry, and fisheries, and its major exports are rubber, timber, pepper, and sago. Communications barely exist. Its history provides its sole romantic aspect: from 1839 until 1946, it was ruled by the White Rajahs of the Brooke family as a private fief. At the end of World War II, it was ceded to Britain by the third Rajah, and became a crown colony. In 1963 it joined Malaysia.

Though the Chinese are in the minority, the only effective political power is held by the Chinese-dominated and communist-infiltrated Sarawak United Peoples Party (SUPP). And Sarawak's Chinese are not particularly happy about Malaysia, particularly in the state's southern area.

"Sarawak's First Division," said a Western intelligence official, "is the most dangerous area of Malaysia." "SUPP's leadership is clean," said the same official, "but from there on down it's almost completely communist-controlled." And there's doubt that the moderate leaders have any say in what SUPP does. Other parties include the Sarawak Alliance, which includes tribesmen, Malays, and some Chinese, but it's nowhere near SUPP's strength. Another party, called Machindia, is also multiracial. It opposes the concept of Malaysia and has no strong leaders.

Behind SUPP in Sarawak are what the British call the Clandestine Communist Organizations (CCO), particularly strong in the First Division and which have now spread their influence up the coast. Early in 1965, for instance, the Malaysian government anounced it was calling in all firearms owned by "non-natives" (Chinese) in the Kanowit district of the Third Division.

Explaining its action, the government said the district recently had been "flooded" by CCO cadres that were busily attempting to subvert the native population. Late in 1964, six Chinese cadres were seized in this district, and their documents showed an instructive, and frightening, parallel with CT methods used during Malaya's emergency.

And in mid-summer, as CCO activities reached a new peak, the government trotted out tactics which proved successful in Malaya's emergency. Police rounded up five thousand Chinese villagers and consigned them to fenced-off camps. "It is clear," a government statement said, "that terrorist outrages were made possible by the active support of the communist organization in the area, and the passive indifference of many other Chinese residents in the vicinity." (The "outrages" cited were a series of attacks in late June, 1965, which left nine dead and four wounded.)

A week later, intelligence sources told newsmen that interrogation of thirty-eight suspected communists had produced evidence indicating that CCO membership in Sarawak included roughly two thousand hard-core members and cadre personnel, plus about twenty-five thousand supporters who would serve the fighting men just as the Min Yuen served the CTs in Malaya during the emergency. Many of the hard-core members were trained in Indonesia, either just across the border in Kalimantan (Indonesian Borneo) or in Java. And there was strong evidence to indicate Indonesian subversives were working closely with the CCO before "confrontation" ended.

If the CCO is ever able to mount a full-scale insurrection, some Western sources doubt Sarawak could be held. Like Sabah, it is enormously underdeveloped, and though the Borneo territories were promised lavish financial aid once Malaysia had come into being, little has actually been programmed.

Further north along the Borneo coast is Sabah, Sarawak's smaller sister. Mountainous and densely forested over most of its 29,388 square miles, Sabah's population is concentrated along the west coast in the farming area. Agriculture is the base of Sabah's economy, just as it is in Sarawak, and the state's principal exports are timber and rubber, as well as a little copra. But while Sarawak's economy has never really prospered, Sabah in the sixties experienced a comfortable boom, based principally on timber sales abroad. The consequent prosperity and full employment was an effective bar to subversion, in contrast to Sarawak.

The third North Borneo state is Brunei, tiny and oil-rich, which opted out of Malaysia on its formation in 1963 and remains a British protectorate complete with expatriate advisers to the Sultan. Despite its tiny size and relative prosperity (which had led to its nickname of "the Shellfare state"), Brunei is the only Borneo area that went through a genuine rebellion. In December, 1962, Sheikh Mahmud Azahari led a short-lived but vicious revolt which was put down only with the aid of three thousand British and Gurkha troops. Azahari, who had been mightily encouraged by Sukarno, unsurprisingly took refuge in Djakarta after the revolt failed.

Linchpin of Malaysia's defense is Britain. Some sources in Kuala Lumpur argue that Britain cannot afford to stay on, pointing out that Britain spends about $280 million a year on the defense of Malaysia, while it repatriates to Britain earnings equaling only a third of that total. Others—and they are in the majority—believe that Britain feels a moral responsibility for Malaysia that cannot be measured in pounds and shillings. In addition, defense help also came from Australia, New Zealand, and a bit from Canada as well. Kuala Lumpur officials naturally resent any implication that the British did all the fighting, and it's true that Malaysian troops were active in Borneo. There were, however, rumors that the Malaysian forces weren't quite as effective as the British. But the Malays fought well during the 1948–60 Emergency and in 1964–65, because they have their own nation, had even more reason to fight effectively.

In terms of total strength, however, Malaysia's armed forces are tiny. The army, air force, and navy together muster only about twenty thousand men. The army has ten infantry battalions, organized into five brigades of varying size. It is basically a defensive force, with few heavy weapons. And austerity is the keynote. There are for instance, no field hospitals: Borneo wounded were treated in civilian hospitals. Military sources rate the average infantryman highly, when he's properly led, and his jungle-warfare capability is well above average. Beyond the infantry outfits, there are two armored car regiments, two artillery battalions, four engineer battalions, and signals, transportation, and maintenance units. Conscription is used to fill the ranks: eight hundred men are taken into the forces every three months, but they are trained for only three months and then assigned to reserve units.

The navy totals about sixteen hundred men, less than the crew of a single U.S. carrier, and splashes about in one frigate and several coastal patrol craft. The air force is even smaller: fourteen hundred men, with a few liaison aircraft and helicopters. Both the air force and the navy are commanded by Commonwealth officers. Because the two services were formed only a few years ago, their officers are young and not yet ready for command. (The army, on the other hand, is commanded by a Malay.)

Backing up the armed forces proper are the national police, with a total strength of thirty-five thousand. Malaysia's police are used for everything from writing parking tickets to pursuing CTs. There are, for instance, eight federal police units of two hundred men apiece that perform such special duties as riot-quashing. The Police Field Forces, organized into six battalions, are used as infantry against CTs and other infiltrators, such as the Indonesians who landed at several points along the Malaya coast in 1964 and 1965. Supplementing PFF action against CTs are the Senoi Praak, a band of 320 aboriginal tribesmen deeply skilled in jungle warfare. And beyond these units is a 44,000-man civil guard force called the Local Defense Corps.

These units performed well against the Indonesians. Though several invading groups managed to get ashore on the Malayan Peninsula, none survived more than a week or two. One of the more sizable incursions, an airdrop of ninety-six paratroopers into the Labis area in 1965 was typical: ninety-two were accounted for almost immediately, and the remainder never surfaced and were presumed killed in landing mishaps. Malaysian officers were more than happy about the results. "The Indonesians," an officer told me, "provided the best possible training exercise. A fast start, quick pressure, then surrender, and we go back to the daily routine."

In late 1965, as Sukarno began to slip from power, the Indonesian "confrontation" began to lose its edge. Landings on the peninsula halted, and the incident rate in Sarawak and Sabah slumped. Though Djakarta continued to promise that confrontation would continue, by mid-1966 the threat had ended.

And as Indonesia's anti-Malaysia policy lost momentum, Malaysia's relations with the Philippines improved accordingly. The Manila government, under incoming President Ferdinand Marcos, took steps to raise the level of diplomatic relations. This included the recognition of Malaysia, which had been denied by President Diosdado Macapagal when Malaysia came into being.

In general, Malaysia's relations with Southeast Asian nations place it right of center, a position unsurprising in view of the experiences during the emergency as well as the innate conservatism of both Malay and Chinese leaders. Singapore, on the other hand, leans to the left in some degree, but there seems little chance of a swing toward alignment with Peking or Hanoi. Both Singapore and Malaysia made efforts in the mid-sixties to have themselves included in the Afro-Asian Bloc, ignoring the fact that Afro-Asia was in a process of mild dissolution.

In Kuala Lumpur and Singapore, there was general realization that the Peking regime represented the greatest single threat to their continued independence. Communist China, on the other hand, evidently had relegated Malaysia to a secondary role among its targets. In comparison to propaganda efforts directed against Thailand and South Vietnam, for instance, Malaysia and Singapore were largely ignored. (Eight months after the expulsion of Singapore from Malaysia, nothing on the subject had been published in the Peking press beyond a statement that the break had occurred.)

The Malayan Communist Party, weakened by the failure of the 1948–60 insurrection, exists in Malaysia today only as an underground operation, and fellow-traveling parties such as those included in Malaysia's Socialist Front and Singapore's Barisan Socialis have little influence. The MCP's military arm is confined to the jungled mountains of the Thai-Malaysia border, where about six battalions have managed to stave off Kuala Lumpur's attempts to wipe them out. Ideologically, it remains closely aligned with the Chinese Communist Party, and there are at least a dozen Malay Chinese in Peking today who serve as liaison between the two groups. Major spokesman for the MCP abroad seems to be the *Malayan Monitor* published in London. And the *Monitor* takes a stand of unwavering opposition to Malaysia, describing the concept vitriolically as a "British plot" to retain control of the former colony. The *Monitor* is banned in Malaysia, and its fame abroad rests largely on the fact that Peking is given to quoting from it liberally and approvingly.

There are no diplomatic relations between China and either Malaysia or Singapore. Peking, however, recognized the Federation of Malaya on its formation in 1957, and a year previous to this, a combined Malaya-Singapore trade delegation visited Peking. (Even today, despite the worsening of relations, there are still many Chinese Communist consumer goods on sale throughout the peninsula.)

Peking all but ignored the steps leading up to the formation of Malaysia in September, 1963, and in the year before Malaysia came into existence made only one direct reference to it. That article was called "Dissect the 'Federation of Malaysia' Plan," which condemned both Britain and the United States for their roles in Malaysia's creation.[10] It seemed something less than coincidental that the MCP itself said nothing about Malaysia until four days after its founding.

Though the MCP, the *Monitor,* and the Chinese press have attacked Malaysia verbally since that time, the frequency of the attacks is not great. In general, emphasis was on Indonesian determination to smash Malaysia, rather than on Malaysia's misdeeds. And with the ending of Indonesia's confrontation policy, direct Chinese propaganda against Malaysia went into an equally slow decline.

More important for the future was the establishment in Peking of the Malayan National Liberation League on January 1, 1966. Previously, the League had had its headquarters in Djakarta, but the anti-Sukarno coup which started on September 30, 1965, forced its removal.

It is headed by one P. V. Sharma, a former president of the Singapore Teachers Union, who was expelled from Singapore in 1952 for subversive activities. The league thus joins other front organizations in Peking, such as the Patriotic Front of Thailand and the South Vietnamese National Liberation Front. If the MNLL follows the usual pattern it will emerge as a refuge and a rostrum for the exiled Malays and overseas Chinese now residing in China. So far, however, little is known of either Sharma's colleagues or policies, beyond his pledge in early 1966 that the league stood firmly behind all and every anti-Malaysia policy.

For Malaysia and Singapore, the future is cloudy at best. British support is dwindling, and within a few years it seems reasonable to expect withdrawal of British troops, throwing the burden of defense upon the tiny Malaysian forces now in existence. The United States so far has been reluctant to assume Britain's responsibilities in the area, and further budget expenditures for Southeast Asia will pass through Congress only with a great deal of protest, in view of the current outlay on Vietnam.

Beyond this is the racial question, even more important to the area's future. It seems fair to say that Malaysia's greatest problem, and perhaps its greatest tragedy, is its plural society. Malay-Chinese antipathy is at base the reason for Malaysia's expulsion of Singapore, and there seems to be little in the way of a solution in view. It is small consolation to realize that the governments in both Kuala Lumpur and Singapore are working better than many observers expected. Indeed, the alternatives to each are more than disagreeable: if the Malay "ultras" succeed in ousting the moderate Tunku, and if Lee Kuan Yew is succeeded by the local communists, race riots would be only a beginning.

Both Lee and the Tunku have shown a degree of willingness to face their mutual problems together. But more than this is needed if Malaysia is to avoid being dragged into the whirlpool of hatred and blood that is Southeast Asia today. China, for the time being, seems content to let Malaysia stew in its own problems. And perhaps that is the most hopeful sign now in sight.

1. Lee's enemies make a habit of calling him "Harry" Lee, but only at their peril. He dropped his English name, for obvious reasons, on his entry into Singapore politics.
2. Originally, the lodge was a jerry-built construction shack perched on a building site in Kuala Lumpur. The Tunku spotted it one day, liked its Malay-style roof, and asked the builder how much a duplicate would cost. The builder put the Tunku off, finished the job, trucked the shack up to Alor Star, and presented the key to the Tunku, who was charmed.
3. Britain retained responsibility for defense and foreign affairs, and internal security was under the wing of the British-dominated Security Council.
4. UMNO, the United Malay National Organization, is the keystone of the ruling Alliance. It represents the Malays and dominates the other Alliance members—the Malaysian Chinese Association (MCA) and the Malaysian Indian Congress (MIC), which stand for the Chinese and Indians in the country.
5. See D. G. E. Hall, *A History of Southeast Asia,* Macmillan & Co. Ltd., London, 1965, second edition, pp. 7 and 9.
6. Quoted in Victor Purcell, *The Chinese in Southeast Asia,* Oxford, London, 1965, p. 235.
7. K. G. Tregonning, *A History of Modern Malaya,* Eastern Universities Press Ltd. for University of London Press Ltd., 1964, p. 180.
8. Francis Starner, "Communists in Malaysia: A Multifront Struggle," included in *The Communist Revolution in Asia,* edited by Robert A. Scalapino, Prentice-Hall, Inc., Englewood Cliffs, N.J., 1965, p. 224.
9. Anthony Short, article in *Malaysia: A Survey,* edited by Wang Gung-wu, Donald Moore Books, London, 1964, p. 153.
10. Pi Wen, article in Shih-Chieh Chih-Shih (World Culture), Number 7, April 10, 1963, Peking.

five

THE
OTHER CRISIS:

Indonesia

Indonesia today is a monument to the intertwined brilliance and folly of one man—President Sukarno. He led his countrymen in the long and eventually successful fight for independence from the Dutch, and in the process became a national hero. In his complex personality, he summed up the assets and debits of all Indonesians. A great speaker, great dreamer, and great lover, he was the very incarnation of the revolutionary. But for all his greatness he was tragically flawed. There are two broad types of revolutionaries: one, the man who leads his people to freedom, then gives way to the technicians who can proceed to build a working nation; the other, the man who in himself has both the ability to lead and to consolidate. Sukarno cared nothing for consolidation, and under his megalomaniacal rule the consolidators were not allowed to function. And today, as Indonesia moves slowly into the post-Sukarno era, it is desperately ill-equipped for progress into the modern world.

Sukarno's legacy, to put it bluntly, is chaos. For Indonesia, obviously, this is tragic, for this huge, sprawling nation is potentially one of the richest countries of the world. Its more than 3,000 islands support a population of an estimated 105 million, making it the fifth most populous nation in the world, and its natural resources are huge. Oil reserves, for instance, are enormous: there is a proven potential of at least 9 billion barrels, and some oilmen predict total reserves are even greater. Production of crude oil averages more than 20 million tons a year, making Indonesia Southeast Asia's greatest oil producer—and oil, unsurprisingly, is the country's single largest earner of foreign exchange. Tin and bauxite reserves are almost equally as vast, and there are limited coal reserves as well. Beyond this are more

[175]

mineral resources: nickel, phosphate, manganese, silver, and gold. Among agricultural resources are rubber (Indonesia in the past produced as much as 40 percent of the world total), tea, and spices. But since 1957, when Sukarno expelled the last of the Dutch technicians whose managerial skills had kept production at reasonable levels, the story has been one of increasing neglect and decreasing output; few Indonesians could be found who had the necessary skills to keep production high. And all Sukarno's flamboyant oratory was not enough to keep the country economically healthy. By the mid-sixties, the outlook was bleak indeed.

In January, 1962, when I first visited Indonesia, Djakarta qualified instantly as the most depressing capital I'd ever seen. At the time, the final quarrel with the Dutch was well under way, and in a brief, bloody sea battle off the coast of Dutch New Guinea (Irian Barat), two small Indonesian warships had been sunk. The streets were full of soldiers and demonstrators, and in the huge parade-ground in the center of the city, volunteers were training to join an invasion of Irian Barat, the last Dutch remaining possession in the old Netherlands East Indies. The Indonesians, of course, did have a case, for The Hague had promised eventually to turn its half of New Guinea over to Indonesia when the Round Table Conference of 1949 ratified Indonesian independence. But no specific time for the turnover had been set, and the Dutch seemed ready to cling to their last Indies outpost for years to come. For Sukarno, the issue was a lifesaver. Plagued by accelerating economic problems, including an almost farcical devaluation of the rupiah, an outside distraction was an obvious way of whipping up support at home. Beyond this, the Irian Barat affair was an equally welcome excuse for seeking foreign arms for Indonesia's poorly armed troops: once the United States made it clear that massive shipments of American weapons were not forthcoming, Sukarno turned to the always-willing Soviet Union and picked up an estimated $1 billion in jets, vehicles, and weapons of every conceivable variety.

Most of these arms had arrived in Indonesia by early 1962, and the threat of a shooting war became painfully clear. The Soviet Union, anxious to consolidate a foothold in Southeast Asia, was prepared to buy its way into Sukarno's esteem by shipping the weapons needed for the exercise in Irian Barat, and the Dutch were clearly outmanned and outgunned. But in Washington, a fresh policy course was adopted with uncharacteristic speed. Ellsworth Bunker, an experienced diplomat, was assigned to act as a special emissary to the Dutch and the Indonesians, and succeeded in getting both sides to accept a temporary United Nations mandate over New Guinea. In time, it was hoped, the Papuans of West New Guinea would make their own choice of allegiance. The upshot, as most cynics had expected, was that Sukarno proceeded to renounce the idea of self-determination and, a year later, graciously accepted Irian Barat from the U.N. as Indonesia's own. But at least the Dutch were off the hook; and from the U.S. point of view, the Soviets had received only a bloody nose for their huge investment.

As it turned out, however, the Soviet repulse merely set the stage for more trouble. Within a year, Sukarno had embarked on what he called a "confrontation" with the newly born nation of Malaysia, and as allies he chose the Communist Chinese—evidently convinced that Russian strength in Asia was not what it seemed to be. And the United States, whatever credit it had built up as a result of its role in 1962, was equally on the outside. More important in the long run was the fact that in Sukarno's preoccupation with foreign policy, he turned his back almost completely on Indonesia's real problem: the increasingly debilitated economy. And thus by 1962 the pattern of what turned out to be the last act in the Sukarno scenario was rapidly becoming clear. I gained, in that brief visit, a scarifyingly clear appreciation of Sukarno the ruler. What never became apparent was Sukarno the man, who still remains, to me at least, something of a puzzle.

The bare facts of his life, however, are accessible. He was born in East Java, near Surabaya, in 1901, the son of a Balinese mother and a Javanese schoolteacher. His sign of the Zodiac is Gemini (the twins), and he has pointed to this on several occasions as symbolic of his dualistic nature. (Sukarno, like almost all Indonesians, is a deeply superstitious man.) After graduation from high school in Surabaya, he went on to Bandung University and graduated in 1925 with an engineering degree.[1] During high school, he became interested in the embryo nationalist movement, and in his Bandung years attracted the frosty attention of the Dutch authorities with a series of strongly nationalistic speeches. By 1927, he was deeply involved in an organization that a year later transformed itself into the Indonesian Nationalist Party (PNI, or Partai Nasional Indonesia). And at about this time, he was developing his own political philosophy, Marhaenism: a system of belief that had much in common with the philosophy of Mao Tse-tung.

His election in late 1928 as chairman of a group of six political parties, including the PNI, intensified the interest of Dutch security officials in him, and a year later they arrested him, with three associates, on charges of plotting a revolt. After a trial, he drew a four-year term (later reduced to two), and while he was in prison, PNI fell apart, to be replaced by two separate organizations. Released from prison in 1931, Sukarno took over leadership of one of PNI's successors and built it into a twenty thousand-member force. Once again, the uneasy Dutch popped Sukarno into prison, and he was not released until the arrival of the Japanese in 1942.

In contrast to other Asian leaders, who spent their periods of imprisonment writing memoirs and essays, Sukarno seems to have remained largely passive during his detention. At any rate, he has talked little about those years since his release, and for that matter has been something less than generous with detail about his role during the war. He did work for the Japanese, and in the immediate postwar years the Dutch did their best to label him a collaborator. It seems more accurate to say, however, that he worked closely in those years with the leaders of the Indonesian underground to maintain and accelerate the nationalist movement. And while Indonesian nationalism did not particularly enrapture the Japanese, it is certain that anticolonialism was regarded with distinct benevolence.

As the Allied pressures on the Japanese increased, Sukarno found himself able to lay more and more stress on nationalistic activities. Japanese formation of a home defense corps in 1943 put arms into Indonesian hands, and the Japanese, faced by steadily more serious defeats, by 1945 had all but dropped whatever opposition had existed previously to Indonesian independence movements. In August, Sukarno and Mohammed Hatta, another leading Indonesian revolutionary, were flown to South Vietnam for final discussions. There, at Japanese regional headquarters in the pleasant hill resort of Dalat, the Indonesian republic became a reality. All that remained was the mere proclamation of it.

But here Sukarno wavered, perhaps suspecting a trap of some sort, perhaps not quite believing the Japanese were finished. By the time he and Hatta returned to Djakarta (then still called Batavia), the Indonesian underground chieftains, led by Sutan Sjahrir, were in full cry: they wanted independence, and they wanted it immediately. Once Sukarno's uncertainty became obvious, he and Hatta were kidnapped by a group of young leftist revolutionaries demanding he act. At this moment, word of the Japanese surrender reached Indonesia, and Sukarno finally moved. On August 17, 1945, the Indonesian republic was proclaimed; Sukarno became president and Hatta vice-president.

Four confusing years intervened, however, before the republic's hold was firm. Threatened by both the Dutch, unable to recognize that history had passed them by, and local communists, who mounted a brace of coups, Indonesia staggered from crisis to crisis. Less than a year after independence, the first communist coup attempt was triggered by Tan Malaka. It failed, and was followed a year later (in July, 1947) by the first of two Dutch "police actions," which forced the collapse of the Sjahrir government but which failed to put an end to the republic. As confusion multiplied, the Partai Komunis Indonesia (PKI) staged an insurrection at Madiun in September, 1948, which was crushed only after bloody fighting by troops under the command of General Abdul Haris Nasution. And then the Dutch, hoping to profit from the post-Madiun uncertainty, mounted their second "police action"—a harsh, efficient operation that produced the fall of the republic's capital of Djogjakarta and the capture of Sukarno and Hatta. To the Dutch, at least, the struggle must have seemed over—but angry resistance continued. And on November 2, 1949, they finally transferred sovereignty to the Indonesian republic at the Round Table Conference at The Hague.

Here was a point, it seemed, at which the consolidation of the revolution's gains should begin. It did not. Proclamation of a new constitution in 1950 did nothing to allay fears of leaders from the outer islands that Java would monopolize both political control and economic revenues. And Sukarno, suspicious of any opposition that seemed likely to diminish his power, began what amounted to a long and drawn-out guerrilla campaign for total control. Governments came and went with increasing speed, nothing was done to accelerate economic progress, and separatist feelings, particularly in the Celebes and Sumatra, were allowed to grow almost unchecked. The PKI, almost totally smashed after the failure of the Madiun revolt, was quietly rebuilding its strength under the leadership of a new secretary-general, D. N. Aidit.

During this period, Indonesian foreign policy had a single major aim: non-alignment. A period of pro-Western sentiment had ended in 1952, and from then on Sukarno began a cautious exploration of relations with the communist world. Communist China, true, had been recognized in 1950, but not until 1953 did relations shift from the polite but chilly stance of the first years. In 1955, Sukarno made a giant step toward an ambition that was to consume him—to become Asia's great neutralist leader.

That first move was the convening of the Bandung Conference in April, 1955, "which brought Indonesia into the forefront of world politics and into the leadership of the Afro-Asian bloc of nations."[2] Nearly all the powers that had achieved independence in post-World War II years were represented there; India's Jawaharlal Nehru, Indonesia's Sukarno, and Communist China's Chou En-lai dominated proceedings. Little of real consequence occurred at Bandung: the resolutions signed with such splendid fanfare were largely forgotten ten years later. But Bandung was enormously significant in one respect: Chou and Sukarno emerged on the world stage, and this twinning of the two big Asian powers was to have many repercussions over the next decade.

Both nations, suitably enough, reached full sovereignty in 1949, and the Indonesians—like other Asians—had known and respected Chinese power for centuries. The first contacts date back to the third, or perhaps even the fourth, century before Christ. These were trade contacts, almost exclusively; there is no evidence indicating China had conquest in mind. And they continued. There is, for instance, a record of a Chinese expedition to northern Sumatra in the first century A.D. to pick up a rhinoceros for the Han emperor's zoo. In addition to trade, Chinese pilgrims stopped off in Sumatra and Java en route to India over the next several centuries. And Chinese court records show that Java dignitaries visited China, bearing the usual tribute, during these years. In 813, for instance, a Javanese envoy presented the emperor with four Negro slaves, parrots, and other tropical birds.

The states represented by these tribute bearers, of course, were small and relatively powerless. The first Indonesian dynasty of real importance was the Madjapahit, which was founded in 1293. Ironically enough, a Chinese fleet was instrumental in its creation. Several years before, Emperor Kublai Khan had sent envoys to Kertanegara, ruler of the East Java state of Singosari, to demand he acknowledge the Khan's suzerainty. Kertanegara was rash enough to refuse, and south from China swarmed an expeditionary force to avenge the insult. By the time the fleet arrived, under Shih Pi, Kertanegara had been slain by a rival, and a son-in-law, Prince Widjaja, persuaded

Shih to support his bid for power. With Chinese aid, he crushed his foes and established the Madjapahit, which lasted for two hundred years and for the first half of its existence dominated the other states in the area, including ports on the Malay peninsula and in Borneo. It was during the Madjapahit that the first Chinese settlers began appearing in the archipelago, first in Sumatra, at Palembang, and later in Java.

Trade and tribute continued over the next several centuries, but there was only one final Chinese armed thrust southward—the huge Ming Dynasty expeditions under the command of the Imperial Eunuch, Cheng Ho. There were seven voyages in all, and the fleet ranged east to the Philippines, south to the Indonesian archipelago, and west as far as India and the eastern coast of Africa. These voyages, though they brought back huge treasures to China, do not seem to have been raiding expeditions; rather, they were intended primarily to spread word of the glory of the Ming. With the end of the early Ming expansionism, China's political interest in Java and Sumatra began to ebb. For the next three hundred years, the Dutch took over the Chinese role. Trade went on, however, and so did Chinese emigration to the Indies.

When the Dutch fleet arrived in 1596, it found small groups of Chinese scattered throughout the islands. Over the first decades the Dutch displayed no special fondness for the Chinese, who were treated as badly as the Indonesians themselves. But after the founding of Batavia (now Djakarta) in 1619, the new Dutch governor-general, Jan Pieterszoon Coen, saw a potential asset in the Chinese and did the best he could to increase emigration. The results were obvious: despite several initial setbacks under Coen's successors, there were eighty thousand Chinese in Batavia alone by 1733. And their numbers continued to increase. "They had in fact," noted one authority, "become necessary to both Dutch and natives as middlemen, and it was no longer possible, even if it had been desirable, to root them out."[3] Early in the nineteenth century, the Chinese had assumed control of the import market as well as the bulk of inland commerce—power still largely in Chinese hands today.

Their economic influence, added to the fact that the Dutch decided to bring the Chinese under their own civil code while maintaining separate courts for Indonesians, contributed to the widespread unpopularity of the Chinese throughout the islands. They played almost no part in the rise of Indonesian nationalism. It was, in fact, only during the rise to influence of the PKI in the early sixties that the Chinese moved into politics to any degree, and then it was via the back door—through finances. Never completely assimilated, never liked, and almost inevitably mistrusted, Chinese in Indonesia today remain very much on the outside. And their isolation, to a great extent, is due to poor political guesswork. The alien Chinese counted on the increasingly pro-Peking stance of the PKI, coupled with Sukarno's increasing fondness for the politics and techniques of Mao Tse-tung, to propel them into a position of major influence. Their judgments were wrong, and a major reason for their defeat—and the consequent strains on Indonesian Chinese—was the bungling of the PKI.

Indonesian communists are in fact a notably luckless crew, in contrast to other Asian parties. While communists in Korea, China, Japan, Vietnam, and Laos have had some notable successes as well as failures, the Indonesian party seems to have had far more than its share of disasters. True, they have managed to shake off previous defeats. But there seems little question that they, and through them Chinese communists as well, have suffered a particularly conspicuous black eye as a result of the premature coup of September 30, 1965.

On the face of it, there appears little reason. From the very beginnings, the PKI found fertile ground in Indonesia. Founded on May 23, 1920, it is Asia's oldest communist party, and in the sixties (if not before) it ranked as the largest communist party (a claimed 2.5 million members) outside the Soviet Union and China. Its nationalistic aspect, almost from the very beginning, made it a lodestone to younger Indonesians seeking radical, immediate change. But only two years after its founding, the PKI began running into problems. A young Sumatran activist named Tan Malaka, an Indonesian of Chinese parentage, did his best to swerve the all-powerful Comintern from its opposition to the Pan-Islam movement, which had powerful appeal in the largely Moslem East Indies. But the Comintern's doctrinaire anti-religious stance precluded any such sympathies, and thus cost the party much of its initial backing. And as the PKI leadership accordingly moved into the control of the radicals, their activities brought them directly under the nervous scrutiny of the Dutch security officials. One by one, the party's leaders were shipped into exile abroad, producing the awkward phenomenon of a party without that most essential of ingredients, continuing and cohesive leadership. Once abroad, the leaders plunged into a struggle for party control, and the often conflicting directives that emerged produced even more confusion at home.

Against this background, the first of the PKI's three great follies materialized. Despite the failure of a general strike scheduled for December, 1925, the PKI clung to its belief that revolution was possible. And in November, 1926, the PKI struck: two hundred armed men seized the telephone and telegraph center in Batavia, cutting the capital off from the outside world. Embarrassingly, however, the populace failed to rise, and within six days the revolution dissolved. The leaders were tucked away in prisons, nine of the men most directly concerned were executed, and the remnants of the PKI faded underground for almost a decade. Tan Malaka himself, as well as more radical leaders such as Alimin Prawirodirdjo and Musso, had been forced to leave Indonesia before the abortive revolt and thus were able to continue pulling strings from abroad. But for all practical purposes, the PKI's effectiveness was nil.

In the early thirties, the PKI remained a negligible force. But in 1935, Musso returned clandestinely with orders to rebuild the party. This time, the thrust was to cooperate—quietly—with the nationalists and concentrate on construction of a common front against the growing threat of Japan. Tan Malaka, in contrast, worked with the Japanese to a degree: "Tan Malaka," explains one source, "saw in Tokyo a lever for ridding the Indies of Dutch rule."[4] This widened the split in the left's leadership to an even greater degree, and the move was to have deep repercussions after World War II.

During the war, in contrast to other communist parties throughout the world, the PKI's contribution to the resistance seems to have been negligible. Small, isolated cells continued to function, but that was about the extent of it; nationalist groups were more effective. But in August, 1945, as the Japanese surrender neared, the PKI reasserted itself, and in the group of young radicals that kidnapped Sukarno on his return from Dalat was a young cadre activist named Dipa Nusantara Aidit, who was to take over the party's leadership nine years later.

Over the next three years, the PKI struggled to improve its position. Tan Malaka slipped even further into disrepute among the more Stalinist leaders, such as Musso, by mounting a fruitless bid for power in mid-1946. His attempt was crushed, and Tan Malaka was jailed. His failure, however, proved to be no lesson at all to Musso. In 1948, almost certainly in conjunction with other communist risings throughout Asia (the Philippines, Malaya, and Burma), the PKI rose in rebellion at Madiun, in central Java. Once again, they were smashed: Musso himself was slain and the rest of the leadership erased. Though the fighting went on for three months, the PKI forces never really had a chance. Once again, Indonesian communists had erred embarrassingly, and once again the party went into eclipse.

Aidit was left to pick up the pieces. And pick them up he did, employing a brilliantly conceived line of strategy that produced the dynamic PKI of the early sixties. His thinking was logical enough: the PKI had learned Sukarno could not be beaten—but perhaps he could be absorbed. Aidit proceeded to attempt just that. For the moment at least, Aidit had caught the tide: "It is the responsibility of each member of the party," he said in 1953, "not only to be a good communist, but also a good nationalist."[5] And through the fifties, the PKI's progress was steady: in both the 1955 and 1957 elections, PKI and PKI-backed candidates prospered.

But the government did not. Caught in a political swamp, a succession of prime ministers staggered through their roles, ignoring the country's multiplying problems in their desperate attempts for political survival. Far above the political hullabaloo floated the beaming face of President Sukarno, flushed from his triumphs on the world stage at Bandung and more interested in the progress of the nation he had brought into existence than in preserving his own eminence. In 1957, after an extensive swing around the world, he came back to earth. Deeply impressed by his look at the achievements of Communist China, and at least mildly interested in the political mess at home, he announced in February of that year that henceforth Indonesia would adopt what he called "guided democracy." Western-style parliamentary democracy thus died a sudden death—in truth it had been ineffectual. And in the same year, as if to emphasize the progress possible under his guidance, he ordered confiscation of the bulk of Dutch properties in Indonesia, a move that only accelerated the country's economic decline. But if Sukarno was confident, others were not.

In February, 1958, almost exactly one year after the proclamation of guided democracy, civil war broke out. Disgusted with both the economic failures and Djakarta's aimless politicking, a group of army leaders and economists formed the Revolutionary Government of the Republic of Indonesia (PRRI, or Peremintah Revolusioner Republik

Indonesia), with headquarters in Padang, Sumatra. It found support in other areas, particularly in secession-minded Celebes, but it failed to catch hold in Java and ill-designed CIA backing was little help. For three years, PRRI held out, but its failure was never in doubt. Moreover, the affair gave Sukarno the pretext he needed to bring the government more completely under his control. He abolished the 1950 constitution and ordered reinstatement of the constitution of 1945, a move that returned a monopoly of power to the presidency and gave him almost all-inclusive authority. Opposition parties were banned and opposition politicians were arrested. By 1961, when the PRRI revolt finally dribbled to an end, Sukarno was in fact "Supreme Leader of the Revolution."

Abroad, Sukarno's flirtation with the communist bloc continued to blossom, though in the late fifties the warm relationship with Communist China frosted over, temporarily. At stake were the 2.5 million overseas Chinese—Indonesia, not without reason, believed they should opt for Indonesian citizenship, while China maintained their right to hold Chinese passports. In an attempt to break Chinese economic influence in the countryside, Sukarno in 1959 ordered "aliens" to close their business establishments in the hamlets, thereby threatening at least four hundred thousand Chinese with the loss of their livelihood. Though the order was never totally implemented, it was a clear signal to Peking that adjustments would have to be sought. Talks were begun, and in 1960 the agreements approved at Bandung five years before were finally put into effect, giving Chinese of dual nationality two years in which to make a final decision as to which passport they wished to carry. During the months leading up to the stalemate, however, Sino-Indonesian relations plunged to an all-time low, and in 1959 nearly one hundred thousand Chinese residents fled Indonesia for the homeland. The signing of the pact, though it did little to repair the basic hostility of Indonesians toward their Chinese neighbors, set the stage for Sukarno's rapidly accelerating slide into the embrace of Peking—and the parallel rise in influence of the PKI.

The PKI, in fact, seized upon the Irian Barat confrontation as the quickest way toward increasing its own influence, and the success of that effort helped propel the PKI into the commanding position it held over the next several years. At the same time the Soviet Union failed to profit from Indonesia's success, and as its influence faded, Sukarno moved within snuggling distance of the Communist Chinese. Thus the Malaysia confrontation was waged by a slightly different set of allies from Djakarta's side.

In the early sixties, Indonesian politics had polarized into what might be described as a teeter-totter arrangement, with the PKI on one end, the armed forces on the other, and Sukarno balancing the structure in the center, first leaning one way, then the other. Within the armed forces, however, there were clumps of PKI sympathizers, notably in the air force, while the PKI's enormous organization included a certain proportion of opportunists seeking to ride PKI coattails into power. It had become transparently clear that the PKI was Indonesia's only effective political party, and many politicians made the necessary adjustments—either by directing their own ineffective followings into alliance with the PKI or by at least making their personal sentiments clear.

Indonesian communists were themselves making adjustments, in accordance with the widening split between Communist China and the Soviet Union. Aidit, whose links with Moscow were long-established, at first seemed reluctant to shift the party's orientation. But others in the leadership saw that their road to power in Djakarta might well lead through Peking, and Aidit nimbly recovered his balance in time to preserve his leadership by moving the PKI onto China's side in the dispute. This shift was paralleled by an increase in the activity of the PKI's Chinese members.

There had been Chinese elements in the PKI, of course, from its beginnings. Tan Malaka himself, as noted earlier, was part Chinese, and the party's postwar hierarchy included two veteran Chinese communists, Tan Ling Djie and Oey Gee Hwat. But popular dislike for Chinese forced these men to keep themselves well in the background. Invaluable organizationally, one of their primary functions was to raise funds through front organizations such as BAPERKI (Badan Permusjawaratan Kewarganegaraan Indonesia, or the Consultative Body on Indonesian Citizenship), which was headed by a former editor of the party's daily paper, Harian Rakjat (*People's Daily*), named Siauw Giok Tjhan. Indonesian Chinese, in general, were only slightly stirred by the triumph of communism in the homeland—but there was, nonetheless, a change in their basic affiliation: to most overseas Chinese, historically, changes in the government at home have meant little. China remains China, whoever rules. And thus BAPERKI began to flourish almost automatically. To the leftists among

Indonesia's Chinese minority, of course, PKI membership was an obvious affiliation.

Though the military remained dubious, Sukarno and the PKI pushed the Malaysia confrontation for all it was worth. For Bung Karno, it was another step en route to fulfillment of his dream of becoming the leader of the new nations. In a typically grandiose Sukarnoism, he announced his discovery that the world was divided between the newly established forces (NEFOS) and the old established forces (OLDEFOS) and in so doing made it clear he was the obvious leader of the NEFOS. In speech after speech, up and down the Indonesian archipelago, he lashed out at Malaysia and the OLDEFOS, which (he charged) were responsible for Malaysia's creation.

Sukarno's opposition to Malaysia hadn't always been so firm. In 1959, Indonesia and Malaya (then less than two years into independence) signed a friendship treaty. And when Tunku Abdul Rahman broached the idea of a Malaysian federation at a Singapore press dinner in 1961, Indonesian Foreign Minister Subandrio indicated his general approval of the idea. But it seems accurate to say that Subandrio was being either thoughtless or something less than frank, for Indonesia had had its eyes on Malaya as far back as 1945, and the political dynamics of Indonesia in the late fifties and early sixties all but required an outside foe. With the Dutch disposed of, Malaya became the next target. And long before Malaysia (uniting Malaya and the old colonies of British Borneo) came into existence on September 16, 1963, Indonesian hostility was apparent. Surprisingly enough, there was a degree of PKI-military unity on Indonesian opposition to Malaysia—though for starkly contrasting reasons.

Sukarno and the PKI, heartily supported by Peking, saw—or at least pretended to see—Malaysia as an imperialist creation, created in order to surround Indonesia with a belt of foes. The armed forces, on the other hand, believed Malaysia would eventually fall under Chinese communist domination because of the power and influence of its resident Chinese. On this unlikely base, confrontation grew into a real threat. Though a series of airborne and seaborne landings on the Malayan peninsula proved total failures, raids across the border of Indonesian Borneo had at least a degree of success—in part because in Sarawak (the southernmost of the three British states) the long-established communist apparatus assisted the raiders.

During this period, China's role in Sukarno's political spectrum was becoming increasingly important. In early 1961, China's foreign minister, Chen Yi, flew into Djakarta to sign a friendship treaty, and a year later, after Aidit and the PKI's first deputy chairman, M. H. Lukman, were brought into Sukarno's cabinet, an Indonesian-Chinese Communist-sponsored rebellion broke out in Brunei, a tiny, oil-rich state in British Borneo. It was smashed rapidly by British troops, reinforced by units flown in from Malaya, but the rebellion crystallized left-wing domestic support for Sukarno and gave Peking a pretext for moving even closer to the Bung.

Subandrio flew off to Peking for talks on Brunei with Chinese Prime Minister Chou En-lai, and the confrontation with Malaysia was on in earnest. In April, 1963, China's State President Liu Shao-chi (at that time, the anointed heir to Mao Tse-tung) flew to Djakarta to seal the bargain. His visit was impressive; I watched the arrival ceremonies at Djakarta's Kamajoran Airport with a degree of skepticism, given the general harsh feelings of Indonesians toward Chinese, and was mildly surprised at the warmth of the welcome. Obviously, Sukarno had made a major effort: truckloads of students had been brought in from the countryside over the previous twenty-four hours, and the streets were lined with cheering youngsters. But it was clear, on close examination of the welcomers, that the cheering section consisted largely of Indonesian Chinese. During the next several days it became apparent that despite Sukarno's lavish series of receptions and parties for Liu, the basic equation had not changed: that while Liu and Sukarno agreed on the principle of united action against NEFOS, a basic suspicion of Chinese policy aims remained among the Indonesian rank and file. And that, of course, was what I reported: an estimate given added impact by severe anti-Chinese riots in Tjirebon and Bandung within two months. For my pains, I was singled out by *Harian Rakjat* as the instigator of the riots. The PKI's estimate of my influence was flattering, but somewhat overstated.

Throughout the rest of 1963, the confrontation against Malaysia escalated. "Ganjang Malaysia" ("Crush Malaysia") was the cry, and the slogan was scrawled across hoardings all over Djakarta. From Peking came the usual shrill exhortations toward greater fierceness and undying support, and the PKI swung ever closer to Peking's side in the Sino-Soviet harangues.

In the spring of 1964, I flew back to Djakarta, assigned to do a story on the PKI as well as on Indonesia's increasingly anti-Western posture. Paying the obligatory courtesy call on Subandrio's spokesman, a malevolent little man named Ganis Harsono, I was shown a collection of my stories on Indonesia. "In your country," he told me, "you have a saying: three strikes and out. Mr. McCabe, this is your third visit to Indonesia." The message was clear.

In early April, I sent a brief advisory cable to New York warning of the possibility of serious riots "in the wake of" a Sukarno address scheduled ten days later. Nine days after the cable had been sent, I was arrested by agents of Indonesian military intelligence.

It was a terribly polite arrest. At 7 A.M., on a Sunday morning, I was awakened by a knock on the door of my room at the Hotel Indonesia. Suffering from the effect of a long, joyous dinner the night before, I opened the door, barked at the boy that all requests for anything should be funneled through the front desk, and went back to sleep. An hour later, the knock was repeated, and this time the nervous room boy was backed up by two Indonesian officers, who shoved an arrest order at me.

But Indonesians, thanks to Allah, tend to be a terribly modest people. After explaining that I must get dressed, I shut the door again, hoping that the prospect of watching a hairy foreigner clothe himself would be too much for Indonesian sensibilities. I was right: they made no effort to force an entrance. So I picked up the phone, called an American diplomat, and told him about the excitement, then proceeded to get dressed.

Twenty-four hours later, I was still at military police head-quarters, vigorously protesting my detention, devouring a series of perfectly adequate, beer-supplemented meals, and reading, for the third time, a book of short stories by Somerset Maugham smuggled in to me by my embassy friend. By this time, it had become embarrassingly clear that Sukarno himself had ordered my arrest, and that I was not to be allowed to cover his speech. Sure enough, within an hour after his talk was completed, I was driven back to the Hotel Indonesia, suffering from nothing more than impatience.

My treatment, in fact, had been extraordinarily mild. The interrogations lasted only two hours and were directed simply toward discovering the source for my prediction of serious disturbances.[6] Once it had become clear that I was not going to cooperate, I was simply left alone. And there the matter rested until U.S. Ambassador Howard Jones was able to make a personal protest to Sukarno. The reason for the arrest was never publicly stated, but after checking local intelligence sources, it became clear that Sukarno had heard rumors of an assassination plot directed against himself. His agents had decided that I had received information along these lines. And my use of the word "wake" in that cable sealed my fate: evidently, a researcher had discovered in a dictionary that "wake" could have funereal overtones.

In any case, the arrest gave Aidit all the excuse he needed to cancel our promised interview, and my story on the PKI accordingly lacked a certain amount of flavor. "You are McCabe of *Newsweek?*" he asked when I braced him after my release. "No no no, you are not a friend of Indonesia." This was unfortunate, because Aidit at this time was busy cementing his alliance with Sukarno—and with the Chinese Communist Party in the bargain. In a February interview with the *Christian Science Monitor*'s Takashi Oka, he said: "In many countries, the main task of the communist party is to overthrow the government. But in Indonesia, if we overthrow the government we overthrow ourselves, and President Sukarno as well, who is a great patriot."

Aidit stated his position well. Sukarno by 1964 had bought the PKI line, and the PKI as well. Over and over, Sukarno pressed his theory of a NASAKOM government; a unity, in other words, of Nationalists (NAS), religious parties (A), and communists (KOM). All told, there were ten parties then allowed to operate. Under the nationalist label, there were four: the Partai Nasional Indonesia (PNI), led by former United Nations Ambassador Ali Sastroamidjojo, which had climbed aboard the PKI bandwagon; Murba, a nationalistic communist party, which included in its leadership Adam Malik; Partindo, best described as further left than the PKI; and IPKI, once the army party but in 1964 dominated by military fellow-travelers. Under the religious banner were five parties: Perti, also leftist; Parkindo, a small and ineffectual Protestant party; Partai Katholik, the weak Catholic party; PSII, a splinter group; and the Nahdlatul Ulama (Moslem Scholars Party), which was the only significant Moslem party but which suffered from indecisive leadership. Under the KOM label, of course, was the PKI.

In 1963 and 1964, the PKI influence in government increased markedly. Into top jobs went Astrawinata, minister of justice, a known PKI member; Oei Tjoe Tat, a key leader of Partindo and the pro-Chinese BAPERKI; and Josef Muda Dalam, minister of finance (and, in effect, Sukarno's bagman), who was closely linked to the PKI. Njoto, the party's second deputy chairman, joined Aidit and Lukman in the cabinet's inner circle. Liaison with China continued to improve: Indonesia's ambassador in Peking was Djawoto, a PKI member; and contributions to the PKI by Indonesian Chinese increased significantly, putting PKI finances in their healthiest state ever. In 1964, the virulence of PKI attacks on "revisionism" (a polite synonym for the Soviet Union) continued to grow, and by fall Sukarno had recognized the Viet Cong and established diplomatic relations with North Korea and North Vietnam.

Despite the general drift leftward, however, there was still a degree of opposition remaining in Djakarta. In October, Subandrio felt called upon to warn against coup-makers in a speech to national police. Behind this was the formation, in September, of the so-called Body for Support of Sukarnoism (BPS), which included both army elements and politicians. In early December, the BPS evidently had picked up momentum sufficient to worry the PKI. In addition, Sukarno's kidney problems had worsened, forcing him to cut back sharply on his public appearances. As word of Sukarno's debility spread, the BPS went into high gear. Led by Third Deputy Premier Chaireul Saleh, a national communist close to the Murba Party and probably the wealthiest man in Indonesia as a result of his governmental manipulations as minister of national resources, BPS by this time had gained a degree of high-level support. Among its key figures was Adam Malik, Murba's leader, minister of trade, and former ambassador to Moscow. BPS also had a degree of support from armed forces chief General Abdul Haris Nasution. But for all its influential members, BPS was essentially a negative force, opposed to the PKI but without a positive alternative. On December 17, 1964, Sukarno banned BPS, bowing to the will of the PKI, whose members had for the past month scrawled "Ganjang BPS" on almost every available wall in Djakarta.

Sukarno excused his move by proclaiming that BPS "showed indications of causing disunity among progressive revolutionary forces, which might endanger the progress of the revolution." But the banning of BPS was a clear victory for the PKI: seven of the country's ten political parties had supported BPS, while only the PKI, the fellow-traveling PNI, and a minor splinter group opposed it. Sukarno's decision created even more doubts among the financial community. The rupiah, which had steadied in its headlong slide at about 9,000 to $1 when it seemed BPS would survive, dropped suddenly to 13,000 to $1 when BPS died.

During 1965, Sukarno's drift leftward continued. He took Indonesia out of the United Nations in January, using Malaysia's assumption of a seat on the Security Council as his excuse. But no other nations followed Indonesia's move: despite China's support, the Bung's pretensions to leadership of the NEFOS seemed conclusively discredited. Sukarno himself compared his move to the Prophet Mohammed's hegira from Mecca to Medina in 622 A.D., explaining that Indonesia was hemmed in by its enemies at the U.N. just as was the Prophet so many years ago.

Through the first half of 1965, the Malaysian confrontation continued to limp along, but the rapid buildup of British troops in Borneo and Malaya had cut sharply into the effectiveness of the raiders. South Vietnam, bolstered by the accelerating numbers of American troops, still had not fallen to the Viet Cong and North Vietnamese, and communist lack of triumph here had a braking effect on general Asian communist momentum. PKI influence continued to expand, however, and Sukarno came to believe that its power, supplemented by the influence of Communist China, constituted his real power base. On August 17, 1965, at the annual Independence Day speech, he announced the formation of a Djakarta-Hanoi-Peking axis.

That, effectively, was Sukarno's last great move. The PKI, armed with the Bung's complete confidence, decided the time had come to smash the army's reactionary leadership. Sukarno's recurrent illnesses, emphasized by his temporary collapse the previous winter, gave added force to Aidit's decision. The coup itself was set for October 5, Armed Forces Day, when PKI-influenced army units would have an excuse to be in the capital. And to reinforce those suborned units, the PKI in early 1965 began training its own paramilitary force, armed with Chinese Communist weapons shipped secretly into the country. An obscure pro-communist lieutenant colonel named Untung, who led a unit of the crack presidential guard (Tjakribirawa), was put in charge of the actual operation. On September 25, just two weeks before the takeover was scheduled to occur, Aidit learned that the army had begun inquiries into the shipments of Chinese arms. He moved up the coup's date to September 30. And thus the stage was set for the PKI's third great error in its history—one that was to result in a purge of communists so huge as to defy attempts at an accounting.

On the night on September 30, Aidit and his key aides drove to

Halim Air Force Base, near Djakarta, where facilities had been arranged by the air force's pro-PKI leader, General Omar Dhani. At 0400 October 1, PKI para-military units sped toward the Djakarta homes of the army's top six leaders, including Nasution, Chief of Staff General Achmad Yani, military intelligence chief General Parman, Strategic Reserve Commander General Suharto, and two others. All but Suharto and Nasution were bagged easily—they were told Sukarno wanted urgently to see them. Instead, they were driven to Halim. There they were turned over to the PKI's female branch, Gerwani, sadistically tortured, and their mutilated bodies dumped into a dry well at Lubang Buaja (Crocodile Hole). Suharto and his family were away from home and thus escaped capture. Nasution's adjutant, who sensed something was wrong, alerted his boss, and Nasution escaped the kidnappers by leaping over his back fence. But he was shot in the leg as he fled, and a daughter was slain.

Three hours later, Djakarta radio broadcast a statement saying that Untung had moved to forestall an army plot to depose Sukarno, adding that the CIA—of course—was behind it all. To bring stability to the country, the broadcast added, a revolutionary council had been formed. Sukarno appeared at Halim during the early morning hours, and it seems clear he had been carefully briefed beforehand, by Aidit, on the coup. Sukarno announced he had temporarily taken over command of the military, and named a replacement for Nasution. The takeover, seemingly, was a success.

It had, however, failed. Suharto and Nasution rallied loyal units and began to move against the outgunned forces led by Untung. Sukarno, learning that both leaders had escaped the PKI net, left Halim for his country retreat at Bogor, after refusing to sign a decree establishing the revolutionary council. Aidit, Lukman, and Dhani flew to central Java, a PKI stronghold, hoping to arrange a mass uprising. But support failed to materialize, and Aidit was captured and executed in mid-November.

The death of Aidit was only one among hundreds of thousands. The PKI's failure set off a wave of killing unparalleled in modern times. Observers who have traveled through Java, Bali, and Sumatra since Gestapu (the September Thirtieth Movement, or Gerakan Tigapuluh September) estimate that at least five hundred thousand died in the aftermath. The Indonesian army was partially responsible for some of the deaths, but the bulk seems to have been carried out privately. For months afterward, streams and rivers in Java were clogged with bodies, and the stench of rotting flesh hung like a pall over hundreds of villages.

Slowly but surely, power slipped from Sukarno's hands. Suharto assumed the nation's leadership, moving with due deliberation in deference to Sukarno's still-strong popularity among the masses. The PKI was banned, to no one's surprise, and hatred of Communist China—and local Chinese as well—flared high. The Chinese embassy in Djakarta was sacked, as were consulates in Medan and other cities, and Chinese shops throughout the archipelago were looted and burned. A series of increasingly angry protests began to flow south from Peking, Chinese aid was shut off, and Peking's technicians were hurriedly recalled. For all practical purposes, diplomatic relations were ended.

Sukarno, however, continued to cling to at least the trappings of power. He was stripped of his lifetime tenure as president, but retained the office itself. But the Malaysian confrontation was called off, and diplomatic relations resumed. In March, 1966, Sukarno was forced to sign over executive power to Suharto. In a broad governmental shakeup, a ruling triumvirate appeared: Suharto, Adam Malik (foreign minister), and the Sultan of Djogjakarta, Hamengku Buwono (minister of economics, finances and development). Sukarno, surprisingly to some, was kept on as president for the time being.

But for Sukarno, the end of the line was approaching. The PKI was crushed, perhaps beyond redemption, though twice before it has managed to revive itself. And Communist China, its hopes for a modern-day tributary state all but dead, confined itself to encouraging formation of an Indonesian government-in-exile in Peking.

Slowly, but with deadly certainty, Indonesia's new leaders zeroed in on Sukarno. In a series of trials of his old associates, evidence of his complicity in the Gestapu affair continued to build up. And though he spoke up angrily on occasion against Indonesia's return to its traditional habits of non-alignment in international affairs, no one seemed to listen. Much more attention was being paid to the economic crisis, which, in mid-1967, seemed to show signs of easing slightly. The Suharto-Malik-Buwono triumvirate appeared to be willing to keep Sukarno around indefinitely, stripped of all titles and responsibilities. The reason for such a policy might well lie in a favorite Sukarno yarn.

Back in the late fifties, as a group of correspondents stood outside his palace in Djakarta, Sukarno emerged to issue a statement, clad as usual in an impeccable uniform. But he was wearing neither socks nor shoes, and one reporter asked the inevitable question. Sukarno stared haughtily for a moment, then replied: "I am discharging electricity." He pointed off into the middle distance. Exactly where he was pointing, an enormous flash of lightning split the clouds. A decade later, with criticism bound to pile up as the new rulers try to deal with the nation's overwhelming problems, Sukarno's final role may well be that of the lightning rod.

1. The Dutch maintained he did not win a degree. For much of the following biographical material on Sukarno, I am indebted to Bruce Grant, author of one of the most lucid books on Indonesia I've read. (Bruce Grant, *Indonesia*, Melbourne University Press, Melbourne, 1964 and 1965.)
2. *Ibid.*, p. 136.
3. J. S. Furnivall, *Netherlands Indies*, Cambridge, 1939 and 1944, quoted in Victor Purcell, *The Chinese in Southeast Asia*, Second Edition, Oxford University Press, London, 1965, pp. 407–8.
4. Arnold C. Brackman, *Indonesian Communism*, Praeger, New York, 1963, p. 38.
5. *Ibid.*, p. 184.
6. That source was a high-ranking Indonesian diplomat stationed at that time in Southeast Asia. A week before my arrival in Djakarta, he had warned a scholar friend that Djakarta would be "dangerous" for foreigners in the next week or two. He was right, as far as I was concerned.

THE
BREAKING STORM:

Summary

For the foreseeable future, China will remain the key factor in Southeast Asian affairs. Unless and until the United States formulates a fresh and effective China policy, American tactics toward both China and Southeast Asia will continue to be as hit-or-miss as they have been for the past two decades. The same is true for the nations of Southeast Asia: preoccupied by the Chinese threat, they haven't yet decided how to cope. The political disintegration that began in China in 1966, accordingly, will have an enormous and continuing impact on both Washington and the capitals of Southeast Asia. In mid-1967, the duration of the struggle was anyone's guess: the sole certainty seemed to be that Peking's foreign policy, for a time at least, would be less representative of the grander delusions of Mao Tse-tung.

China's turmoil is, in general terms, simply another manifestation of the flux that has pervaded Southeast Asia since 1945. There are, after all, common pressures at work: nationalism, communism, poverty, shaky leadership, and shakier economies. And in varying degree, every Southeast Asian nation shares with China the sick manifestations of those pressures: wars, riots, strikes, governmental collapses, and hunger. The record is bleak.

Through the first half of the sixties, the basic issue was plain. Southeast Asia has become the cockpit of conflict between the United States and China. American gropings for a policy boiled down essentially to a simplistic containment of China, and no better solution seemed at hand. By late 1966, however, the Peking government went into a tailspin; partially because of its own paranoiac fears that the United States intended invasion, but more because of a catastrophic series of domestic political and economic errors. In any case—and this was of overriding importance—Washington's containment policy seemed clearly outdated.

Now, the time for fresh thinking on Asia has arrived. Long-held U.S. policy assumptions no longer apply. And even long-range policy planning, predicated as it was on the conclusion that a Maoist society would continue to dominate China, must be thoroughly overhauled, in order to be able to deal with a broader spectrum of contingencies. Over the long run, China can be expected to continue its *drang nach suden,* but during the next few years, Peking's riven leadership must necessarily concentrate on restoring internal order and control, however loudly they may vow to carry on their efforts to export revolution.

Thus American policy makers now have an opportunity to reshape policy, to scrap the errors of the past, and build a policy for the future—to try, as Harvard's Professor John K. Fairbank said in late 1965, to bring China into the world. (And, it might be added, to speed Southeast Asia's progress along the same path.)

Toward China and Southeast Asia, Washington has pursued contrasting policies. In Southeast Asia, the United States has labored to support the principles of self-determination and independence, and to encourage the growth of democratic, non-communist states. Inevitably the policy was selective, and shocking errors were made, but its thrust was basically positive. Toward China, however, policy was almost precisely the opposite: the key words were containment, isolation, and hostility. What were the gains? Until 1959, China was able to obtain much of its needs from the Soviet Union, which rudely ignored the American trade ban, and while that assistance shrank to almost nothing by 1965, Peking was able to attain a reasonable momentum. American hostility was not enough to deter China from the series of foreign policy adventures—and successes—that marked the years up through 1964. And the United States, during those years, was China's chief propaganda target—the great foe, as Peking put it, of progressive nations everywhere.

It must be pointed out, however, that such a role was inescapable. Nationalists in Asia and elsewhere long ago came to realize the usefulness of a major external threat as a spur to national unity. For the Chinese Communists, the United States filled that role admirably, and their choice was clear as long ago as 1949 when Mao took power in Peking. It is not generally realized, for instance, that American diplomats, including Ambassador John Leighton Stuart, stayed at their posts as the communist armies moved south, driving Chiang's Kuomintang troops before them. These men were under instructions to contact the communist leaders and attempt to arrange a *modus vivendi*. Diplomats of other nations, including those of the Soviet Union, fled to Japan and Hong Kong. But the Americans stayed on, only to be sharply rebuffed. There was ample reason: Washington had after all supported Chiang Kai-shek against the communists all the way.

From China's point of view, the tone of U.S.-China relations was struck in 1949. But Mao Tse-tung was a captive of ideology, the United States was not. Nevertheless, the United States replied in kind: hate for hate, hostility for hostility. Both sides were prisoners of their own preconceptions. And of the two, the United States at times seemed even more rigid. In 1956 and 1957, for example, when China twice invited groups of American newsmen to visit China, Washington flatly prohibited any such thing. The United States had decided to play a waiting game, counting on the emergence of new leaders, and Secretary of State John Foster Dulles evidently felt that allowing U.S. newsmen to visit China might rock that boat.

Late in 1963, however, policy changes seemed to be in the air. There were strong reports that a modification of the total ban on trade with China was being studied. And in a December speech in San Francisco, Assistant Secretary of State Roger Hilsman made it clear that present hostility no longer predicated future hatred. For a time, nothing more happened: it became known that Hilsman's speech had been conceived with the approval of President Kennedy, and that with Kennedy's assassination, the impetus for change had dwindled. But through the next several years, there came surface indications that some change was indeed under way: scholars, businessmen, doctors, and scientists joined newsmen on the list of those cleared for travel to China by the State Department. There was no positive response from China, however: as far as Peking was concerned, the door had been slammed shut in 1957.

To its credit, Washington continued its efforts. In April, 1966, Secretary of State Dean Rusk said that while the United States did not "expect that for the time being the Chinese communists will seize upon these avenues of contact," he did believe that "contact and communication are not incompatible with a firm policy of containment." And Ambassador to Japan, U. Alexis Johnson, speaking to a group of Japanese businessmen in February, 1967, said: "I would hope that those forces in China which want to move from a reliance on outworn shibboleths and doctrines which have repeatedly demonstrated their failure, to dealing with their own internal problems and external relations in a practical way, will ultimately prevail. When that day comes, I can assure you that they will find the United States responsive. Indeed, that is our goal."

The slow modification of American policy vis-à-vis China was paralleled, to a degree, by alterations in Washington's thinking about Southeast Asia. Here, there were glaring exceptions to a basically positive approach. Sukarno's Indonesia and Sihanouk's Cambodia, for instance, were kept at arm's length—and even further as anti-American trends gained momentum. As the United States lost ground, Communist China gained, and vice-versa.

Vietnam is, beyond doubt, the most compelling example of this interaction. Peking recognized Ho Chi Minh's government in 1950, provided weapons and supplies for the war against the French, and played an important role in the Geneva conference ending that war in 1954. Since then, China has expanded its assistance—though not yet to the point of entering physically into Ho's war against the United States. It has, on the contrary, seemed perfectly content to let the North Vietnamese try to pull Chinese chestnuts out of the fire—and there is good reason to suspect relations between Hanoi and Peking accordingly are not as close as they seem from abroad. In 1954, the United States replaced France as the major external power in South Vietnam, and the consequences of that ill-thought-out decision have been discussed in detail. Vietnam, clearly, is the point of uneasy confrontation between China and America: communist victory there will inevitably lead, under present circumstances, into similarly agonizing confrontations over the coming decades.

Elsewhere in Southeast Asia, the conflict has been more diffused. Washington's always-qualified support for Cambodia ebbed steadily over the sixties as Sihanouk led his nation into China's corner. But in Laos, once the Americans abandoned their overenthusiastic backing of the Lao right-wing, a fragile equilibrium was established: one that for the time being profits both Washington and Peking. Thailand and Malaysia have enjoyed solid U.S. support, and although neither nation is free of the danger of communist-backed insurrection, China's efforts to fan the flames have had, so far, little result. Burma has clung, with great determination, to its policy of non-alignment—

aided by at least a degree of tacit consent to this line from both China and the United States. In Indonesia, of course, China suffered the greatest foreign policy defeat in the history of the communist regime. The United States had backed Sukarno in earlier years, then had looked on helplessly as Sukarno, following Sihanouk's example, brought his country's policies into alignment with those of Peking. But Sukarno moved too far too fast: since October, 1965, Indonesia has struggled back toward non-alignment and seems a good bet to reach this goal. The turn of events in Indonesia stands, for the moment at least, as significant validation of Washington's wait-and-see policy.

In its dealings with these nations, however, the United States has tended to act in an anti-communist context. True, militant communism has proved itself a genuine danger in the area: the history of events since 1945 provides ample evidence of this fact. But in its concentration on the problems posed by communism, Washington too often has ignored a second problem. Time and again, my Asian friends have told me that Americans display little or no understanding of Asian nationalism—and this factor, to me, stands out as the single most important key to what makes Asia tick. With the single exception of Thailand, which never came under colonial rule, the post-'45 revolution was given meaning and momentum by nationalistic aims, not communist drives. Communists took over many Asian revolutions in part because of superior organizational techniques, in part because they displayed the necessary militancy, and *only* in part because of any broad ideological attraction that communist ideas possessed. As these revolutions progressed, genuine nationalists were swallowed up by their communist counterparts. This was particularly true in Vietnam, Indonesia, and China.

One of my Saigon friends summed up Vietnamese nationalism this way: "You Americans are experts at analyzing our problems. You point to our weaknesses, and we have many. But you do not understand Vietnam and the Vietnamese. We have been invaded and conquered in the past, we have been divided for more than a decade, but we will never be beaten down. In South Vietnam, we aren't all democrats; in North Vietnam, they aren't all communists. We are, first of all, Vietnamese nationalists; we are one people. And no Chinese or American can ever change this." He spoke for many in Vietnam, and elsewhere in Southeast Asia as well.

And the Vietnamese, in particular, are solidly aware of the

second great problem of Southeast Asia—China. In the spring of 1964, Nguyen Khanh put it this way: "Our enemy is not only the Viet Cong. Behind them are the Chinese communists, who now influence North Vietnam." And then he added: "The only nation that can oppose the Chinese communists is the United States." Other Asians agree: Thais, Laotians, and Indonesians among others have made their sentiments clear to me on many occasions. "Someone must shoulder the burden of rescuing South Vietnam," Malaysian MP Ali bin Haji Ahmad told me. "If South Vietnam falls, the communists will be that much stronger." Malaysia, of course, is well aware of the dangers: the communist revolt there lasted twelve years. Malaysian Finance Minister Tan Siew Sin, an overseas Chinese, summed it up in a 1965 interview: "Without American assistance, Southeast Asia would go communist."

To most Southeast Asians, China is both the historic threat and the present danger. But the struggle for power in Peking of 1966–67 puzzled Asians perhaps even more than Westerners. Out of long and often scarifying experience, the peoples around China's periphery have come to respect and fear the Chinese. China, after all, has dominated events in Asia for many centuries. Its population has always been far larger than any other Asian nation, and at present rates of increase, there will be 1 billion mainland Chinese by 1985. As other Asians know, the Chinese in general are pragmatic, hard-working, and highly intelligent: the Chinese nuclear explosion of 1964 surprised only a few of my friends, though it did give them pause. And 1964, for that matter, had been a splendid year for the Peking government.

That first nuclear explosion was only one of a series of solid gains that included significant foreign policy advances in Africa and Latin America, a steadily accelerating swing toward China in Indonesia, genuine economic progress at home, and recognition by one of the long-haughty European powers—the France of Charles de Gaulle. But a year later, Chinese prestige was sadly tarnished. Peking's efforts to promote the second Afro-Asian conference had failed miserably, and the footholds in Indonesia, Africa, Cuba, and the rest of Latin America had been all but destroyed. In part, this was a reflection of the bungling of China's leaders: Chou En-lai's statement that Africa "was ripe for revolution" had a distinctly disturbing impact on Africa's leaders, for instance. The exchange of ambassadors with France had failed to produce any particular results. Trade, for example, stayed at pre-recognition levels, and there was increasing unhappiness in Paris about the move. ("Stay firm," a high-ranking French China specialist told me in 1966. "Do not make the stupidity of recognizing Peking.")

In the summer of 1967, as Mao's Great Proletarian Cultural Revolution continued to throb, Asians and Westerners alike were incredulous. Clearly, Mao was attempting to rivet his philosophy of revolution on China for decades to come; just as clearly, he had judged his comrades and found many of them wanting. There was no other explanation for the disgrace of once-favored leaders such as Peng Chen, Liu Shao-chi, Teng Hsiao-ping, Ho Lung, and Chu Teh; the list of victims seemed endless. The Chinese Communist Party itself was in severe difficulties: disgraced province leaders were trying to build their own bases of power, disobeying Peking's commands and in many cases clashing with pro-Mao forces. From many of China's major cities—Shanghai, Nanking, Canton, Wuhan—came reports of bloody clashes for control. The effect on foreign Communist parties was enormous: the Japanese communists, for instance, formally broke long-cherished ties with their Chinese counterparts, and North Korea's communist government edged steadily away from Peking. Over the short run, it seemed clear, China's ability to influence affairs abroad were sure to ebb.

China's long-term policies toward Southeast Asia, however, inevitably will remain unchanged. I doubt that even Mao planned overt military conquest of Southeast Asia; I have seen no evidence in his pronouncements, or in those of other government spokesmen, that such was the intention. But China does want to ensure that its border areas are under total domination. (The 1962 invasion of India was intended, in large part, to bolster security on China's Southwest flank of the Aksai Chin plateau, which, intersected by a vitally important military highway, lies across the Himalayas from north India.) Beyond this, China feels it needs a series of buffer states along its southern boundaries; states that not only serve as shock absorbers against what Peking sees as the ever-present Western threat, but that in addition provide the food and raw materials that are vitally necessary for the growth of a strong and dominant China. Consider the following: "Southeast Asia supplies approximately 90 percent of the world's crude rubber, 60 percent of its tin, and 80 percent of its copra and cocoanut oil. It is the world's largest exporter of rice, quinine, kapok, teak, pepper, and tapioca flour, and it also exports sizable quantities of sugar, tea, coffee, tobacco, sisal, fruits, natural resins and gums, petroleum, iron ore, and bauxite."[1] Southeast Asia's political and economic importance to China cannot be overestimated.

The problem is not one of China *per se:* few in Southeast Asia, or the West, for that matter, quarrel with the fact that great powers almost automatically develop spheres of influence. And a less threatening China would stir little concern. But Communist China's policies, from 1949 onward, gave every indication that China intended to overthrow existing governments and replace them with puppet regimes subservient to Peking's policies, and, more than that, to compress Southeast Asia into the cruel and stifling ideological straitjacket that Mao believes is a vital ingredient for national progress.

The results of this policy became evident in China itself in 1966; in this sense, there would seem to be ample reason for containment, if only to spare Southeast Asia the same agonies.

But the Chinese turmoil, which can be used to justify present American policy toward China, also opens the door for a new, more positive approach to this enormous and potentially powerful nation. Fresh policies, of course, are enormously difficult to develop— but it is unthinkable that the United States should meet any post-Mao government with the same old hostility, compounded by fear and ignorance. It is far past time, for instance, to forget that diplomatic recognition implies approval. It might be well to offer recognition to China, if only to put the onus for refusal on China rather than the United States.

Washington has already begun efforts to widen communication with China: a host of passports has been validated for travel to the mainland, when and if visas are forthcoming from Peking. But much more could be done along this line: American diplomats, for instance, should be encouraged to try to develop informal contacts with Chinese representatives abroad, instead of being forced to ignore officially their presence. At Warsaw, true enough, the Sino-American talks continue. But the meetings are strained and formal and, so far, largely unproductive. Surely the base for the Warsaw talks could be broadened so that American officials in other world capitals can at least make an attempt to develop similar discussions.

The question of aid to China inevitably will trigger loud Congressional protests, but it deserves serious study. Not many years ago, the United States offered to sell grain at cost to a hungry Communist China: the offer was scornfully rejected—but the effect of the offer wasn't lost on other Asians. And to judge from the vehemence of China's retort to the offer, it seems reasonable to assume the offer had a great deal of impact in Peking as well.

One of the more important Sino-American policy issues is the two-China question: can the United States, in other words, afford to recognize both the Peking regime and Chiang Kai-shek's Kuomintang government on Taiwan? Since 1962, the two-China issue has been debated in the United States; it has, moreover, been firmly rejected by both Taipei and Peking, each of whom contends there is no other legal Chinese government. The fact is, however, that there are indeed two Chinas, and that any realistic foreign policy must be based on this truth. For all practical purposes, the United States long ago recognized this fact: the American Consulate-General in Hong Kong functions in many ways as the equivalent of a U.S. Embassy in Peking. Among the younger Foreign Service officers, I've met none who even pretends to believe that Chiang's aging government rules China, although some senior officials still seem to cling to this illusion. In any case, the question of "two Chinas" almost certainly won't live much longer than Chiang Kai-shek himself: Taiwan is destined to become part of China once more, and only the timing is uncertain.

Communist China stands indicted by its own statements since 1949 as a distinct threat to the peace of Asia. It is clear that if the United States had not stood firm in the years after World War II, China would be much more a preoccupation to the West than it is today. In interviews conducted over five years from Rangoon to Djakarta to Manila, I have found general Asian support for this U.S. stand. But containment no longer applies, any more than NATO's outdated premises apply. China is changing, and the United States must adjust its policies to meet this change, and this challenge.

For the United States, the development of an effective China policy must go hand in hand with the building of an effective Asian strategy. In this context, it is worth noting that American policy in Asia began to take on added dimensions some years ago, specifically in the support of Southeast Asia's several regional institutions.

Probably the most important of these is the U.N.'s Economic Commission for Asia and the Far East (ECAFE), a prime mover behind the multinational effort to develop the huge potential resources of the Mekong River. Despite war in Vietnam and Laos, despite the break in diplomatic relations between Cambodia and two

(Thailand and South Vietnam) of the other three prime members of the Mekong Committee,[2] the project continues to make progress. Dams are being built, hydroelectric power plants are being developed, and irrigation and navigation projects are well under way.

In 1965, ECAFE played a key role in bringing the multimillion-dollar Asian Development Bank into existence. The United States pledged $200 million toward the funding of the ADB, an amount matched by Japan, and smaller Asian nations chipped in to the level of their abilities. Authorized capital of the bank is $1 billion, though initial levels will be somewhat smaller. ADB represented a long step toward developing a spirit of Asian unity, and continuing Western support will prove of enormous value. Closely allied to ECAFE's aims is the Colombo Plan, a loosely coordinated effort that involves most Asian nations, as well as Commonwealth countries and the United States. Limited in scope, it represents a largely successful attempt to promote regional cooperation on developmental problems.

Several Southeast Asian nations came to realize the value of building up regional economic cooperation on their own long ago: in 1961, for example, the Philippines, Thailand, and Malaya (which later became Malaysia), formed the Association of Southeast Asia (ASA). After a bright start, ASA was shelved as a result of Indonesia's "confrontation" of Malaysia, but Sukarno's fall from power brought about ASA's reactivation. And in May, 1967, Indonesia and the Philippines laid the foundation for a new regional organization which is expected to include Thailand, Malaysia, and Singapore as well. To my mind, this is the only valid sort of regional thinking, for regionalism *imposed* by the west, such as that represented by the moribund Southeast Asia Treaty Organization, is fruitless.

SEATO, organized in 1954 by former Secretary of State John Foster Dulles to act as an Asian counterpart of the North Atlantic Treaty Organization, shares NATO's dubious future. Several members, notably France and Pakistan, have all but dropped out, and SEATO has never been much more than a convenient method of funneling Western military aid to Thailand. Inevitably, SEATO will have to be redesigned if it is to become effective, and there must be broader and more active participation by Southeast Asian nations themselves. It might be well to consider the reshaping of the entire system of U.S. alliances in Asia, for that matter. It is clear that Canada, Japan, South Korea, Australia, New Zealand and, to a lesser degree, the lands of Latin America that border on the Pacific, have a common interest in

Asian peace and development. Perhaps a Pacific Development Bank, involving these countries, some day will come to act in concert with its Asian counterpart.

In all these efforts, the United States can play an enormously important role, and in fact it is already helping, in some degree. Hopefully, this participation will increase: Southeast Asia has proven itself an area of rapid and dramatic change, and the United States, in its own best interests, must be prepared to assist in further transformation. Many of Asia's first-generation revolutionary leaders have already left the scene, more will depart—as either victims or heroes —over the next several years. Given the nearly incredible rate of technological progress in the West, there will be more and more techniques available that, if properly applied, can help Southeast Asia make the necessary giant strides toward economic progress. Here again, the United States should be ready to assist. Indeed, a basis exists: in April, 1965, President Johnson urged the nations of Southeast Asia to join in an "expanded cooperative effort for development," to which he pledged an American investment of $1 billion. His decision was greeted by China and North Vietnam as a propaganda gimmick, an attempt to buy the United States out of the war, and indeed there was some truth to the accusation. More important, however, is the fact that the offer was largely sincere: it opens another door to Asian development, on a truly gigantic scale.

In its concentration on fostering Asian development, the United States has largely ignored communist North Vietnam, which has been lumped together with China as "the enemy." Yet there are differences between the two capitals; both Hanoi and Peking have their own hawk-dove problems. As Dr. Donald Zagoria has pointed out,[3] Peking has displayed more intransigence than Hanoi on the question of a negotiated settlement in Vietnam. "North Vietnam, " he wrote in 1966, "has a clearly more limited interest, namely, the unification of Vietnam under communist hegemony." And because of this, he added, negotiations under certain conditions are more attractive to Hanoi than is generally believed. In the coming years, the question of specifically including Hanoi in some of the development projects might be well worth study.

The complicated relationship between China and North Vietnam, in fact, is a reflection of the rapidly changing nature of communism. China, in its deliberate exacerbation of the Sino-Soviet split, has helped speed the passing of international communism: the old bogey of the communist monolith is dying a remarkably untidy death. In the Soviet Union, Stalin's rigid economic policies are being discarded— and replaced by a system that reeks of capitalism. Moscow's hold over the Eastern European countries is fast dissolving: socialism in one country is replacing socialist unity. And in China, Mao's attempt to preserve pure Marx-Leninism played a major part in creating the turmoil of 1966–67.

The implications of these changes have not been lost on the leaders of Southeast Asia. In one sense, a Maoist victory in China is almost irrelevant: for Southeast Asia, the Chinese threat will remain a reality whether it is communist, nationalist, or mugwump. China's nuclear weapons program is a deep concern, and the Great Prole-tarian Cultural Revolution, intelligence sources report, has not been allowed to reach into Peking's nuclear and missile projects. In June, 1967, China exploded its first hydrogen bomb, well ahead of sched-ule. There were ominous reports it been dropped from an aircraft, indicating that work on a delivery system was well advanced. By 1974, Western military intelligence sources have said, the Chinese probably will have intercontinental ballistic missiles, and IRBM's should be in production by 1969 or 1970. Long before then, China's power struggle should have ended.

Here, three broad possibilities now face the United States: a Maoist China dedicated to his ideals of Asian hegemony; a revisionist but still nationalistic China, led by men who opposed Mao's policies but remain aggressive communists; or a neutralist China, still suspi-cious of the West but essentially moving along the path trod by the Soviet Union. However pleasant the third possibility may seem, its chances of immediate realization are slim. Washington, I believe, must cope with an intransigent China for the foreseeable future. A strong but flexible stance toward China thus becomes vital, and any oppor-tunity to bring China in from the cold should be seized. Just as important is an even more determined effort to help the nations of Southeast Asia to build up their strength, individually and collectively, to a degree that will allow them to stand firm against the historic danger from the north. The war in Vietnam erupted at least in part because of a series of short-sighted American policy blunders that made South Vietnam seem an easy target: I can conceive of no one in the United States eager for more Vietnams in the years ahead.

And it is of overriding importance that Americans learn to see China as it really is: not a drooling monster eager to devour the world, not a milling mass of mindless peasants, impotent and will-less, but an appallingly naïve, fiercely nationalistic nation beset by enormous problems. Its drive to the south can be justified, by many Chinese at least, by simple historical precedent; it is a traditional exercise in solving traditional problems. And the United States must learn to deal with the thrust realistically, on a basis of knowledge and wisdom, rather than the combination of ignorance and spasm response that has too often characterized past policy.

American involvement in Asia, to me at least, is both necessary and inevitable. Necessary because only the United States is strong enough, and disinterested enough, to help Asia to progress; inevitable because we are, in truth, a Pacific nation, and a stable, self-sufficient, and progressive Asia is clearly in the best interests of the nations of Asia and the United States as well. For the Pacific, after all, is our last frontier on earth: it is up to us to try to help make it truly pacific.

1. A. Doak Barnett, *Communist China and Asia,* Harper & Brothers, New York, 1960, p. 302.
2. The fourth member is Laos.
3. Donald Zagoria, "China's Crisis of Foreign Policy," *New York Times Magazine,* May 1, 1966.

Suggested Reading—General

Barnett, A. Doak. *Communist China and Asia: Challenge to American Policy.* New York: Harper, for the Council on Foreign Relations, 1960.

Blum, Robert. *The United States and China in World Affairs,* ed. A. Doak Barnett. New York: McGraw-Hill, 1966.

Bone, Robert C. *Contemporary Southeast Asia.* New York: Random House, 1962.

Boyd, R. G. *Communist China's Foreign Policy.* New York: Praeger, 1962.

Brimmell, J. H. *Communism in South East Asia: A Political Analysis.* London: Oxford University Press, 1959.

Buchan, Alastair (ed.). *China and the Peace of Asia.* Studies in International Security: 9. London: Chatto & Windus, for The Institute for Strategic Studies, 1965.

Butwell, Richard. *Southeast Asia Today—and Tomorrow.* New York: Praeger, 1961.

Chatham House Study Group. *Collective Defence in South East Asia.* London: Royal Institute of International Affairs, 1956.

Crozier, Brian. *South-east Asia in Turmoil.* London: Penguin, 1965.

Du Bois, Cora. *Social Forces in Southeast Asia.* Minneapolis: University of Minnesota Press, 1949.

Fifield, Russell H. *The Diplomacy of Southeast Asia, 1945–1958.* New York: Harper, 1958, pp. 167–229.

Fisher, C. A. *South-East Asia: A Social, Economic and Political Geography.* London: Methuen, 1964.

Fitzgerald, C. P. *The Chinese View of Their Place in the World.* London: Oxford University Press, 1964.

Griffith, Brigadier General Samuel B., II. *Peking and People's Wars.* New York: Praeger, 1966.

Hall, D. G. E. *A History of South-East Asia,* 2d ed. New York: Macmillan, 1964.

Harrison, Brian. *A Short History of South-East Asia.* London: Macmillan; New York: St. Martin's Press, 1955.

Hinton, Harold C. *China's Relations With Burma and Vietnam.* New York: Institute of Pacific Relations, 1958.

Kennedy, D. E. *The Security of Southern Asia.* Studies in International Security: 8. London: Chatto & Windus, for The Institute of Strategic Studies, 1965.

King, John Kerry. *Southeast Asia in Perspective.* New York: Macmillan, 1956.

Levy, Roger, Lacam, Guy, and Roth, Andrew. *French Interests and Policies in the Far East.* New York: Institute of Pacific Relations, 1941.

McLean, Charles B. *Soviet Strategies in Southeast Asia: An Exploration of Eastern Policy Under Lenin and Stalin.* Princeton, N.J.: Princeton University Press, 1966.

Montgomery, John D. *The Politics of Foreign Aid: American Experience in Southeast Asia.* New York: Praeger, 1962.

————. *China, Vietnam and the United States.* Washington: Public Affairs Press, 1966.

Purcell, Victor. *The Chinese in South-east Asia.* London: Oxford University Press, 1951.

Reischauer, Edwin, and Fairbank, John K. *East Asia: The Great Tradition.* 2 vols. Boston: Houghton Mifflin, 1958, 1960–65.

Scalapino, Robert A. (ed.). *The Communist Revolution in Asia.* Englewood Cliffs, New Jersey: Prentice Hall, 1965.

Thompson, Virginia, and Adloff, Richard. *Minority Problems in Southeast Asia.* Stanford: Stanford University Press, 1955.

Williams, Lea E. *The Future of the Overseas Chinese in Southeast Asia.* New York: McGraw-Hill, 1966.

Wint, Guy (ed.). *Asia: A Handbook.* New York: Praeger, 1966.

Wolf, Charles, Jr. *Foreign Aid: Theory and Practice in Southeast Asia.* Princeton, N.J.: Princeton University Press, 1960.

Vietnam

Browne, Malcolm W. *The New Face of War.* Indianapolis: Bobbs-Merrill, 1965.

Burchett, Wilfred G. *The Furtive War: The United States in Vietnam and Laos.* New York: International Publishers Co., Inc., 1963.

————. *Vietnam: Inside Story of the Guerrilla War.* New York: International Publishers, 1965.

Buttinger, Joseph. *The Smaller Dragon.* New York: Praeger, 1958.

Cady, John F. *The Roots of French Imperialism in Eastern Asia.* Ithaca, N.Y.: American Historical Association, Cornell University Press, 1954.

Truong Chinh. *Primer for Revolt. The Communist Takeover in Viet-Nam.* With an Introduction by Bernard B. Fall. New York: Praeger, 1963.

Ennis, Thomas E. *French Policy and Developments in Indochina.* Chicago: University of Chicago Press, 1936.

Fall, Bernard B. *Street Without Joy.* Harrisburg, Pa.: Stackpole, 1961.

————. *The Two Viet-Nams.* New York: Praeger, 1963; rev. 1964.

————. *Viet-Nam Witness; 1953–66.* New York: Praeger, 1966.

Groslier, Bernard P. *The Art of Indochina, Including Thailand, Vietnam, Laos and Cambodia.* New York: Crown Publishers, 1962.

Halberstam, David. *The Making of a Quagmire.* New York: Random House, 1965.

Hickey, Gerald G. *Village in Vietnam.* New Haven: Yale University Press, 1964.

Hammer, Ellen J. *The Struggle for Indochina.* Stanford: Stanford University Press, 1954.

Honey, P. I. (ed.). *North Vietnam Today.* New York: Praeger, 1962.

Lacouture, Jean. *Vietnam: Between Two Truces.* New York: Random House, 1966.

Lancaster, Donald. *The Emancipation of French Indochina.* London: Oxford University Press, 1961.

Mecklin, John. *Mission in Torment.* New York: Doubleday, 1965.

Pike, Douglas. *Viet Cong.* Cambridge: MIT Press, 1966.

Roy, Jules. *The Battle of Dienbienphu.* London: Faber and Faber, 1965.

Sacks, I. Milton. "Marxism in Viet Nam." *Marxism in Southeast Asia,* ed. Frank Trager, pp. 102–170. Stanford: Stanford University Press, 1959, p. 102–170.

Scigliano, Robert G. *South Vietnam: Nation Under Stress.* Boston: Houghton Mifflin, 1963.

Shaplen, Robert. *The Last Revolution.* New York: Harper and Row, 1965.

Tanham, George K. *Communist Revolutionary Warfare: The Vietminh in Indochina.* New York: Praeger, 1961.

United States, Department of State, Bureau of Public Affairs, Office of Public Service, *A Threat to the Peace: North Vietnam's Effort to Conquer South Vietnam.* Washington, D.C.: Government Printing Office, 1961.

Vietnam News Agency. *Ten Years of Fighting and Building of the Vietnamese People's Army.* Hanoi: Foreign Languages Publishing House, 1955.

Viet Nam Lao Dong Party. *Thirty Years of Struggle of the Party,* Book I. Hanoi: Foreign Languages Publishing House, 1960.

Vo Nguyen Giap. *People's War, People's Army: The Viet Cong Insurrection Manual for Under-developed Countries.* New York: Praeger, 1962.

Cambodia

Burchett, Wilfred G. *Mekong Upstream.* Hanoi: Red River Publishing House, 1957.

Herz, Martin F. *A Short History of Cambodia.* London: Atlantic Books, Stevens & Sons, Ltd., 1958.

Mayer, Charles (ed.). *Cambodge.* Phnom Penh: Le Ministère de L'Information, 1962.

Steinberg, David J., a.o., *Cambodia: Its People, Its Society, Its Culture.* New Haven: Human Relations Area Files Press, 1957.

Laos

Berval, Rene de, et al. *Kingdom of Laos: The Land of the Million Elephants and of the White Parasol.* Saigon: France-Asie, 1959.

Dommen, Arthur J. *Conflict in Laos.* New York: Praeger, 1964.

Halpern, Joel M. *Aspects of Village Life and Culture Change in Laos.* New York: Council on Economic and Cultural Affairs, 1958.

———. *The Role of the Chinese in Laos Society.* Santa Monica, California: Rand Corp., 1960.

Le Bar, Frank M., and Suddard, Adrienne, eds. *Laos: Its People, Its Society, Its Culture.* New Haven: Human Relations Area Files Press, 1960.

Laos. R. 4935, Reference Division, Central Office of Information, London, 1961.

Simmonds, E. H. S. "Independence and Political Rivalry in Laos, 1945–1961."

Sisouk na Champassak. *Storm Over Laos.* New York: Praeger, 1961.

Wolfkill, Grant, and Rose, Jerry A. *Reported To Be Alive.* New York: Simon and Schuster, 1965.

Thailand

Benedict, Ruth F. *Thai Culture and Behavior.* Ithaca, N.Y.: (Southeast Asia Program, Cornell University, Data Paper No. 4.), 1952.

Blanchard, Wendell A. O. *Thailand: Its People, Its Society, Its Culture.* New Haven: HRAF Press, 1957.

Coughlin, Richard J. *Double Identity: The Chinese in Modern Thailand.* Hong Kong and London: Oxford University Press, 1960.

Darling, Frank. *Thailand and the United States.* Washington: Public Affairs Press, 1965.

de Young, John. *Village Life in Modern Thailand.* Berkeley: University of California Press, 1955.

Ingram, James C. *Economic Change in Thailand since 1850.* Stanford: Stanford University Press, 1955.

Pendleton, Robert L., et al. *Thailand: Aspects of Landscape and Life.* New York: Duell, Sloan & Pearce, 1962.

Vella, Walter F. *The Impact of the West on Government in Thailand.* (University of California Publications in Political Science, vol. IV, No. 3.) Berkeley and Los Angeles: University of California Press, 1955.

Wales, Horace G. Quaritch. *Ancient Siamese Government and Administration.* London: Bernard Quaritch, 1934.

Wilson, David A. *Politics in Thailand.* Ithaca, N.Y.: Cornell University Press, 1962.

Burma

Butwell, Richard. *U Nu of Burma.* Stanford: Stanford University Press, 1963.

Cady, John F. *A History of Modern Burma.* Ithaca, N.Y.: Cornell University Press, 1958.

Dobby, E. H. G. *Southeast Asia.* 2nd ed. New York: John Wiley, 1951.

Hall, D. G. E. *Burma.* London: Hutchinson's University Library, 1950.

———. *Europe and Burma.* London: Oxford University Press, 1945.

Johnstone, William C. *Burma's Foreign Policy: A Study in Neutralism.* Cambridge, Mass.: Harvard University Press, 1963.

Mi Mi Khaing. *Burmese Family.* Calcutta: Longmans, Green, 1946.

Khin, U. *U Hla Pe's Narrative of the Japanese Occupation of Burma.* (Southeast Asia Program, Cornell University, Data Paper No. 41.) Ithaca, N.Y.: 1961.

Pye, Lucian W. *Politics, Personality and Nation Building: Burma's Search for Identity.* New Haven: Yale University Press, 1962.

Tinker, Hugh. *The Union of Burma.* London: Oxford University Press, 1956.

Trager, Frank N. *Burma—From Kingdom to Republic.* New York: Praeger, 1966.

Walinsky, Louis J. *Economic Development in Burma, 1951–1960.* New York: Twentieth Century Fund, 1962.

Woodman, Dorothy. *The Making of Burma.* London: Cresset Press, 1962.

Malaysia

Allen, G. C., and Donnithorne, Audrey G. *Western Enterprise in Indonesia and Malaya.* New York: Macmillan, 1957.

Cowan, Charles Donald. *Nineteenth Century Malaya: The Origins of British Political Control.* London and New York: Oxford University Press, 1961.

Emerson, Rupert. *Malaysia: A Study in Direct and Indirect Rule.* New York: Macmillan, 1937.

Great Britain. *Malaysia: Agreement Concluded Between the United Kingdom of Great Britain and Northern Ireland, the Federation of Malaya, North Borneo, Sarawak and Singapore.* Comnd. 2094. London: H.M. Stationery Office, 1963.

Hanrahan, Gene Z. *The Communist Struggle in Malaya.* New York: Institute of Pacific Relations, International Secretariat, 1954.

Kennedy, J. A. *History of Malaya, A.D. 1400–1959.* New York: St. Martin's Press, 1962.

MacDonald, Malcolm. *Borneo People.* New York: Knopf, 1958.

McKie, Ronald. *Malaysia in Focus.* Sydney: Angus & Robertson, Ltd., 1963.

Miller, Harry. *The Communist Menace in Malaya.* New York: Praeger, 1954.

Mills, Lennox A. *British Rule in Eastern Asia.* London: Oxford University Press, 1942.

———. *Malaya: A Political and Economic Appraisal.* Minneapolis: University of Minnesota Press, 1958.

Purcell, Victor. *The Chinese in Malaya.* London: Oxford University Press, 1948.

———. *Malaysia.* London: Thames and Hudson, Ltd., 1965.

Pye, Lucian W. *Guerrilla Communism in Malaya: Its Social and Political Meaning.* Princeton, N.J.: Princeton University Press, 1956.

Silcock, Thomas H. *Readings in Malayan Economics.* Singapore: Donald Moore for Eastern Universities Press, 1961.

Smith, T. E. *The Background to Malaysia.* (Chatham House Memorandum, September 1963.) London and Fair Lawn, N.J.: Oxford University Press, 1963.

Tregonning, K. G. *A History of Modern Malaya.* Eastern University Press Ltd. for University of London Press Ltd., 1964.

————. *North Borneo*. H.M. Stationery Office, London, 1960.

Winstedt, Sir Richard O. *Malaya and Its History*. 5th ed. London: Hutchinson's University Library, 1958.

————. *The Malays: A Cultural History*. Rev. ed. London: Routledge & Kegan Paul, Ltd., 1950.

Wang Gung Wu, ed. *Malaysia, A Survey*. London: Donald Moore Books, 1964.

Wurtzburg, Charles Edward. *Raffles of the Eastern Isles*. London: Hodder & Stoughton, 1954.

Indonesia

Allen, George C. and Donnithorne, Audrey G. *Western Enterprise in Indonesia and Malaya*. London and New York: Macmillan, 1957.

Brackman, Arnold C. *Indonesian Communism: A History*. New York: Praeger, 1963.

————. *Southeast Asia's Second Front*. New York: Praeger, 1966.

Feith, Herbert. *The Decline of Constitutional Democracy in Indonesia*. Ithaca, N.Y.: Cornell University Press, 1962.

Fischer, Louis. *The Story of Indonesia*. New York: Harper, 1959.

Grant, Bruce. *Indonesia*. Melbourne: University Press, 1964.

Hanna, Willard A. *Bung Karno's Indonesia*. New York: American Universities Field Staff, 1960.

Higgins, Benjamin H. *Indonesia's Economic Stabilization and Development*. New York: Institute of Pacific Relations, 1957.

Kahin, George McT. "Indonesia." *Major Governments of Asia*, ed. Kahin. 2nd ed. Ithaca, N.Y.: Cornell University Press, 1963.

————. *Nationalism and Revolution in Indonesia*. Ithaca, N.Y.: Cornell University Press, 1952.

Legge, J. D. *Central Authority and Regional Autonomy in Indonesia: A Study in Local Administration, 1950–1960*. Ithaca, N.Y.: Cornell University Press, 1961.

McVey, Ruth T. *The Rise of Indonesian Communism*, Ithaca, N.Y.: Cornell University Press, 1965.

Paauw, Douglas S. *Financing Economic Development: The Indonesian Case*. Glencoe, Ill.: Free Press, 1960.

Schrieke, B. J. O. *Indonesian Sociological Studies*, 2 vols. The Hague and Bandung: van Hoeve, 1957.

Soedjatmoko. *An Approach to Indonesian History: Towards an Open Future*. (Cornell Modern Indonesia Project, Translation Series.) Ithaca, N.Y.: 1960.

Sukarno. *Toward Freedom and the Dignity of Man*. Djakarta: Department of Foreign Affairs, 1961.

Sutter, John O. *Indonesianisasi: Politics in a Changing Economy, 1940–1955.* (Southeast Asia Program, Cornell University, Data Paper No. 36.) Ithaca, N.Y.: 1959.

United States Economic Survey Team to Indonesia. *Indonesia: Perspective and Proposals for United States Economic Aid; A Report to the President of the United States.* (Yale University, Southeast Asia Studies, Special Publication.) New Haven, Conn.: 1962.

van Niel, Robert. *The Emergence of the Modern Indonesian Elite.* Chicago and The Hague: Quadrangle and van Hoeve, 1960.

Wertheim, W. F. *Indonesian Society in Transition.* 2nd ed. The Hague and Bandung: van Hoeve, 1959.

Willmott, Donald E. *The National Status of the Chinese in Indonesia, 1900–1958.* (Cornell Modern Indonesia Project, Monograph Series.) Ithaca, N.Y.: 1961.

INDEX

About the Author

Robert Karr McCabe is a Midwesterner who first went to the Far East in 1957 and never completely returned. Born in Minneapolis in 1929, he was graduated from Dartmouth College and, before joining *Newsweek* in 1962, worked for *The Wall Street Journal, Stars and Stripes,* and the *New York World-Telegram.* After five years in Hong Kong, where he was *Newsweek*'s bureau chief, he returned to the United States in 1966 as an associate editor of the magazine. In early 1967, he became foreign news editor of the Public Broadcast Laboratory. With his wife, Inger, and three children, Kari, Alexander, and Marit, he lives in Manhattan.